Hollywood's Indian

10/23/00

Dear Betty,

   Thanks so much for the hospitality, collegiality, and efficiency.

   — Pete Rollins

Hollywood's Indian

The Portrayal of the Native American in Film

Peter C. Rollins and John E. O'Connor, Editors

THE UNIVERSITY PRESS OF KENTUCKY

Publication of this volume was made possible in part
by a grant from the National Endowment for the Humanities.

Scholarly publisher for the Commonwealth,
serving Bellarmine College, Berea College, Centre
College of Kentucky, Eastern Kentucky University,
The Filson Club Historical Society, Georgetown College,
Kentucky Historical Society, Kentucky State University,
Morehead State University, Murray State University,
Northern Kentucky University, Transylvania University,
University of Kentucky, University of Louisville,
and Western Kentucky University.
All rights reserved

Editorial and Sales Offices: The University Press of Kentucky
663 South Limestone Street, Lexington, Kentucky 40508–4008

02 01 00 99   5 4 3 2

Library of Congress Cataloging-in-Publication Data

Hollywood's Indian : the portrayal of the Native American in film /
     Peter C. Rollins and John E. O'Connor, editors.
          p.   cm.
     Includes bibliographical references and index.
     ISBN 0–8131–2044–6 (cloth : alk. paper)
     1. Indians in motion pictures.   I. Rollins, Peter C.
II. O'Connor, John E.
PN1995.9.I48H66   1998
791.43´6520397—dc21   97–30062
ISBN 0–8131–0952–3 (pbk: alk. paper)

To Ray and Pat Browne—
pioneers in the study
of the popular-culture images
that shape our lives

Contents

Foreword

The image of the American Indian, more than that of any other ethnic group, has been shaped by films. Why? Because the characteristics that define the American Indian are dramatically conveyed by this powerful twentieth-century medium. All American ethnic groups, of course, are defined—stereotyped, if you will—by Hollywood, but no other provides the opportunity to convey that image in a narrative form in terms of rapid physical movement, exotic appearance, violent confrontation, and a spirituality rooted in the natural environment.

Such characteristics attracted European and American observers long before the advent of film. The image of the Indian in dramatic, violent, and exotic terms was incorporated in the reports of missionaries and soldiers, in philosophic treatises, in histories, and in the first American bestsellers, the captivity narratives of the seventeenth and eighteenth centuries. Although the image of the Indian varied in these early descriptions, one is struck by the tone of admiration and frequent references to honor and nobility even in the context of cruelty and savagery.

The present collection of essays illustrates the widely varying trends and depictions of the American Indian in films. Among those trends are the change from the Indian's being portrayed as savage opponent to that of being portrayed as wronged victim or generous host. More recently there has been a dramatic shift from white actors portraying Indians to Indian actors (finally) portraying Indians. How much better for us all—Indians and whites—that the Indian activist Russell Means has finally found his metier as an actor (as Chingachgook) in *The Last of the Mohicans* and as the narrator in Disney's *Pocahontas*. Means' Sioux continue, as in history, to lord it over their traditional enemies (as in *Dances With Wolves*, in which Wes Studi provides a stunning image of the evil Pawnee in contrast to the idyllic and peace-loving Sioux).

I believe that the film industry, because of its ability to define the Indian past in dramatic cinematic terms, helped promote the recovery of the contemporary Indian in the early and mid-twentieth century and the renaissance of the Indian—particularly in art and literature—in the most recent decades of the century. Motion pictures did this first by not letting the Indian identity be absorbed into the larger American society as just another—and tiny—ethnic minority, and, second, by reminding other Americans of the worthy character of the Indian adversaries of the other principal *dramatis personae* of American history, the frontiersmen and pioneers who form the subject of the current debate over the "new" and "old" Western history. Although the reforms of the New Deal period by Indian Affairs commissioner John Collier did not derive directly from the presentation of the Indian on film, the successful passage of such reforms and their retention by succeeding congresses may well have owed much to the continuing presence of the American Indian—whether as villain, victim, hero, or worthy foe—in America's movie houses and thus in the American popular imagination.

The viewer of imaginative re-creations of the Indian-white past may be better off than the viewer of documentary films, or "docudramas," that have assumed a growing importance. The viewer of *Little Big Man* or *The Last of the Mohicans* will rarely forget that the representation of the past that he is seeing is the product of an artist, or series of artists, working with an admittedly incomplete record of the past. In the preface to *The Unredeemed Captive: A Family Story from Early America,* John Demos, discusses his conversion to narrative history, which had become almost extinct among professional historians, and he attributes "special inspiration" to fictional portrayals of the Indian—in particular, to Brian Moore's *Black Robe.* Viewers of films claiming the authority of a documentary or docudrama, such as *Annie Mae—Brave Hearted Woman* (about an activist killed during the 1973 occupation of Wounded Knee), on the other hand, too often assume the historical reality of the representation no matter how ideologically distorted or historically unsupported it may be. Better than the many contemporary, politically tinged documentaries is a clearly imaginative film such as *Powwow Highway.* Incorporating stereotypes of greedy white mining companies and "puppet" tribal governments, it focuses on a dramatic trip in a battered car from North Dakota to New Mexico in which the traditional personalities of its present-day Indian protagonists emerge in the context of contemporary American life.

Scholars endlessly debate the question of objectivity in history, sometimes, as a consequence, forgetting to write history itself. Literary scholars have carried the debate to the extremes of doubting the objective existence of a physical reality. In such a climate the imaginative channel to reality provided the viewer by film is, as they say, "privileged." As Gore

Vidal has pointed out in his *Screening History*, the history we believe we "know" is the history presented in film. Vidal would prefer an earlier era when the novel conveyed the reality of the past, but he recognizes that this era cannot be recovered by either historians or novelists in a time when the public prefers to see—rather than read about—the past.

Critics of film as well as of literature will find any number of objections to works produced in either form. Mark Twain railed against Fenimore Cooper's "literary offenses," but, as Jeffrey Walker rightly points out, Twain's criticism is "a tour de force in the history of American humor" rather than "serious literary criticism." Critics can easily find similar incorrect or anomalous details in any number of Indian films. Others will apply questionable abstractions, such as "collective wish-fulfillment patterns," in interpreting Indian films. Still others will use the past to comment on the present (for example, *Soldier Blue* or *Little Big Man*, which allude to the Vietnam War). Few will agree on what films truly represent the American Indian, but no one should be deterred from debating the question. The "historical reality"—if one can accept the concept at all—will always remain elusive, speculative, and controversial. The filmmaker can legitimately stand with the historian and the novelist in asserting equal claims to representing the American Indian.

—WILCOMB E. WASHBURN
Smithsonian Institution

Acknowledgments

This collection began as a special issue of *Film & History: An Interdisciplinary Journal of Film and Television Studies* 23.1–4 (1993). The issue proved to be very popular in college classrooms, and we were thus inspired to add new material to fill out the portrait and to produce a text that would serve the classroom with a broader spectrum of offerings.

Two authors, Eric Gary Anderson and Michael J. Riley, began their research from scratch at the editors' urging at a Tulsa, Oklahoma meeting of the Southwest/Texas Regional Popular Culture/American Culture Association. The resulting articles on *Powwow Highway* and *The Vanishing American* are excellent contributions to this collection, revealing the high standards of young scholars today.

John O'Connor's essay "The White Man's Indian" is taken from his book *The Hollywood Indian* (1980) and is here published with the permission of the New Jersey State Museum, publisher of the lavishly illustrated text.

Robert Baird's essay on *Dances With Wolves* has appeared previously in the *Michigan Academician* (25:2 [1993]: 133–46) and in an excellent book Edited by Elizabeth Bird, *Dressing in Feathers: The Construction of the Indian in American Popular Culture* (Westview Press, 1996: 195–209). This expanded version is published with their permission.

Pauline Turner Strong's essay at the end of this collection was, in a different form, published previously in *Cultural Anthropology* 11.3 (1996): 405–24 and is here published with the permission of the American Anthropological Association.

Many thanks to the editors, readers, and assistants who have made *Film & History* such a success over the last twenty-four years; more recently, we extend thanks to Kim Marotta, Shirley Bechtel, and Cecilia Austell, who provided last-minute help to bring this collection for completion. Those curious for more information about *Film & History* should consult its Web site: http://h-net2.msu.edu/~filmhis/. Paul Fleming of

Oklahoma State University deserves special thanks for his contributions to the success of Film & History in the area of layout and design.

Ray and Pat Browne deserve our praise and thanks for fostering these kinds of studies in popular media when they were new and controversial. The controversy is over, but we remember their pioneering spirit as we go forward with our work of cultural analysis.

The Study of Hollywood's Indian
Still on a Scholarly Frontier?

The 1992 Columbian quincentenary set into motion a reconsideration of the place of the Native American in our historical memory. A more recent eruption of interest (and controversy) has focused on a proposed Disney historical theme park in Haymarket, Virginia. A local newspaper speculated on how the Native American might be included in a controversial Disney version of history, giving ample evidence of the distance Americans still need to travel along the path toward understanding: "The theme park concept probably never penetrated the thick skulls or shadowy minds of the prehistoric men who once dragged their knuckles across what is now present-day Haymarket. Certainly, no caveman ever grunted Disney. According to some local historians, the Walt Disney Co. regards the legacy of those primal progenitors with equal indifference." The writer ridiculed the notion that Disney might consider the Native American site as important. This troglodytic attitude received immediate and ardent condemnation; indeed, the Internet-based academic discussion group of the Popular Culture/American Culture Association *h-pcaaca*@msu.edu) lit up. Wilkie Leith, a George Mason University student, found it difficult to curb her anger and asked for confirmation from the list: "My intention here is to see if others find this issue outrageous. . . . Is anyone interested in a full-scale protest against both the paper and Disney? Or am I just— overreacting?"

At the opposite extreme of the spectrum of attitudes toward Native Americans is a project being advertised by *Reader's Digest*. While promoting a five million dollar grand prize in a special sweepstakes, the powerful media giant offered a volume entitled *Through Indian Eyes*. No author, editor, or creator was cited in connection with the book offer. Instead, the brochure promised a plethora of romantic insights:

> As you will see, it is a bittersweet story filled to the brimming with a love of nature and the land. . . . The Indian sees time not as an elusive river that flows relentlessly in one direction, but as a deep and eternal lake on which past and present mingle. . . . What was it like riding with Plains hunters in pursuit of buffalo? Watching the coming of the Iron Horse and the pandemonium of the Gold Rush? Fighting the good battle, answering the call of Crazy Horse, Sitting Bull, Geronimo? And what must it have been like to dream the lost dream of a land before the strangers came?

Here empathy for a lost cause spills over into sentimentality and revives timeworn, romantic notions of a "passing West." (American history students will remember that this kind of romanticism was once directed *against* Native Americans. In 1832, President Andrew Jackson—in defiance of the Supreme Court's decision in *Cherokee Nation v. Georgia* case—used just such a portrait to justify his "Trail of Tears" approach to preserving—putatively—edenic Native Americans from civilization's "infections.")

Although contemporary ignorance and stereotypes in popular culture certainly deserve condemnation, those of us who study the visual media need to go farther down the trail of this legacy. And the trail leads west to Los Angeles where, since the silent era, the Native American experience has been molded into melodramatic formulas to attract audiences. This collection attempts to examine Hollywood's image, what we call "Hollywood's Indian"—its construction, its aesthetics, its major productions, its impact, and its future.

We asked Ted Jojola (University of New Mexico) to survey recent cinematic productions and to give us his impressions. He reports that the Native American community is disappointed with the meager attempts to portray life as actually lived by his people. The community is especially outraged that non-Indian actors (for example, Raquel Welch, who plays the starring role in *The Legend of Walks Far Woman* [1984]) have such prominence in films ostensibly sympathetic to the Native American dilemma.

Many readers, including the editors, have heard of semiunderground films like *Powwow Highway* (1989), but have difficulty placing them within a general pattern. Jojola performs a useful task by linking such commercially minor (but culturally important) films to a broader context. Also, his sensitivity to how such films can run amok is enlightening. He asks a pointed question: Do Native Americans themselves need to be

Figure I.1. *Removal of the Civilized Tribes to Indian Territory* (now Oklahoma). Mural painting by Elizabeth Janes, 1939. Courtesy of the Archives and Manuscripts Division, Oklahoma Historical Society.

"reawakened" to appreciate their own heritage? Jojola also points out excesses in what he labels "Indian Sympathy Films," productions capitalizing on the success of *Dances With Wolves. The Last of the Mohicans* and *Geronimo* do not fare well under Jojola's scrutiny. Jojola concludes, "as long as Native actors are assigned roles controlled by non-Natives, the image will remain revisionist."

As John O'Connor's essay demonstrates, there are institutional approaches to studying the image. Since 1980, when O'Connor surveyed the Native American media image for the New Jersey State Museum, too few scholars have pondered one of his methodological insights, namely that "Hollywood is presumably not filled with Indian haters intent on using their power to put down the natives. One need only observe how quickly a director or a studio might switch from portraying a 'bloodthirsty' to a 'noble savage' if the market seems to call for it. Far from purposeful distortion, significant elements of the Indian image can be explained best through analyzing various technical—and business—related production decisions that may never have been considered in terms of their effect on the screen image." With these factors in mind, O'Connor examines the myth of the frontier in American history, a myth in which the Hollywood Indian became subsumed within a definition of Americanness through struggle. O'Connor stresses the temptation in visual media to create polarized antagonists (black hats) and protagonists (white hats) for "entertainment value." Furthermore, Hollywood's limited notion of "action" often requires a set of jaws to be punched. In recent blockbusters, those jaws tend to be Arabic, as in the Arnold Schwarzenegger film *True Lies;* during the studio era, those jaws often belonged to stereotyped bands of

Odeon Theatre

Thursday and Friday, Jan. 13-14

William Desmond
IN
A BROADWAY COWBOY

HE KILLED SIX INDIANS
AFTER LUNCH EVERY DAY—

That is, when he was a matinee idol playing western "leads"
But you ought to see him as a real cowboy
without the grease paint.

You'll Smile, Laugh, Chuckle and Roar.

Here's a pippin comedy drama, peppy,
spicy and zippy.

Here's a refreshing romance, gay as a
cocktail, breezy as the prairie and as funny
as the first joke that ever tickled your
funny bone.

Don't miss it!   *Don't miss it!*

Figure I.2. Revision of the image begins here. Courtesy of the Archives and Manuscripts Division, Oklahoma Historical Society.

whoopin' and hollerin' Hollywood Indians. Finally, O'Connor reminds us that, at least for the last fifty years or so, there have been few power bases in the political arena from which Native Americans could bring pressure on Hollywood. In the struggle to interpret the frontier past, the Native American dimension has been the least defended—and hence the most vulnerable—of images.

Clearly, some paradoxes O'Connor highlights for the early days of film continue. Ted Turner financed the making of an ambitious documentary entitled *The Native Americans* (1994). This six-hour special aggressively attacked the racial legacy in America since the Age of Discovery; it is a noble effort for which Turner deserves praise. On the other hand, in 1993, television viewers were regaled with pictures of Ted Turner and his athletic wife doing "the Tomahawk chop" for the Atlanta Braves, a demeaning gesture that some advocates protested. This is the same man who presented the made-for-TV *Geronimo* and *Broken Chain*. The Turner example is an updating of the paradox O'Connor identifies, further complicating our notion of how Hollywood and the larger media culture use, refine, and rewrite the Native American story and image for mass consumption. Finally, the Turner broadcast empire shows more cowboy-and-Indian shoot-'em-ups than any other media conglomerate. These contrasts in imagery point to the need for a business and institutional approach to image development, an approach begun by O'Connor in 1980, but one that later researchers have not pursued sufficiently.

The United States is not the only market for Westerns or the only country that fantasizes about its native peoples. Hannu Salmi is a teacher of history at the University of Turku in Finland who has speculated on the international popularity of the movie Western. His essay on "The Indian of the North" reminds us that Native Americans always have been part of a worldwide population of indigenous peoples encroached upon by an expanding European civilization. In the process, these "backward" people became the objects of fable and fantasy.

Salmi is one of the few authors in this collection to invoke the name of Frederick Jackson Turner, the apparently forgotten titan of "frontier studies" who, in 1893, made his announcement that the frontier had finally closed and that a phase of the American cultural life and character had ended. From Salmi's Finnish film analysis emerges a fascinating parallel between east–west cultural contrasts in the United States and south–north tensions in Finland. Evidently, Finland's South can be seen as a parallel to America's "civilized" East, whereas northern life is perceived as closer to nature. Because the Lapp peoples appear to live where there is more freedom, more honesty, they have become overladen with cultural

Figure I.3. Even the historical record can confuse: Geronimo at the wheel? Courtesy of the Archives and Manuscripts Division, Oklahoma Historical Society.

projections by Finland's moviemakers and their audiences. Salmi concludes, "As there is an ideal West in American cinema, there is an ideal North in the Finnish mind and film, the Wild North which is a sort of unattainable happy milieu for the modern nervous citizen."

Frederick Jackson Turner's approach to American history took root during the 1920s, a time when Americans were looking for alternative lifestyles. The "lost generation" explored aesthetic frontiers in Paris; "new women" explored professional and sexual frontiers; and even Sinclair Lewis's American prototype, George Babbitt, flirted briefly with a bohemian alternative to Zenith's bourgeois lifestyle. Such pervasive discontent with Establishment culture fostered sympathy for alternative visions. Yet an epic contemporary film about the collision between Indian and white cultures, *The Vanishing American* (1925), drew pessimistic conclusions about the future of a people, once free, denied their birthright as Americans even after valiant military service during World War I. Although the movie attempted to be sympathetic toward the Indian, its Social Darwinian assumptions predicated a "struggle for existence" and a (bogus) theory of racial evolution that would doom the Indian to extinction. The ideology of the day made it impossible for even those sympathetic to envision constructive alternatives for the future. As Michael Riley (Roswell Museum, New Mexico) concludes, Native Americans are not only trapped by history, "but are forever trapped in the history of film."

The Vanishing American was only the beginning of a series of confusing messages from Hollywood.

For millions of viewers, John Ford is synonymous with the Western genre—along with his favorite actor, John Wayne. Ken Nolley (Willamette University) examines the career of John Ford in relation to the American West. Ford would be the first to defend his portrait of the Native American, but Nolley finds the legendary director's artistic record to be entangled in Hollywood traditions. Fortunately, Ford's later films made a serious effort to transcend Hollywood imagery—indeed, to condemn the tragic heritage of America's racial stereotypes.

Westward expansion involved a deadly culture war. Frank Manchel (University of Vermont) explores a fundamental clash in world views between Euro-Americans and Native Americans: our pioneers saw the West as empty and the Native Americans as obstacles to their Manifest Destiny, whereas Native Americans lacked a sense of "real" property that might have protected their claims to the putatively "open" lands of what was known as Indian Territory. By focusing on Delmer Daves's *Broken Arrow* (1950), Manchel highlights the conflict between the colliding cultures—not only during the nineteenth-century period of initial contact but as remembered by our celluloid history. The use of "historical inaccuracies" as clues to the distortion of vision is especially valuable in this test case, as is Manchel's discussion of specific scenes in the film to prove his broader arguments. *Broken Arrow* has previously been identified as a progressive step in the treatment of Native Americans in film; Manchel questions the conventional wisdom.

John A. Sandos (University of Redlands) has used the novel (1960) and film (1969) versions of *Tell Them Willie Boy Is Here* to study what he and his colleague Larry E. Burgess call "Indian-hating in popular culture." It is their hope that a case-study approach will convince filmmakers that there is drama and style in an authentic Native American perspective. The storytelling art of the Native American would be, in their eyes, a refreshing and innovative approach to the West's real story, tapping new cultural conventions and providing an opportunity for Hollywood to "discard the conventional mask it has shown toward Native Americans and craft a commercial film that truly mirrors an American society with Indians in it." Unfortunately, there must be audiences ready to appreciate such work and lending institutions motivated to exploit the commercial potential before such a desirable shift in perspectives can happen. The Sandos and Burgess study is a good beginning, providing filmmakers—perhaps even Robert Redford and his Sundance Films—with both a basic narrative and a fresh philosophical orientation.

Margo Kasdan (San Francisco State University) and Susan Tavernetti (De Anza College) have gone back to *Little Big Man* (1970) and reconsidered its treatment of Native Americans. Kasdan and Tavernetti find severe limits to the film's generosity—that, in fact, the film perpetuates negative images just when it attempts to transcend stereotypes. Yet, seen from a distance of time, the film scholars applaud *Little Big Man* for making some progress. When *Dances With Wolves* appeared, exultant reviewers seemed to have forgotten this wonderful film by Arthur Penn (starring a young Dustin Hoffman); yet it is hard to believe that the Kevin Costner blockbuster could have been made until after the successful "demystification" efforts of Penn's parody.

Growing up in Oklahoma can foster a special perspective on the Native American experience. Robert Baird (University of Illinois), of mixed Native American and European ancestry, is an Oklahoma-born film scholar with Hollywood experience. From 1984 to 1986, he worked as a post-production editor on fourteen films, including Cannon Films' *Breakin'* and *Delta Force* and Alan Rudolph's independent feature *Trouble in Mind*. Baird brings special insights to bear in his sophisticated study of *Dances With Wolves*.

Ted Jojola believes that *Powwow Highway* "came closest to revealing the 'modern' Indian-self" of any contemporary film. Yet the movie failed at the box office; later, it gained popularity as a favorite video rental, building an underground audience among Native Americans. In his interpretive essay, Eric Gary Anderson (Oklahoma State University) savors both the sense of seriousness and play that characterize the film—a mixed bag of cultural statement, parody, and adventure. *Powwow Highway* is unusual because it adopts the perspective of the Native American in ways that can nonetheless reach a white audience: "Part western, part picaresque road film, part buddy movie, part comedy, part action (or adventure) film, and part repository of American popular culture image and allusions, *Powwow Highway* Americanizes Native Americans and Native Americanizes the movies, while at the same time respecting the sacred traditions of both the Hollywood Western and the Cheyenne Indians." Little wonder that, despite its limitations, this creative and playful production is so popular with Native Americans—especially younger viewers.

Some scholars trace the image of the Native American back to the many, long (some would say tedious) novels of James Fenimore Cooper. Most middle-aged American Studies scholars cut their teeth on Henry Nash Smith's landmark book *Virgin Land* (1950), where Cooper is considered in great detail as a purveyor of the "myth" of the American West. (For strangers to the book, it should be noted that Smith did not use the

Figure I.4. Nostalgia within nostalgia: the 1936 version yielded
adventure for 10 cents. Courtesy of the Archives and Manuscripts
Division, Oklahoma Historical Society.

word "myth" in a pejorative sense.) For this collection, Jeffrey Walker
(Oklahoma State University) examines the details of Cooper's vision of
the West as found in the literary and cinematic renderings of *The Last of
the Mohicans* (1826/1992). Walker found that the press kit for the 1992
film version touts the production as a work of reverence. Director Michael
Mann claims that *"The Last of the Mohicans* is probably the first film I
saw as a child. It was a black-and-white, 16mm print, and I must have
been three or four—it's the first sense memory I have of a motion picture." (Mann here refers to the Randolph Scott version of 1936.) Walker
takes the position that Mann should have spent less time indulging his
childhood memories and more time reading Cooper's literary classic. Yet
Walker finds not only the recent cinematic version of *The Last of the
Mohicans* to be lacking, but that all Hollywood treatments of this classic
frontier novel—each in its own way—have violated Cooper's plot, characterization, and world view. As early as 1920, Hollywood was imposing
its vision of "entertainment" on the American classic. Michael Mann's
rendering in 1992 is particularly vexing to the Cooper scholar; Walker
notes with exasperation that "of all the many revisions of Cooper's novel
. . . Mann's decision to turn *The Last of the Mohicans* primarily into a love
story and to ignore the essence of the Native-American theme is the strangest and most damaging plot twist of all . . . [and misses] the essential
theme and flavor of Cooper's classic tale." As often happens in the history
of filmmaking, enormous resources have been wasted in a production

Figure I.5. Cooper's or Mann's epic? Daniel Day-Lewis as Hawk-eye in *The Last of the Mohicans*. Courtesy of the Museum of Modern Art/Film Stills Archive.

that could have both popularized a classic American novel and helped us to understand the cultural conflicts on the frontier during America's colonial era.

In 1995, two major films for children featured Hollywood Indians. Disney's *Pocahontas* and Columbia's *The Indian in the Cupboard* were both moneymakers and spawned many spinoff products, which inspired Pauline Turner Strong (University of Texas-Austin) to consider both the images presented and the spinoff "commodification" in dolls, games, and a fascinating CD-ROM. Many of the derivative objects and softwares are well-meaning, but, Strong warns, "destabilizing stereotypes is tricky, as others easily rush in to fill the void." For example, on the surface, the *Pocahontas* song "Colors of the Wind" is innocuous, perhaps even helpful, in its promotion of empathy for nature. Yet Strong is concerned by other messages from the film: "what is the exotic, sensual, copyrighted Pocahontas if not the mascot for a feminine, earthy, conciliatory New Age spirituality?" As in so many cases throughout the Hollywood Indian's history, filmmakers have rediscovered their own "lost innocence" vicariously through another Hollywood Indian. Both *The Indian in the Cupboard* and *Pocahontas* suffer from the chokehold of Hollywood aesthetic constraints. Strong concludes, "They are rife with tensions and ironies exemplifying the limitations of serious cultural critique in an artistic environment devoted to the marketing of dreams."

What do we know at this stage about the Hollywood Indian? Please tread the trails to new horizons of scholarship suggested in the pages to follow. Each essay moves out in a different direction, but—taken collectively—they suggest deeper insights into a vital part of our cultural heritage. Whether we condemn the Disney version, ignore the *Reader's Digest* special offer, or applaud or deplore Ted Turner's series *The Native Americans*, clearly our understanding of the connections between the Hollywood Indian and the true heritage of Native Americans is a scholarly frontier worthy of exploration. Film and television have inscribed our nation's memory with so many misconceptions. We hope that media scholarship, followed by critical viewing and discussion in our classrooms, will lead to a more humane future for us all.

Absurd Reality II
Hollywood Goes to the Indians

When McMurphy, the character portrayed by actor Jack Nicholson in the fivefold Oscar-winning movie *One Flew Over the Cuckoo's Nest* (1975), prods a mute Indian Chief (played by Indian actor Will Sampson) into pronouncing "ahh juicyfruit," what the audience heard was far removed from the stereotypical "hows," "ughs," and "kemosabes" of tinsel moviedom. "Well goddamn, Chief," counters McMurphy. "And they all think you're deaf and dumb. Jesus Christ, you fooled them Chief, you fooled them. . . . You fooled 'em all!" In that simple and fleeting scene, a new generation of hope and anticipation was heralded among Native American moviegoers. Long the downtrodden victims of escapist shoot-'em-and bang-'em-up Westerns, Native Americans were ready for a new cinematic treatment—one that was real and contemporary.

Native Americans had grown accustomed to the film tradition of warpaint and warbonnets. When inventor Thomas Alva Edison premiered the kinetoscope at the 1893 Chicago Columbian World's Exposition by showing the exotic *Hopi Snake Dance*, few would have predicted that this kind of depiction would persist into contemporary times. Its longevity, though, is explained by the persistence of myth and symbol. The Indian became a genuine American symbol whose distorted origins are attributed to the folklore of Christopher Columbus when he "discovered" the "New World." Since then the film industry, or Hollywood, has never allowed Native America to forget it.

The Hollywood Indian is a mythological being who exists nowhere but within the fertile imaginations of its movie actors, producers, and directors. The preponderance of such movie images have reduced native people to ignoble stereotypes. From the novel, to the curious, to the exotic, image after image languished deeper and deeper into a Technicolor sunset. By the time of the 1950s John Wayne B-Westerns, such images droned into the native psyche. The only remedy from such images was a laughter, for these portrayals were too surreal and too removed from the reservation or urban Indian experience to be taken seriously.

In the face of the exotic and primitive, non-Indians had drawn on their own preconceptions and experiences to appropriate selectively elements of the Indian. The consequent image was a subjective interpretation, the purpose of which was to corroborate the outsider's viewpoint. This process is called revisionism, and it, more often than not, entails recasting native people away and apart from their own social and community realities. In an ironic turnabout, Native people eventually began to act and behave like their movie counterparts, often in order to gain a meager subsistence from the tourist trade. In that sense, they were reduced to mere props for commercial gain.

However, beginning in 1968, with the establishment of the American Indian Movement (AIM), much of this misrepresentation was to change. The occupation of Alcatraz Prison in 1969, of the Bureau of Indian Affairs headquarters in 1972, and of Wounded Knee in 1973 followed in rapid succession. These were bloody struggles that many Native Americans consider to be every bit as profound as the political dissolution of the Soviet Union or the dismantling of the Berlin Wall. They served to bring the attention of the modern Native's plight to mainstream America.

Such activism did not escape the big screen. Hollywood scriptwriters jumped onto the bandwagon with such epics as *Tell Them Willie Boy Is Here* (1969), *Soldier Blue* (1970), *A Man Called Horse* (1970), *Little Big Man* (1970), *Return of a Man Called Horse* (1976), and *Triumphs of a Man Called Horse* (1982). *Little Big Man* in fact, established a milestone in Hollywood cinema as the result of its three-dimensional character portrayal of Sioux people. This included what is perhaps one of the finest acting roles ever done by an Indian actor, Dan George, who portrayed Old Lodge Skins.

Indian activism, however, was subtly transformed toward unmitigated militancy with the production of Vietnam War–based movies. Movies such as *Flap, or Nobody Loves a Drunken Indian* (1970), *Journey Through Rosebud* (1972), *Billy Jack* (1971), *The Trial of Billy Jack* (1974), and *Billy Jack Goes to Washington* (1977) revised the message of Indian activism to an even more bizarre level. Native Americans were portrayed as ex-Vietnam veterans whose anti-American behavior despoiled their common sense. Herein was the ultimate blend of aboriginal nitro and glycerin.

The first premonition of "Red Power" decay came shortly after actor Marlon Brando set up a cameo for the Apache urban-Indian actress Sacheen Little Feather as the stand-in for his rejection of the 1973 Best Actor Academy Award for *The Godfather*. Later in 1973 "Ms. Littlefeather," as she was called, earned herself even more notoriety as the Pocahontas-in-the-buff activist in a nude October spread in *Playboy*. Within the context of puritanical America, this unfortunate feature became the ultimate form of image denigration.

Around this time, the famous "Keep America Beautiful" teary Indian (Cherokee actor Iron Eyes Cody) and the Mazola Margarine corn maiden (Chiricahua Apache actress Tenaya Torrez) commercials were being run on television. These stereotyped images and their environmental messages etched themselves indelibly into the minds of millions of householders. The "trashless wilderness" and "corn, or what us Indians call maize" became the forerunners of the New Age ecology movement.

Because such imagery was so heavily invested in American popular culture, gifted Native actors like the Creek Will Sampson (1935–1988) and Salish Chief Dan George (1899–1982) continued to be relegated to second billings in films like *The Outlaw Josey Wales* (1976, also starring Navajo actress Geraldine Keams), and *Buffalo Bill and the Indians, or Sitting Bull's History Lesson* (1976). The same fate befell others like Mohawk actor Jay Silverheels (1912–1980), who was widely recognized as Tonto in *The Lone Ranger* and who went on in 1979 to be the first Native actor awarded a star on the Hollywood Walk of Fame.

In spite of these shortfalls, the Native presence was posed for a major, albeit short-lived, breakthrough in the film industry. The Indian Actor's Workshop was begun in the early 1960s and was followed in turn by the establishment of the American Indian Registry for the Performing Arts in the 1980s. Both organizations were committed to promoting Native actors in Native roles. This momentum, which came as a result of advocacy among the ranks of senior Native actors, slowed to a lumbering pace with the untimely deaths of Sampson, George, and Silverheels. It left an enormous vacuum within the professional ranks of the Screen Actors Guild.

So, in spite of Hollywood's attempts to "correct the record," the movies of this period all basically had one thing in common—"Indians" in the leading role were played by non-Indians. A few films like *House Made of Dawn* (1987, starring Pueblo actor Larry Littlebird), *When the Legends Die* (1972, featuring "the Ute tribe"), and *The White Dawn* (1975, featuring "the Eskimo People") attempted to turn the tide. Unfortunately, the films earned the most meager of receipts. This in turn guaranteed that a movie cast by and about Native Americans was a losing investment. Producers and directors continued to seek the box-office appeal of "name recognition" instead. When the casting really mattered—as in the film *Running Brave* (1983, starring Robby Benson), which was about the life of the Sioux sprinter Billy Mills, a 1964 Tokyo Olympic gold metalist—non-Indians continued to preempt Indian actors. Ditto for *Windwalker* (1980), whose lead Indian part was preempted by a British actor, Trevor Howard.

The absurdity of casting non-Indians reached its pinnacle in the mid-1980s. In the opening sequence of *The Legend of Walks Far Woman* (1984), a legendary Sioux woman warrior, Walks Far Woman—played by buxom Raquel Welch—plummets over a hundred-foot precipice and stands up looking rather ridiculous and totally unscathed. In *Outrageous Fortune* (1987), actor George Carlin continues the brainless tradition by playing a hippie Indian scout. "That's my main gig," exclaims Carlin as he badgers actresses Bette Midler and Shelley Long,—"genuine Indian shit. . . . "

By the early 1990s, that "genuine Indian shit" had come full circle. What should have happened, a sequel to *Cuckoo's Nest*—a full-featured realistic and contemporary performance about and by an Indian—occurred with *Powwow Highway* (1989). Given an unexpected second life as a rental video, the acting of a then-unknown Mohawk Indian actor, Gary Farmer, came closest to revealing the "modern" Indian-self, much in the same light that Indian producer Bob Hicks attempted to pioneer in *Return to the Country* (1982). Yet although Farmer, as Philbert Bono, is believable to Indians and non-Indians alike, he is still cast as a sidekick to the main actor, A. Martinez. In this film a Vietnam vet, Buddy Red Bow, trails through a cultural and spiritual reawakening while Bono is reduced to a kind of bankrupt Indian trickster. The problem with *Powwow Highway* is that it suffered from a predictable activist storyline that froze solid sometime in the early 1970s. In spite of this flaw, Hollywood was suddenly enamored of the novelty of the multicultural drumbeat—Indians played by Indians.

Another variation on this Hollywood multicultural love affair was *Thunderheart* (1992, starring Oneida actor Graham Greene). Although technically superior to another B-movie, *Journey Through Rosebud* (1972), it managed to rehash a basic plot of the naive half-breed who stumbles upon reservation graft and corruption. But the original conception of this ploy had already been hatched in *Tell Them Willie Boy Is Here* (1969). In that film, a Paiute Indian returns to the reservation to expose the evil machinations of the non-Indian agent.

In *Thunderheart*, the plot is updated so that the blame is shifted to corrupt tribal government officials. Its screenplay was loosely based on the real-life murder of a Native activist, Anna Mae Aquash (played by Sheila Tousey, a Menominee of the Stockbridge and Munsee tribes). In spite of its casting achievement, the film nonetheless went on to demonstrate

Figure 1.1. Sex symbol (Raquel Welch) as Indian: Non-Natives pitched to white audiences? Courtesy of the Museum of Modern Art/Film Stills Archive.

that a non-Native actor cast as a "wannabe" can still walk away completely unscathed from an unpalatable and unresolvable situation.

But the finest example of this wannabe syndrome, as well as being one of the premier reincarnation film of all times, is *Dances With Wolves.* Winner of seven Academy Awards, including Best Picture for 1990, the story is a remarkable clone of *Little Big Man* (1970). Both films used the backdrop of the historic Lakota and Cheyenne wars. Both typecast the Lakota and Cheyenne as hero tribes, victimized by their common arch-enemies, the U.S. Cavalry, and "those damn Pawnees!" However, unlike *Little Big Man*, which reveled in its pointed anti-Vietnam War message, *Dances With Wolves* was devoid of any redeeming social merits. Rather, it was apolitical and subconsciously plied its appeal by professing a simple New Age homily about peace and Mother Earth.

Nonetheless, as a result of its box-office appeal, *Dances With Wolves* accomplished what few other Western films have done. It ushered forth a new wave of Indian sympathy films and unleashed another dose of Indian hysteria among revisionist historians. For example, films like *War Party* (1990) and *Clearcut* (1991) attempted to place the Indian into a contemporary framework. But unlike *Powwow Highway*, the plots of these films were as surreal and bizarre as a Salvador Dali painting. Rather, both films were, more or less, classic in the manner in which they were depicted as psychodramas. Native actors finally got to act out unabashed their colonially induced angst, although that depiction still gets mixed reviews even among Native moviegoers.

Not to be left out, the TV industry also attempted to remake bestselling novels into prime-time movies. ABC-TV's *The Son of the Morning Star* debuted to uninspired TV viewers in 1991. *Lonesome Dove* (1991) fared a little better, and there was great anticipation for the made-for-TV screen adaptation of Modoc writer Michael Dorris's *The Broken Cord* (1992). Unfortunately, TV producers preempted Native actors with non-Indian actors and, as a consequence, the staged overall effect remained dull and staid.

The most contentious example of a non-Native production was yet to come. It occurred in the screenplay adaptation of mystery novelist Tony Hillerman's *Dark Wind* (1992). Non-Native actor Lou Diamond Phillips was cast as the central character, Navajo policeman Chee, while the six-foot-plus Gary Farmer was miscast as a five-foot-tall, more or less, Hopi policeman. Both the odd combination of actors and the spiritually offensive aspects of the storyline resulted in official protests being lodged by both the Navajo and Hopi tribal governments. Fearing legal reprisal, its makers pulled the film out of the American market and floated it among the die-hard, Karl May-reared moviegoers of Europe instead.

But it was now 1992, and this quincentennial celebration was supposed to be a banner year for indigenous peoples. The reality of political correctness, however, turned it into a categorical revisionist bust instead. Neither of the celebratory films *1492* nor *Christopher Columbus: The*

Discovery broke any box-office records or changed any minds about Native people. In fact, if it proved anything, it really did reinforce the old adage that immortal gods don't shit from the sky. Even though attempts were made to draw moviegoers to the exotic pull of the undiscovered New World, the mind's eye proved far more compelling.

Hollywood continued to remain mired in mythmaking. If any strides were to be had, they usually resulted from the work of a few well-placed Native consultants. In this manner, Native playwrights and cultural experts were finally given the opportunity to add a tribal precision and to insert snippets of real Native languages, rather than the usual made-up ones.

The Black Robe (1991) was one of the first representatives of such an attempt. A story about a Jesuit missionary among the warring Huron, Algonquin, and Iroquois tribes, it attempted to debunk the idea that all Native people lived among one another in blissful harmony. Its mistake, though, was to depict a contemporary pan-Indian powwow in 1634 and to insinuate that the only kind of Indian sex was doggie-style intercourse. Another film inspired by Native consultants was the forgettable *Geronimo: An American Hero* (1993). The portrayal of Geronimo by Wes Studi attempted to revamp the warring Apache into a gentler and kinder mystic chief. But the fact of the matter is that because Geronimo has been cast in so many fierce roles, everyone has genuinely forgotten how to deal with the humanization of such a legend. In spite of all their efforts, Geronimo remains, well, Geronimo. ABC-TV's own cartoon rendition of Geronimoo in the *Cowboys of Moo Mesa* was far more interesting and honest.

The most intriguing effort of this cycle, however, was the *The Last of the Mohicans* (1992). This film was a fusion of fact and fiction. The fact was supplied by Native consultants, the fiction by James Fenimore Cooper. At the symbolic center of this film was American Indian Movement activist Russell Means. Means was cast as Chingachgook, a marathon-running sidekick of Hawk-eye, played by non-Indian Daniel Day-Lewis. Although Cherokee actor Wes Studi, playing the Huron villain Magua, ultimately stole the show, the cooptation of a militant AIM founder was the cinematic milestone.

Means's presence resounded with the same activist overtones found in his predecessor, Sacheen Little Feather, a full two decades earlier. Both came to uncertain terms with Hollywood and both were hopelessly seduced by its power. Means followed his debut by playing a Navajo medicine man in *Natural Born Killers* (1994)—prompting some Navajo people to perform curing ceremonies to exorcise the offensive imagery—and, in 1995, Means lent his voice to Chief Powhatan in the animated Disney production of *Pocahontas*. Although it was deeply flawed, Means nevertheless proclaimed *Pocahontas* to be "the finest movie ever made about Indians in Hollywood."

Accolades also continue to be garnered for docudramas produced by independent cable channels like the Discovery Channel and Turner Broadcasting System. Productions like *How the West Was Lost* (1993), *The Native Americans: Behind the Legends, Beyond the Myths* (1994), *The Broken Chain* (1994) and *Lakota Woman* (1995) graced the airwaves. They allowed playwrights like Hanay Geiogamah (Kiowa) and emerging native actors such as Tantoo Cardinal (Cree), Rodney Grant (Winnebago) and Floyd Westerman (Dakota) to have their fifteen minutes of fame.

Nonetheless, the most interesting storylines went largely unnoticed. Ironically, a far more honest portrayal, and one that really came to grips with what the popular image of Indians is all about, is in the *Addams Family Values* (1993). Although never acknowledged as such, this film comes closer to exposing the psyche of Indian Hollywood than most of the so-called "authentic" Indian portrayals. Wednesday, played by Christina Ricci, turns the role of Pocahontas upside down. In her poignant diatribe during the summer-camp Thanksgiving pageant, she exposes the hypocrisy and racism of America in a matter of a few fleeting snippets, something that most Indian sympathy movies fail to do in an hour and a half.

The biggest sleeper, though, was a 1995 film, *The Indian in the Cupboard* (starring another previously unknown Cherokee actor, Litefoot). Disdained by the Pulitzer Prize-winning film critic Roger Ebert for its lack of "entertainment" value, the film successfully explored the deconstruction of the cowboy-and-Indian myth from the naive perspective of two skeptical, adolescent boys. That dialog rightly belonged to non-Indians. In that sense, the film exhibited far more integrity than the trite children's book on which the screenplay was remotely based.

The only glimmer of a true Native presence comes in the form of TV serials. CBS's *Northern Exposure* set the scene for casting a few fleeting cameos, as Native actors were allowed to portray themselves as genuine contemporaries. The presence of another self-made Native actress, Elaine Miles, gave a distinctive sensibility in contrast to the machinations of an otherwise Anglo and neurotic Alaskan community. Her unchanging, stoic delivery, though, eventually began to wear as thin as the tundra. And any advances made by *Northern Exposure* were summarily undone by CBS's other TV serial, *Dr. Quinn, Medicine Woman*—an awful, awful apologist's series done in a historical revisionist tradition. Far more interesting, but unfortunately unavailable to American audiences, was a Canadian TV serial called *North of 60*. Native actors and Native writers collaborated with the

Figure 1.2. Dr. Quinn (Jane Seymour), medicine woman, with Sully (Joe Lando), friend of Cloud Dancing. Courtesy of the Museum of Modern Art/Film Stills Archive.

Canadian Broadcast Corporation to produce this series, set in the Northwest Territory of Canada, which dissected the sociological ins and outs of a small Native woodlands community. Central to the theme was a real-live staging of the escalating interpersonal relationships of Native and non-Native alike.

But the indictment of American television, vis-à-vis our enlightened northern neighbor, is no more evident than the *Star Trek* series and its various spin-offs. For example, in a special episode of *Star Trek: The Next Generation* entitled "Journey's End" (1994), Native actor Tom Jackson of *North of 60* fame is recast as the space-age shaman of a futuristic Taos Pueblo space colony. Throughout this episode he is adorned with Taiwan Indian beads, becoming the New Age mentor to the rebellious space academy cadet Wesley Crusher. In the final minutes, however, his Native character is summarily dismissed and replaced by the "true" wisdom of an alien time traveler—who, of course, is played by a white actor.

In yet another version, the 1996 season premier episode, "Basics, Part II," of *Star Trek: Voyager*—which cast Chicano actor Robert Beltran as the wannabe Native American space rebel, Chakotay—reveals how Captain Janeway and her crew can be stranded on a Class-M planet and still have the audacity to keep referring to its indigenous inhabitants as "aliens!" Moreover, Chakotay bumbles his way through his "Indianness" by exclaiming in a fit of exasperation, "I must be the only Indian in the world who can't start a fire by rubbing two sticks together." He ultimately transcends his Indian impotence by breaking the "ugh" alien tribe language barrier with Indian signing and saves the day by rescuing poor shipmate Kes, who endures being tossed around like a piece of delicious sex fruit, back and forth, between two virile bucks. It is appropriation at its best—or worst—and demonstrates conclusively that America is neither ready for science-fact nor any other kind of Native fact, for that matter. The idea was already dismissed in the 1989 premier episode of CBS's *Saturday Night with Connie Chung*. A defiant Marlon Brando did not instill a sense of optimism when he lamented his failure to convince Hollywood to produce a film about the darker legacy of United States policies and Indian genocide.

All in all, it appears that another cycle of Indian sympathy films will have to wane before Native America can claim its "own" Hollywood imagery. In reality, very little of what has transpired over this century is groundbreaking. Such invention will only come when a bona fide Native director or producer breaks into the ranks of Hollywood, hopefully to challenge the conventional credos of the industry from within. By happenstance, the first step was taken quietly during the 1992 quincentennial hoopla, when the Native American Producer's Alliance was born. It remains to be seen if its activities will gain fruition in repatriating the Indian image back to a Native one. So long as Native people are assigned roles that are controlled by non-Natives, that image will remain unequal and revisionist.

Filmography

A Man Called Horse. 1970. National General Pictures. Directed by Elliot Silverstein. The first film of a trilogy that depicted the life of an Englishman among his adopted Sioux tribe. Although it was billed as the most accurate movie depiction of Sioux tribal customs, the director filled the screen with fabricated sensational and revolting rituals of the rites of passage. The formula must have worked. The public devoured it in several sequels even before the advent of New Agers.

Addams Family Values. 1993. Paramount. Directed by Barry Sonnenfeld. A zany sequel to the *Addams Family.* The parody of "the first Thanksgiving" at Camp Chippewa is hilariously scripted and poignant at the same time.

Billy Jack. 1971. Warner Brothers. Directed by T.C. Frank (a pseudonym of actor Tom Laughlin). The first film of a trilogy that depicted a karate wielding, half-Indian, Vietnam War hero who takes justice into his own hands in the face of reservation-life adversity. The movie contains one of the best one-liners in the Indian-image business: "We communicate with him Indian-style. When we need him, somehow he's there."

Billy Jack Goes to Washington. 1977. Taylor-Laughlin Distributors. Directed by T.C. Frank. Second sequel to *Billy Jack.*

Black Robe. 1991. Goldwyn. Directed by Bruce Beresford. A historical revisionist movie that attempts to spread the onus of Indian genocide among the Jesuits, smallpox and the warring Algonquin, Huron and Iroquoian tribes. Superb on woodlands architecture; weak on plot.

Broken Cord. 1992. Made for TV. Directed by Ken Olin. Based on the bestselling memoir *The Broken Cord* by Native author Michael Dorris. The story depicts the real-life story of a Fetal Alcohol Syndrome child who was adopted at an early age by the author.

Buffalo Bill and the Indians, or Sitting Bull's History Lesson. 1976. United Artists. Directed by Robert Altman. The story of a film that almost could. Director Altman attempts to weave a complex storyline on one of America's most sensationalistic, albeit banal, showman, William F. Cody. Even historians get lost quickly in this quirky version of circus history.

Christopher Columbus—The Discovery. Warner Bros. 1992. Directed by John Glen. French actor George Corraface attempts to be a wannabe Columbus as Marlon Brando's performance as Torquemada, the inquisitor, sinks like the *Santa Maria.* The best performance is turned in by a pregnant rat that scurries down the anchor rope to swim ashore and colonize the New World.

Clearcut. 1991. Northern Arts. Directed by Richard Bugajski. A brutal film that is evenly divided between its native protagonists and antagonists. Two Native people succeed in manifesting elements of terrorism, emoting from the frustrations of a dejected non-Indian lawyer whose stay to suspend the clearcutting of tribal woodlands is overruled.

Dances With Wolves. 1990. Orion. Directed by Kevin Costner. Winner of seven

Academy Awards, including Best Picture for 1990. Extraordinary cinematography overwhelms what is a mushy, formulaic, romantic plot at best. Lakotas adopt an Anglo, Civil War–decorated soldier into their tribal band. He repays the honor by repatriating an Anglo woman, kidnapped and later adopted by the tribe, from the impending throes of physical and cultural genocide.

Dark Wind. 1992. Carolco Pictures. Directed by Patrick Markey. Based on the Navajo-based action novel by author Tony Hillerman. It was the first, and perhaps the last, attempt to bring to cinema the persona of Navajo policeman Jim Chee. Estranged by the politics of the Hopi/Navajo Land Dispute, the production of the film was controversial among both the Navajo and Hopi tribal governments from the beginning. The plot, frankly, is rather unimaginative and certainly not worth spilling any bureaucratic ink over. It was released only in Europe, although it is available on video in the United States.

Dr. Quinn, Medicine Woman. 1993–. CBS-TV. Follow the machinations of a non-Indian doctor as portrayed in frontier America. Episodes attempt to explore the fragile interrelationships of the townspeople and the Indians. The bigger mystery is who actually watches this series in the first place.

Flap or Nobody Loves a Drunken Indian. 1970. Warner Brothers. Directed by Carol Reed. A dejected Indian, Flapping Eagle, played by actor Anthony Quinn, attempts to find a "place in the sun" for his castaway people. The original title of *Nobody Loves a Drunken Indian* raised howls of protest among Native people in the Southwest for its racist overtones. One of the first Hollywood films to present a pan-Indian theme.

Geronimo: An American Hero. 1993. Columbia. Directed by Walter Hill. Cherokee actor Wes Studi blazes the revisionist saddle as Apache chief Geronimo. The film attempts to switch the stereotyped image of Geronimo as outlaw into a genuine American folk hero. Instead, it accomplishes neither, leaving the viewer to ponder the rest of revisionist American history.

Godfather. 1972. Paramount. Directed by Francis Ford Coppola. Incidental to the Hollywood Indian, but star Marlon Brando used the rejection of his Best Actor Academy award to catapult then little-known Indian actress, Sacheen Little Feather, to notoriety as a *Playboy* Pocahontas.

House Made of Dawn. 1987. Firebird Productions. Independent. Directed by Richardson Morse. Adapted from the Pulitzer Prize-winning novel, *House Made of Dawn*, written by Kiowa novelist N. Scott Momaday. This film comes closest to being a cult film among Indian movie fanatics because of its use of Native backdrops and actors. Produced outside of Hollywood circles and too early for video technology, it saw very limited play and distribution. No Indian filmography, however, is complete without this one.

Indian in the Cupboard. 1995. Kennedy/Marshall Company and Scholastic Productions. Directed by Frank Oz. This film is loosely based on the children's book *The Indian in the Cupboard*, written by Lynne Reid Banks. The book is demeaning to Native culture, but the movie is exceptionally brilliant. The film blurs the lines of distinction between education and entertainment. Its

Internet site was remarkable unto itself and featured real Iroquois people writing about their culture to the non-Native audience.

Journey Through Rosebud. 1971. GSF. Directed by Tom Gries. An itinerant draft dodger meets a Vietnam vet on the Rosebud Indian Reservation. Together they combat graft and corruption in the reservation. One of the first formula films with such a theme.

Last of the Mohicans. 1992. Twentieth Century Fox. Directed by Michael Mann. Based on the early romantic novel *The Last of the Mohicans* by James Fenimore Cooper. Director Mann weaves a tale of romance and revenge during the French and Indian War of 1757. Unfortunately, the efforts to weave historical fact with creative fiction fell somewhat short of a memorable story. The film also premieres AIM activist Russell Means as Chingachgook, an interesting contemporary Indian milestone in itself.

Legend of Walks Far Woman. 1984. Made for TV. The film is focused on the exploits of actress Raquel Welch as the legendary Sioux woman warrior Walks Far Woman. Both the actress and the movie, however, are a mismatch from the beginning. One of those movies that should have never been made.

Little Big Man. 1970. National General. Directed by Arthur Penn. A 121–year-old man relates his life among the Cheyenne tribe. Indian actor Chief Dan George, who plays Old Lodge Skins, is mentioned for an Academy Award. This yarn plays all aspects of the Western myth including one of the most, if not the best, dramatic reenactments of Custer's massacres.

Lonesome Dove. 1991. CBS-TV. Directed by Simon Wincer. This week-long TV miniseries featured the exploits of two ex-Texas Rangers herding cattle from Texas to Montana. Indians were definitely the backdrop along every mile of this arduous and totally forgettable adventure.

Natural Born Killers. 1994. Warner Bros. Directed by Oliver Stone. The film is filled, wall-to-wall, with Route 66 Indian trading-post imagery. One situation is staged around a dances-with-tornado sequence at Shiprock, New Mexico (where, such a phenomena has never been witnessed). But the film is most memorable for the sacrilegious performance by Russell Means as a Navajo medicine man.

North of 60. Canadian Broadcasting Corporation. 1993. Directed by David Lynch. Situated in an isolated northern Canadian community, the series attempts to portray the problems of two cultures, white and Dene, trying to live together. The production features Native actors and writers, a refreshing departure from the U.S. television industry.

Northern Exposure. 1989–95. CBS-TV. A popular weekly that follows the machinations of a urbanite, Jewish doctor stuck in rural Cicely, Alaska. Natives get plenty of bit roles and add tremendously to the ambiance of the setting. Occasionally, a Native-based storyline is developed.

One Flew Over the Cuckoo's Nest. 1975. Fantasy/United Artists. Directed by Milos Forman. Features one of the most important contemporary roles played by an Indian actor. Will Sampson, the mute "Chief," who hasn't spoken for twelve years, becomes the metaphor for hope in an otherwise insane environment of a mental asylum. His depiction finally breaks the Indian stereotype.

Outlaw Josey Wales. 1976. Malpaso/Warner Brothers. Directed by Clint Eastwood. Based on the first novel by Forrest Carter, *The Rebel Outlaw: Josey Wales*. Chief Dan George and Navajo actress Geraldine Keams shine in this story about a farmer turned wrathful avenger.

Outrageous Fortune. 1987. Touchstone Pictures. Directed by Arthur Hiller. A zany comedy chase-adventure that goes nowhere fast. Features elements of Pueblo Indians in the plot. Some of the scenes were filmed in the Pueblo of Isleta, New Mexico. Maybe one of its only redeeming aspects.

Pocahontas. 1995. Disney Productions. Directed by Mike Gabriel and Eric Goldberg. A revisionist history of an American myth. The English Governor Ratcliffe of the ill-fated Virginia Colony is transposed as a gold-hungry Spanish conquistador. Mattel's Ken and Barbie are transposed as John Smith and Pocahontas. Activist Russell Means is the voice of a wannabe Chief Powhatan. A serious omission is the lack of the standard film disclaimer that all characters and their resemblance are fiction.

Powwow Highway. 1989. Warner Brothers. Directed by Jonathan Wacks. A sleeper B-film that catches almost every critic off guard. Features the debut of then unknown Mohawk Indian actor Gary Farmer in an acclaimed contemporary Indian role. Unfortunately, the plot focusing on the machinations of an Indian Vietnam vet seeking justice is caught in an irrevocable time-warp.

Return of a Man Called Horse. 1976. United Artists. Directed by Irvin Kershner. Sequel to *A Man Called Horse*.

Return to the Country. 1982. Independent. Directed by Bob Hicks. The only example of a wide-screen 35mm film produced by an Indian director. This short treatment parodies the Bureau of "White" Affairs. It's the ultimate fantasy film for Native activists.

Running Brave. 1983. Englander/Buena Vista. Directed by J.S. Everett. Based on the biography of the Sioux 1964 Olympic gold medalist Billy Mills. This had the potential of being a *Rocky*, but fell flat because of the casting.

Saturday Night with Connie Chung. 1989. CBS-TV. Interview between Connie Chung and Marlon Brando. Brando bemoans his failure to get Hollywood to finance a movie about the genocide of Indian people by the United States government.

Soldier Blue. 1970. Avco Embassy. Directed by Ralph Nelson. Adapted from a novel by Theodore V. Olsen describing the massacre of a defenseless village of Cheyenne Indians by forces under the command of Colonel Chivington in 1864. The movie successfully engenders the anti-Vietnam sentiment of that era.

Son of the Morning Star. 1991. ABC-TV. Directed by Mike Robe. A made-for-TV drama based on the fictionalized historical study *Son of Morning Star: Custer and the Little Bighorn*, by Evan S. Connell. The series attempts to paint a factual, first-hand account of the life of George Armstrong Custer but fails because of its own storytelling and mythmaking.

Star Trek: The Next Generation. "Journey's End." 1994. NBC-TV. In this New Agey episode, a space cadet is mentored by a tribal shaman, played by Native actor Tom Jackson. The novelty here is that a futuristic space colony, dubbed Taos (after the centuries-old Earth village, Taos Pueblo, New Mexico), still has Indians wearing braids and made-in-Taiwan jewelry.

Star Trek: Voyager. "Basics Part II." 1996. FOX-TV. Another of the knock-off series spawned from the prolific *Star Trek* seed, this particular episode successfully captures the worst elements of native image appropriation. Chakotay, the wannabe Indian, touts his ethnic "stuff" by rescuing a Ramona-esque Kes and the *Voyager* crew from a tribe of primitive "aliens."

Tell Them Willie Boy Is Here. 1969. Universal. Directed by Abraham Polonsky. One of the first movies to attempt to present Indian reservation graft and corruption in a more or less contemporary manner. The plot serves to establish a formula of the returning Indian-turned-renegade, which will be repeated oft after.

Thunderheart. 1992. TriStar. Directed by Michael Apted. Loosely based on the tragedy of Native activist Anna Mae Aquash, the film resurrects the plot of the urban Indian who returns to his reservation. There he unravels corruption among the infamous tribal chairman's goon squad and learns enough about his cultural values to escape from it for good.

Trial of Billy Jack. 1974. Taylor-Laughlin Distributors. Directed by T.C. Frank. The sequel to *Billy Jack.*

Triumphs of a Man Called Horse. 1982. Redwing–Transpacific Media–Hesperia/Jensen Farley. Directed by John Hough. Third and final remake, thank goodness, of *A Man Called Horse.*

War Party. 1990. Hemdale. Directed by Franc Roddam. A staged reenactment of an Indian war party at a county fair goes awry. Someone loaded real bullets instead of blanks. But wait—the plot gets more ethereal as the white community attempts to avenge the deaths caused by the unwary Indian actors by mounting an old-fashioned posse. It's déjà vu, Indian style, as the posse pursues its hapless fugitives.

When the Legends Die. 1972. Sagaponack/Fox. Directed by Stuart Millar. An orphaned fourteen-year-old Indian boy is educated as he competes in the Indian rodeo circuit. A basic human-interest story that was filmed with the cooperation of the Ute tribe.

White Dawn. 1975. Paramount. Directed by Philip Kaufman. Based on a historical incident, the movie relates the story of three nineteenth-century sailors who were separated from their whaling ship. They are adopted by an Eskimo clan from Baffin Island who soon grow weary of their insatiable demands. Not a film with a happy ending, and one that has not received adequate recognition for its extensive use of Eskimo dialog.

Windwalker. 1980. Pacific International. Directed by Thomas E. Ballard. A copycat film that glorifies yet another Indian legend. This film billed itself as the most authentic Indian-legend movie ever made. And it even uses the Cheyenne and Crow languages with subtitles to add legitimacy to this hollow boast.

The White Man's Indian

An Institutional Approach

The most obvious explanation for the Native American's Hollywood image is that the producers, directors, screenwriters, and everyone else associated with the movie industry have inherited a long intellectual and artistic tradition. The perceptions that Europeans and Americans have had of the Native American were both emotional and contradictory. Either an enemy or a friend, he was never an ordinary human being accepted on his own terms. As Robert Berkhofer explains in his book *The White Man's Indian: Images of the American Indian from Columbus to the Present* (1977), the dominant view of the Indians has reflected primarily what the white man thought of himself.

As the positive concept of the "Noble Savage" took shape, especially in eighteenth-century France, it was conceived as evidence to support the arguments of Enlightenment philosophers like Rousseau. Paris-bound thinkers believed that people would be better off as children of nature, free of the prejudices and conventions imposed by such established European institutions as the monarchy and the church. The negative view of many of the captivity narratives common in the literature of the New England Puritans proved to the faithful that the forces of the Devil were alive and at work in the dark forests of America. Berkhofer argues that from the first contacts of the European explorers, white men tended to generalize about Indians rather than discriminate among individual tribes, to describe Indians primarily in terms of how they differed from whites, and to incorporate strict moral judgments in their descriptions of Indian life. This judgmental approach has proved true in prose, painting, and documentary photography—in every art form that chose the Indian as its subject, including film. Consider, for example, the characteristic view of the Indians' relationship to the land. The view that the Indian impeded progress because he lacked the ambition and "good sense" the whites used in developing the American landscape has prevailed throughout our history. Movies and television, the popular art forms of today, continue to present images of Native Americans that speak more about the current interests of the dominant culture than they do about the Indians.

As war clouds rose overseas in the late 1930s and early 1940s and the dominant American culture sought to reaffirm its traditional patriotic values, the negative stereotype of the Indian (a traditional enemy) served a broader purpose in films such as *Drums Along the Mohawk* (1939) and *They Died With Their Boots On* (1941). Thirty years later, with America embroiled in a different kind of war—and millions of its citizens challenging the government's policies—the movies reflected its divided consciousness. In films of the 1960s and 1970s like *Tell Them Willie Boy Is Here* (1969) and *Little Big Man* (1970), Berkhofer perceives that "the Indian became a mere substitute for the oppressed black or hippie white youth alienated from the modern mainstream of American society".

One must take care, however, in drawing generalizations. Even with the gradual shift in public interests and values, certain plot formulas have persisted. The Indian raids, for example, on the stagecoach (*Orphans of the Plains* [1912], *Stagecoach* [1939], *Dakota Incident* [1956]), on the wagon train (*Covered Wagon* [1923], *Wagon Wheels* [1934], *Wagonmaster* [1950]), on the heralds of technological progress (*Iron Horse* [1924], *Union Pacific* [1939], *Western Union* [1941]), and on the peaceful frontier homestead (*The Heritage of the Desert* [1924], *The Searchers* [1956], *Ulzana's Raid* [1972]) have changed little. There have been cycles of Indian pictures such as the string of sympathetic films that followed *Broken Arrow* (1950), but at times a romanticized, even glorified, image could coexist with the vicious one. In 1936, for example, when most screen Indians were the essence of cruelest savagery, Twentieth Century-Fox made the fourth screen version of the idyllic Indian drama *Ramona*, starring Loretta Young.

Even in the very early days, when small production companies churned out two-reel westerns weekly for the nickelodeon trade, a patron might leave one movie house where he had just seen a sympathetic—though not necessarily accurate—Indian drama and walk into another theatre where the natives on the screen were totally inhuman. Thomas Ince's *Heart of an Indian* (1912), for example, allowed that some Indians might be sensitive people; but D.W. Griffith's *The Battle at Elderbush Gulch* (1914), though it showed the provocation for battle, presented the Indians as absolute savages—they even wanted to steal Mae Marsh's puppy dogs to kill and eat in a ritual sacrifice. Another common Indian image was the comic one in Western spoofs like Charlie Chase's *Uncovered Wagon* (1920), the Marx Brothers' *Go West!* (1940) and Mel Brooks's *Blazing Saddles* (1974). Over the last ten years a series of film documen-

Figure 2.1. Two children of Nature, Esther LeBarr and White Parker, in *The Daughter of Dawn* (1912). Courtesy of the Oklahoma Historical Society.

taries and docudramas, especially those made for television, have taken strides toward presenting the Indians more on their own terms, but by and large the Hollywood product continues to present the white man's Indian.

The serious scholarship of historians, anthropologists, and other professionals should have helped to dispel the assumptions that tainted the popular concepts of Native Americans. But the conclusions of Helen Hunt Jackson's landmark history *Century of Dishonor* (1881) and such detailed studies of tribal life as those by Steward (1938) and Eggan (1955) were painfully slow in finding their way into school textbooks and into the broader culture.

Filmmakers who perceive the Indians through the distorted lens of the broader culture will invariably produce movies filled with twisted images. However, in spite of a more or less subtle racial bias, Hollywood is presumably not filled with Indian-haters intent on using their power to put down the natives. One need only observe how quickly a director or a studio might switch from portraying a "bloodthirsty" to a "noble savage" if the market seems to call for it. Far from purposeful distortion, significant elements of the Indian image can be explained best through analyzing various technical and business-related production decisions that may never have been considered in terms of their affect on the screen image.

Film is a collaborative art. It requires the creative contributions of dozens of people, who will subtly—sometimes unconsciously—alter the movie's message or the way it is presented. Moreover, although almost any artist would be happy to sell work—to that extent commercial concerns may influence all art—the huge monetary investments necessary to produce a feature film make art and commerce inseparable. If producers, set designers, script writers, cinematographers, directors, and actors want to practice their craft, the films they make must earn a profit. Therefore, the creative process involved in producing a Hollywood movie demands the artistic judgment of a team of professionals and its utmost effort to make the film appeal to the broadest possible audience. The poet, the painter, and (to some extent) the novelist may escape these pressures. In some ways, they complicate the analysis of film art more than the other forms, but they are indispensable to understanding a film's point of view.

To simplify analysis I have grouped some of these production factors into three general areas: dramatic considerations, commercial considerations, and political considerations. These designations are imprecise. Certain elements of filmmaking may fit as well into two or three of the categories, whereas others may not fit easily into any. Such divisions, however, may make the artistic, financial, political and other forces that influence the artistic process easier to understand.

The influence of such production factors is not unique to movies about Native Americans. The three types of considerations figure in the production of every Hollywood film. A similar analysis would be fruitful in studying gangster movies or science fiction films. Of significance in analyzing films about Native Americans is the way in which seemingly unrelated production decisions may have superseded interest in historical accuracy or cultural integrity and how they may have dictated the image of the Indian in particular films.

In many ways, film is a literary form. Like a novel, a play, or any other narrative structure, its purpose is to tell a story. The filmmaker (a composite of all the collaborators), like the novelist and the playwright, must resolve questions of format, structure, and the relationships of characters so that they are comprehensible to the audience. A good filmmaker, like any other artist, will try to solve these problems so that they illuminate some aspect of the human condition. Rather than use words on a page or paints on a palette, the filmmaker works with a complex combination of images projected on a screen, and the demands of this medium influence the dramatic language used to tell the story. This is especially evident in films that have been adapted from another form. *Massacre* (1934) began as a book-length journalistic exposé of the state of Indian affairs in the early 1930s. A well-organized and effective book, it dealt with reservation life, unemployment, inadequate medical care, and other problems. The filmmakers had to create a different structure using fictional characters with whom the audience might identify. Walter Edmunds's novel *Drums Along the Mohawk* was a bestseller in the 1930s. Though some regard it as a classic of historical fiction, the structure did not lend itself to the movies. The story of how the Iroquois "destructives" had terrorized the farmers of the Mohawk Valley year after year was long and episodic. In some ways its drawn-out descriptions of successive attacks must have given the reader a sense of desperation similar to what the colonists must have felt. Moguls at the studio decreed that the film script needed tightening and careful pacing to allow a series of lesser climaxes to lead up to a single major climax that would end the film on a positive note.

Whether told in a book or on film, every story has a point of view. Establishing any point of view, especially a complex one, may be more difficult in film than in print. One reason for this difficulty is that film-making conventions discourage the use of a narrator, preferring that characters develop the plot and point of view through dialog. Only two of the films discussed here use narration. They use it sparingly, and, as the study of the manuscripts at Twentieth Century-Fox indicates, the narration by Tom Jeffords that begins and ends *Broken Arrow* was a device decided on at the last minute. The visual medium lends itself well to describing the landscape or the ambience, but communicating the personality of a character becomes difficult. Without a narrator, the audience's perception of what the characters say and do (and what other characters say about them) is all there is to delineate their personalities. This restriction helps to explain why, even with some narration, Arthur Penn's *Little Big Man* fails to capture the subtle characterization of Old Lodge Skins that Thomas Berger achieves in his novel.

Communicating with images can be more difficult than with words. Images are more open to misinterpretation by the viewer taking in the message on a sensual and emotional level, and at a predetermined rate, in contrast to the basically intellectual, self-paced process of reading a book. Camera angles, composition, lighting, editing, and a host of other factors can influence the viewer's unconscious perception. Imagine how difficult it was to develop characterizations before the innovation of sound. For example, the makers of *The Vanishing American* (1926) had to try to match Zane Grey's skillfully written characterizations working only with pictures and a few subtitles. Of course, even in the silent era the film-maker may have provided a musical score for the theater pianist to play along with the film, or he might have tinted the images on the screen to suggest a mood, as D.W. Griffith did for *America* (1924). But the development of synchronized sound and Technicolor further complicated the process of producing and decoding movies. For example, might the funeral scene in *Massacre* have had a different tone if Hal Wallis had allowed it to be screened with the sounds of weeping and sobbing Indians in the background? In *Drums Along the Mohawk*, would the Indians have seemed so menacing if their painted faces and the farmhouses they set on fire had been filmed in black and white instead of color?

With few exceptions, Indians have come to the screen most often in films about the American West. As Will Wright points out in his *Sixguns and Society: A Structural Study of the Western* (1975), Western films have a mythology and a method all their own. Wright makes it clear that although the Western has several standard plot variations, its popularity with filmmakers (and other artists) over the years depends mainly on the human conflicts involved in life on the critical edge between wilderness and civilization. Whenever this drama allows the full development of an Indian character so that the viewer gets to know him, the film almost always induces some empathy. But little time has been spent in developing the screen personalities of Indians. They become flat characters, relatively nondescript evil forces that help establish an atmosphere of tension within which the cattle ranchers, the townspeople, the stagecoach riders, the outlaws, the sheepherders, the cavalry officers, the schoolmarms, and the barmaids can relate to one another. As another scholar of the Western, John Cawelti, puts it: "The western formula seems to prescribe that the Indian be a part of the setting to a greater extent than he is ever a character in his own right. The reason for this is twofold: to give the Indian a more complex role would increase the moral ambiguity of the story and thereby blur the sharp dramatic conflicts; and, second, if the Indian represented a significant way of life rather than a declining savagery, it would be far more difficult to resolve the story with a reaffirmation of the values of modern society" (p. 38).

Therefore, the demands of dramatic structure and visual communication may have shaped the Indian image in Western movies as much as the traditional myths about which Robert Berkhofer has written. In fact, it seems clear that translation into a visual medium, where characters with complex personalities and subtle motivations are harder to portray than simple good guys and bad guys, accentuated the dichotomy between the bloodthirsty and the noble savage that Berkhofer traced back to the beginnings of the white man's experience in America.

Let us move on to commercial considerations. For the longest time, Hollywood businessmen reasoned that films had to appeal to the broadest possible audience. In some ways this exaggerated the impact of such dramatic considerations as narrative structure and point of view. For a mass audience, for example, the dramatic situations should be straightforward and unconfused. Typically, the audience could easily decide which characters were good and which were evil (white hats or black?). In the studio tradition, "moral ambiguities" were kept to a minimum. (*Devil's Doorway* [1949], a film that played up complex moral questions related to race and prejudice, is a rare exception to an almost ironclad Hollywood rule.)

The same was true for stereotypes of all kinds, particularly for Native Americans. Moviegoers came to expect Indians to be presented in a characteristic way. The designers of Indian movie costumes have generally given little attention to the actual dress of the tribes. Language elements, cultural beliefs, and religious rituals of one tribe have been attributed to others—or, more often, invented on the set. Frequently, Native American actors have been denied roles as Indians in favor of non-Indian actors whom the producers thought "looked better." Not many Americans noticed: where the finer points of Indian culture and history are concerned, moviegoers have never been particularly discriminating.

Especially in Western films, the bloodthirsty, war-crazed Indian has been Hollywood's stock in trade. Something different on the screen might distract the audience from the theme of the film. Distract it too often, and it will not be entertained—and selling entertainment is the name of the game. From time to time the stereotype even had to be reinforced. For *Geronimo* (1939), for example, it was thought that Native American actor Chief Thundercloud would not live up to the public's expectations of a menacing savage. Not only did the makeup artists take on the project of making him look the part, the publicity department prepared a series of photos for the press that showed the transformation.

It is interesting that the attempt to satisfy the total public usually led to a Hollywood film including some element, however small, of explanation for the Indian's brutal behavior. Therefore any viewer of *America* or

Drums Along the Mohawk who might find it hard to believe in such blood-thirsty Indians could rationalize that the Tory leaders (played by Lionel Barrymore and John Carradine) had whipped the "ignorant natives" into their frenzy. No one could doubt that the Indian was the enemy in *They Died With Their Boots On*, but the film allowed a grudging respect for Crazy Horse (Anthony Quinn) and stressed the fact that white men had broken their treaty and provoked the Indians' final resort to the warpath.

One reason that westerns have enjoyed such long-term popularity is that they include lots of action, and the Indians have always served such scenes well. On the other hand, peace-loving Indians make for little excitement. Even in a sympathetic movie, such as *The Vanishing American*, the obligatory battle serves as a climax. The coming of sound further emphasized the excitement of the Indian attack. The war whoops screeched by the Indians in *Massacre* allowed the studio's sound engineers sensational use of their relatively new medium. The publicity material for *Geronimo* suggested that exhibitors play an Indian sound-effects record in their theater lobbies, with tom-toms and war cries to reinforce the impression that the movie being shown inside was action-packed and replete with exotic sounds of a primitive West.

The publicity efforts the studios mounted deserve special attention. Although it may be impossible to determine how much impact such "exploitation campaigns" had on the success or failure of any picture, the studios certainly viewed them as a necessary part of the business. Ironically, in suggesting ways that exhibitors might get public attention for their shows, sometimes the publicity "press books" presented ideas at odds with the theme of the movie itself.

Commercial considerations also help to explain the evolving Indian image. Over time the American movie audience has changed. Since the movies began a financial comeback in the early 1960s, producers have decided that the typical American moviegoer is younger and better educated than his counterpart of the 1930s or 1940s. As a result, audiences want movies to do more than merely entertain. The old stereotypes are less likely to convince today though new cliches seem to have taken their place. And, although pressure groups have always tried to control the presentation of particular images in the movies, Indian activists have only achieved any real clout in the last decade or two.

The bottom line of a successful movie, as in any other commercial venture, can be found on the profit-and-loss statement. Low production and distribution costs will make the breakeven point easier to reach, and the cost of producing Western movies with Indians can be minimal. For example, sets could be put together inexpensively and extras found on the reservation for far less than union scale. The unavailability of most studio financial records makes it impossible to speak with any precision about the actual costs or profits. It is clear, however, that major productions shot on location with large casts of well-known actors become costly. Cost overruns for location shooting on *Cheyenne Autumn* (1964) necessitated the elimination of many scenes, and they may have contributed to the film's artistic and commercial failure.

Finally, a significant percentage of the Hollywood film industry's income since the 1930s has come from foreign sales. A film such as *Tell Them Willie Boy Is Here* could make up for some of its disappointing domestic sales by becoming a hit for European and Third World audiences.

Many would argue that every Hollywood film is a political document. As Soviet films have characteristically excoriated the czarist regime and extolled the Communist Revolution, the Hollywood movie industry—imbued as it is with the capitalist ethic—has supported the political and economic systems on which it relies. Although the process of filmmaking and the role of government may differ considerably, the product is much the same. Apart from this general orientation, however, political factors have influenced the shape of what reaches the screen in more specific ways.

At times political and commercial factors could coincide. When Warner Brothers' early 1930s films of social consciousness, such as *Massacre*, supported the National Recovery Administration and the New Deal that Franklin D. Roosevelt offered the American public, they expressed in part the liberal political point of view that prevailed in Hollywood. But the moviemakers also hoped that their films would ride on the wave of positive popular opinion that accompanied the new president's efforts to kickstart a stalled economy. As the American people began to renew their hope in the future, Hollywood movies helped to feed their growing confidence in the new administration.

In another era, when a studio reasoned that assistance from the U.S. War Department could be a crucial element in keeping down production costs, the military's production suggestions could be a great influence. Nothing could be more political than the way in which Warner Brothers tried to convince the U.S. army that it should help make *They Died With Their Boots On*. The movie's producers heard suggestions from many quarters about various elements of their project on the portrayal of the Indians, for example. But the only recommendations that seem to have received close attention were the War Department's ideas on how to portray the U.S. military.

A different type of a political influence may have shaped D.W. Griffith's work on *America,* especially the Indians' role in that film.

Figure 2.2. White oppression in *Tell Them Willie Boy Is Here* (with Robert Redford and Robert Blake) drew Third World crowds. Courtesy of the Museum of Modern Art/Film Stills Archive.

Griffith's papers suggest that he and others on his production staff were sensitive to the demands of various patriotic organizations concerned about the images that got to the screen. The Indians were the only group they could portray as "heavies" without inviting the political wrath of the cultural establishment. In an interview for the recent images of Indians television series, director King Vidor noted that although many minorities and ethnic groups had "lobbies" in Hollywood to protect their movie image, no one spoke for the Indians. Perhaps the ultimate irony is that in Western films, where Indians most often appear, producers have always had to consider the demands of the American Humane Society about the treatment of the horses—yet the Native Americans are not treated with nearly as much politesse.

International politics could play a part too. As Twentieth Century-Fox prepared *Drums Along the Mohawk* for release in 1939, decision-makers tried to weigh the impact such a film could have on current tensions in Europe. Might Germany read a popular film that played up the long-forgotten hatred and resentments associated with the American Revolution as a sign that the alliance between the United States and Great Britain was perhaps not so secure? This conclusion would be less likely if, as in the film, Indians and American Tories were the enemy portrayed and no British officers were shown.

Most recently, political influence found its way into movies of the late 1960s and early 1970s in the form of Indian allegories of the American experience in Southeast Asia. The Indian movies made then, such as *Little Big Man* and *Soldier Blue* (both 1970), films that indicted the American Army for practicing genocide on the Native American, were partly the expressions of the producers' and directors' feelings about Vietnam. Even more important, however, they were commercial products aimed at the moviegoing public of young adults who, by profitable coincidence, also represented the age group most deeply involved in the antiwar movement.

Some of the films discussed here offer striking contrasts and similarities. *The Vanishing American* and *Broken Arrow* present a "noble savage" stereotype, while *Drums along the Mohawk* deals with the era of the American Revolution, and its production was fraught with worries about how to portray the British as an enemy. Interesting similarities exist in the ways that *The Vanishing American, Massacre,* and *Tell Them Willie Boy Is Here* address the pressures of reservation life, even though the contemporary styles of filmmaking (in the silent era, the early sound era, and the era of the independent producer, respectively) differ considerably. *They Died with Their Boots On* and *Little Big Man,* made almost thirty years apart, sharply contrast in their views of the United States military and their Indian enemies at times (1941 and 1970) when war was much on the mind of the American public. The producers of other films, such as *Devil's Doorway* and *Cheyenne Autumn,* bent over backward to sympathize with the Indians' plight, but they did nothing to correct Hollywood's characteristic carelessness in portraying historical events and the complexity of Native American cultures. In spite of the forces that changed the shape of the movie business over the past three-quarters of a century and transformed the precise nature of the stereotypes, Hollywood Indians are still far from real.

Works Cited

Berger, Thomas. *Little Big Man*. New York: Dial Press, 1964.

Berkhofer, Robert F. *The White Man's Indian: Images of the American Indian from Columbus to the Present*. New York: Random House, 1977.

Cawelti, John. *The Six-gun Mystique*. Bowling Green, Ohio: Popular Culture Press, 1978.

Edmunds, Walter. *Drums Along the Mohawk*. Boston: Little, Brown, 1936.

Eggan, Fred. *Social Anthropology of North American Tribes*. Chicago: University of Chicago Press, 1955.

Gessner, Robert. *Massacre*. New York: Jonathan Cope and Harrison Smith, 1931.

Grey, Zane. *The Vanishing American*. New York: Harper, 1925.

Jackson, Helen Hunt. *A Century of Dishonor*. New York: Little, Brown, 1881.

Steward, Julian Haynes. *Basin-Plateau Aboriginal Socio-Political Groups*. Washington, D.C.: U.S. Government Printing Office, 1938.

Wright, Will. *Sixguns and Society: A Structural Study of the Western*. Berkeley: University of California Press, 1975.

The Indian of the North
Western Traditions and Finnish Indians

"American social development has been continually beginning over again on the frontier," wrote Frederick Jackson Turner in 1893. "This expansion westward with its new opportunities, its continuous touch with the simplicity of primitive society, furnish the forces dominating American character" (184). According to Turner, the frontier was "the meeting point between savagery and civilization" (184). "American character" was, in other words, born out of a contradiction, a duality. "Primitive society" and its "savagery," although not parts of this character, were essential raw material, or "forces," for its rebirth. The encounter between "civilized men" and "savages" was therefore a key question for the American identity.

These ideas are relevant not only to the American Western but also to Western fiction in general, including Finnish westerns where modes of narration and filmic traditions meet ethnic problems and national challenges. In order to accomplish this task, however, it is necessary to take a closer look at the ideology and structure of both American and European Westerns. Since Turner's time, our view of the American West has strongly based on polarities. It can even be argued that Turner's ideas of American history have formed an ideological basis also for the representation of Indians, inasmuch as the "savages" were only raw material for construction of the American "character."

"At the frontier the environment is at first too strong for the man," Turner continues, "he must accept the conditions which it furnishes, or perish, and so he fits himself into the Indian clearings and follows the Indian trails" (185). As we see, the opposition must be overcome in order to find the way to "effective Americanization" (185). But from an ethnic viewpoint, Turner concludes with a dilemma: the following of "the Indian trails" may lead to a regenerated identity, but only after a violent confrontation.

Self-evidently, this encounter has been one of the central themes of Western fiction as well. As Jean Wagner has pointed out, there seems to be a close connection between the Turnerian conception of American history and Western fiction. Wagner has seen Westerns as cultural artifacts through which American society has sought its identity in the spirit of Turner's thesis (252–263). Some Western scholars, among them Jim Kitses and Will Wright, have regarded Turner's conflict between civilization and savagery also as the primary dichotomy of the Western (Kitses 11, Wright 142). This central opposition can also be interpreted geographically, east and west. Turner pays almost no attention to the north-south dimension. We may argue that the tension between north and south was a historical trauma that Turner tries to minimize. The same seems to be valid for Westerns, too, which are typically constructed around a movement from east to west.

Western movies have often been characterized as American cinema par excellence and as stories about the history of the American West (Kitses 8). Will Wright has written, "Although Western novels reach a large and faithful audience, it is through the movies that the myth has become part of the cultural language by which America understands itself" (Wright 12). Yet this myth has spoken not only to Americans, but also to millions of other people around the world. And this universal popularity is due not to global interest in American history, but rather to the fact that Westerns carry elements that evoke emotions and reflections from other local perspectives as well. Westerns have provided a milieu also for national storytelling in France and Italy, in Japan and India, in the former Soviet Union and Germany—and even in Finland.

Most of the non-American Westerns have been made in Italy; the Cinecittà studios produced more than four hundred Westerns between 1964 and 1970 (Frayling 256). The central figure for the birth of this overwhelming production was Sergio Leone. After his *Fistful of Dollars* (*Per un pugno di dollari*, 1964) the studio invested heavily in the mass-production of what became known as "spaghetti westerns" (Leone 37).

When Cinecittà produced its first Westerns, they were made to look as American as possible (Frayling 58). This cultural impersonation was not entirely successful, however, since there were Italian and European features that could not be handled within American parameters. The opposition between east and west, for example, seems to be totally absent.[1] Instead, Italian Westerns stress the polarity between north and south. Leone's *Fistful of Dollars* opens with a scene that was repeated numerous times in the later films: a gringo appears from nowhere in a Mexican village. This basic scene has been interpreted as a reflection of inner social conflict within Italy: the gap between the rich north and the poor south, imaged in the confrontation between a superior fast-handed gringo and the poor Mexicans, who are permitted only a minor role in the narrative (Baudry 55–56, Nowell-Smith 147). In the late 1960s, the protagonist more often became a Mexican bandit, not a gringo. This shift has been construed as a change to "the political spaghetti western" (Salmi, *Synteesi* 62).

It may, in other words, be asserted that, in relation to the national audience, spaghetti westerns dealt with a highly relevant issue by articulating tensions of domestic social conflict. The ethnic minorities of the Italian society, however, do not usually appear in spaghetti westerns. If we take these films to be a component of national cultural debate, there seems to be no ethnic problem within Italian society that could arouse the need to use the Western imagery of Indians as a metaphor for national minorities. On the other hand, the inner social conflict between northerners and southerners offered a problem appropriate for metaphorical Western narration.[2]

If we read spaghetti westerns as metaphors of Italian society, it does not mean that this articulation was always conscious—nor that they would have been perceived as such metaphors by the public. Nonetheless, we may still presume that these Westerns played a specific role in the construction of Italian national identity, although in a different way than in the United States. Before World War I and under the Fascist regime, Italian films often accentuated the theme of geographical expansion. For Italians, the geographical direction of this frontier of expansion was not the open prairie in the west, but the open sea, the Mediterranean to the south. Such well-known imperialist films as *Cabiria* (1914) by Giovanni Pastrone or *Scipione l'Africano* (1937) by Carmine Gallone are both staged on this southern frontier. Their central dilemma is between those who are inside the community and those who are outside, reminiscent of the manner in which Romans used to distinguish themselves from the "barbarians." This arrangement illustrates the way R.D. Grillo has defined the logic of nationalist thinking: "The national process establishes a difference between 'Us' and 'Them' which signifies the essential unity of 'Us' as insiders against 'Them' as outsiders" (Grillo 25). Therefore, the encounter between the Romans and the North Africans takes the major role in the narrative, culminating in a demonstration of superiority of Italians compared to outsiders.

It seems that after the collapse of the Mussolini regime this setting was displaced by inner conflicts. Postwar films in Italy aimed at structuring national identity not by contrasting Italians with other peoples and

other nations, but by focusing attention on the lack of economic and social balance within the society. It was no longer relevant to talk about the
"essential unity of 'Us'" because there was no "Us." This adaptation of the
perspective and signification of westerns' polarities resembles the developments in Finnish cinema.

The comparison of this Italian development to the history of American (or Finnish) cinema is not altogether without risks. There are many
historical and cultural differences rendering such an attempt difficult.
First and foremost, Western fiction has played a unique role in American
society, and comparisons to any other country would be hazardous. In
the American historical consiousness, expansion westward has taken on a
special meaning. According to Turner, the American identity was born
out of the experience of the simple life on the frontier. The encounter
between "civilization" and "savagery" could not be a threat to national
identity (as in the Italian case); it was necessary for its development.

Feature films have been made in Finland since 1907, when *The Moon-
shine Distillers* (*Salaviinanpolttajat*) premiered in Helsinki. To date, about
950 full-length Finnish feature films have been completed. Although the
volume of Finnish cinema has not been particularly large, for decades
production was organized according to the American example. The Finnish
studio era lasted approximately from 1935 to 1963. There were three
major companies dominating filmmaking: Suomen Filmiteollisuus, Suomi-
Filmi, and (from 1950 onward) Fennada-Filmi. During this period, there
were many attempts to produce genre films in the American mold. Compared to the total volume of production, the number of these attempts
was low; domestic genres, such as lumberjack films and the so-called
rillumarei comedies, were more fertile.

Most of the American-style films were made after World War II, during the last decades of the Finnish studio era. These years were also the
most productive ones. In Finnish society in general, the period from the
late 1940s to the early 1960s was one of reconstruction, political stabiliza-
tion, and restoration of national self-confidence. Increasing affluence
during the 1950s saw the gradual withdrawal of rationing, which had remained in effect since the war. 1952 marked a turning point of sorts, with
the payment of the last reparations to the USSR,[3] the hosting of the Olympic Games in Helsinki, and the crowning of Armi Kuusela as Miss Universe. The Finnish people had rediscovered their national pride.

There is no doubt that films played a major role in creating this reborn "Finnishness." Many of the films of this period still occupy an important place in the mental landscape of the Finnish people: *People in
the Summer Night* (*Ihmiset suviyössä*, 1948), *Rob the Robber* (*Rosvo*

Roope, 1949), *The Ten Men from Härmä* (*Härmästä poikia kymmenen*, 1950), *At the Rovaniemi Fair* (*Rovaniemen markkinoilla*, 1951), *The White Reindeer* (*Valkoinen peura*, 1952), and *The Unknown Soldier* (*Tuntematon sotilas*, 1955). Among the many directors who were involved in representing these collective dreams were Edvin Laine, Ville Salminen, Roland af Hällström, Ilmari Unho, Hannu Leminen, and Aarne Tarkas.

Aarne Tarkas (1923–76) was the most active filmmaker of the last studio years. He aimed to appeal to public taste by applying American formulas to the Finnish context. He tried Western patterns also, and directed three full-length Finnish Westerns: *The Wild North* (*Villi Pohjola*, 1955), *The Gold of the Wild North* (*Villin Pohjolan kulta*, 1963), and *The Secret Valley of the Wild North* (*Villin Pohjolan salattu laakso*, 1963). These films were iconographically and narratively descendants of the American Western, but they were located in Finland's mythical wild north. In addition to this trilogy, the history of the Finnish Western also includes two comedies produced by Spede Pasanen, *Speedy Gonzales* (1970) and *The Unhangables* (*Hirttämättömät*, 1971).[4]

Finnish Westerns have been called an "absurdity" and a "conceptual impossibility" (Bagh 3), but in fact, the Western tradition seems to have offered many features compatible to Finnish cinema. Finland has an ethnic minority, the Lapps, who have long been under pressure from the dominant culture to migrate further north. During the seventeenth century, the Lapps still inhabited central Finland, but, in the course of time, they have been pushed to the north, not to reservations but to more difficult conditions. It is therefore no wonder that a geographical opposition is as central to Finnish cinema as it is to American cinema, although it goes between north and south, rather than between east and west. This polarity is nearer to the American equivalent than the Italian one, and the geographical duality is also matched by other significant oppositions.

Crucially, the duality civilization/savagery also operates in the Finnish context. The population in Finland is highly concentrated in the southern parts of the country: the south is both the industrial and the cultural center, containing the biggest cities. We can modify the scheme of Kitses (11) to Finnish cinema and present some central polarities:

North	*South*
savagery	civilization
freedom	restrictions
nature	culture
tradition	change
honesty	compromises

Figure 3.1. Indians of the North in *Secret Valley of the Wild North* (1963). Courtesy of the Finnish Film Archive.

We should not, however, go much further in the listing of polarities: the categories are usually not so immanent and coherent as the categorizations would suggest. There are also other oppositions in Finnish cinema that do not seem to fit into this scheme—for example, light–darkness. To complicate matters, the north can be a place of both never-ending day and never-ending night. This binarity is due to Finland's peri-Arctic location. In summer the day is long, and in winter it is short. In northern Finland, this polarity is at its strongest.

There is an extensive array of Finnish films dealing with this northern–southern connection. It seems that this dimension became especially relevant after World War II, probably due to the postwar dynamics in society: people started to move to big towns in the south and the payment of reparations led to the reorganization of industry. As the standard of living increased, especially in the urban centers, economic growth generated contradictions. (Parallels to this societal imbalance can be drawn with the social confrontations in postwar Italian cinema.) In addition to social changes, it must be kept in mind that the postwar decades in Finland were also a period of intellectual reorientation and identity-building: in addressing these polarities, the cinema was simultaneously addressing basic problems of the national psyche. During the 1930s and 1940s, this psyche had been oriented to the east.[5] After the war this was no longer so.

Instead, after World War II, there were many film types relating to new orientations (e.g., the *rillumarei* comedies, Ostrobothnia films). Lapland was frequently taken as a central location, but foreign locations and foreign characters also appeared on the screen much more than before. The problem of ethnic minorities was handled frequently in the movies, too; this was something completely different from the war period, when the cinema had usually stressed the homogeneity of society.

The contradiction between north and south was especially taken up in the so-called *rillumarei* comedies. This Finnish genre was born in 1951, with the release of Jorma Nortimo's *At the Rovaniemi Fair*. The critics, who expected only nationally elevating, high-culture works of arts, were shocked by the unsophisticated humor and popular lightness of this film. Nevertheless, the film was an enormous success and was followed by similar comedies. *At the Rovaniemi Fair* told a story of three men who left the fussy life of the south and traveled singing to the north in order to pan for gold and enjoy their freedom.[6] Maybe the critics were also astonished by the open rejection of society: work was a highly emphasized value in an economy driven by the need to pay reparations. The heroes of the *rillumarei* comedies openly rejected this contemporary national ethic.

At the Rovaniemi Fair was succeeded by a series of films that became favorites with audiences; for example *Mr. Coolman from the Wild West* (*Lännen lokarin veli*, 1951), *The Girl from Muhos* (*Muhoksen Mimmi*, 1952), *Adventure in Morocco* (*Rantasalmen sulttaani*, 1953), *Esa "Flies" to Kuopio* (*Lentävä Kalakukko*, 1953) and *Hei, Trala-lala-lalaa* (*Hei, rillumarei!*, 1954). *Mr. Coolman from the Wild West* had nothing to do with the Wild West or Westerns, but it described the adventures of an emigrant who returns to Finland from the United States. All these films emphasized the possibility of a lifestyle different from the postwar, urban adjustment. The contrasting element was sometimes the simple nature of northern Finland, sometimes foreign cultures.

In the *rillumarei* comedies, and also in some other comedies of the 1950s such as *Pete and Runt on the Trail of the Abominable Snowman* (*Pekka ja Pätkä lumimiehen jäljillä*, 1954), the events were located in northern Finland, but the natives of the north, the Lapps, were seen only in minor roles. They were a kind of *typage*, reproducing cultural stereotypes and playing only a supporting function in the narrative, not as individuals but as a group (cf. Naremore 25). Some films, however, were made during this period that intentionally focused on Lappish exoticism and also offered Lapps as protagonists. Such films were especially *Maaret—Daughter of the Fells* (*Maaret—tunturien tyttö*, 1947) by Valentin Vaala, *Arctic Fury* (*Aila—Pohjolan tytär*, 1951) by Jack Witikka, and *The White Reindeer* (*Valkoinen peura*, 1952) by Erik Blomberg. Even here, however, the Lapp characters were not portrayed by natives, but by southern actors (such as Eila Pehkonen and Mirjami Kuosmanen). The basic setting in *Maaret—Daughter of the Fells* resembles the later *rillumarei* comedies: the leading male character is a surgeon from Helsinki (played by Olavi Reimas) who, after a nervous breakdown, escapes to the north and finds a balanced life. The contradiction between north and south is as clearly presented in *Arctic Fury* and *The White Reindeer*. Rather than the social aspects of this contradiction, however, what is foregrounded is Lappish exoticism.

In Finnish films, the journey to the north leads the protagonists into serious rethinking of identity. The Arctic milieu is a zone between nature and culture and, thus, similar to the idea of the American frontier. In the Western tradition, a typical incarnation of the frontier life is the settler-farmer who comes to the wilderness and starts to cultivate the open land. In the Finnish literary tradition, there is a quite similar character, an ex-tenant farmer who moves to the difficult and ascetic circumstances of the northern backwoods in order to start a life of his own. In this tradition, the wilderness represents a threat not in the form of Indians, but in the form of hostile natural conditions. The cultivation of land is hard in the north, where summers are short and nights are cold. One of the basic scenes shows us the settler trying to reclaim the frosty swampland and make it into a fertile field. A typical filmic representation of this theme is *The Toilers of Rantasuo* (*Rantasuon raatajat*, 1942) by Orvo Saarikivi.

Although settlers in American and Finnish films have differences, they have also interesting similarities. In both cases, the myth of a settler is bound to the elevation of national self-confidence and to the creation of a national identity. But what is missing in the Finnish films is the strong individualism of the Americans, derived from the thinking of the eighteenth-century Enlightenment. The character of the Finnish settler was created during the nationalistic upheaval of the nineteenth century. Nationalists as J.L. Runeberg and Zachris Topelius established the prototype of the Finnish citizen, who was depicted as humble, slow-thinking, hard-working, reticent, God-fearing and always obedient. Later, however, other mental images were created, especially through the provincial scope during the twentieth century. For example, in the Ostrobothnia fiction,[7] there were many representations of freedom-loving peasants who were always willing to protest against social injustice. This fiction, usually located in the nineteenth century (that is, prior to Finnish political sovereignty), included not only literature but also opera and film and reflected the thinking of the Finnish independence movement during the first decades of the twentieth century (Laine 65).

As we have seen, therefore, a series of interesting parallels can be identified between American and Finnish films. Interestingly enough, The Wild North films by Aarne Tarkas are consciously based on these parallels. Already in the first film of the series, features of the Western and of the Finnish setting are blended, but this mixture goes much further in the subsequent movies.

The Wild North (1955) is a Western pastiche. In the beginning, Karin Turkka (Elina Pohjanpää) arrives in a little town called Utopila in order to find out who has killed her father. Before his death, Turkka had found a profitable gold mine. The people of Utopila believe Tundra-Tauno (Tapio Rautavaara) to have been guilty of the murder, and he had to escape to the backwoods to avoid being lynched. Two years have passed, but the real murderers still have not found the gold mine. Karin Turkka sets out to kill Tundra-Tauno, but when she discovers that he is innocent, the two join forces to fight against the real criminals, the sheriff and the mayor of Utopila.

The Wild North fuses Western-style scenes and settings with modern features, such as technology (airplanes, cars). With respect to its narrative structure, the film is quite near to the contemporary American Western. It reminds us of the "transition theme" in the categorization of Will Wright (74–85), and has some common elements, for example, with Nicholas Ray's *Johnny Guitar* (1954).

The critics of the daily press had difficulties in understanding this Finnish variation of the Western. It was usually seen as a parody, but as a failure, in which the skills of the filmmakers did not quite reach the standards of a decent comedy. The characterization as parody may be valid for the few first minutes of the film but, after this beginning, there are scarcely any parodic elements. Tarkas was actually irritated by the label "parody." Later he wrote:

> It would have been reasonable to expect that an alert critic would have noticed the comment at the beginning of the film that everything happens in a fantasy world which is a pure product of the imagination without any real basis. Nobody argues that, for example, Tarzan novels were jungle parodies. There are many similar examples. Let us think only of James Hilton's "secret valley" Shangri La, somewhere

in the highlands of Tibet, where people live hundreds of years. In his books, Jules Verne travelled to the moon and under the sea, and they were not labeled as parodies. Dante himself went to purgatory and inferno. So why could not one Tarkas visit the Wild North, which is a sort of unattainable happy milieu for the modern, nervous citizen. (16)

In the last sentence, Tarkas clearly reveals the binary basis of his thinking. The south was the center of modernity and "unnatural" life, whereas the north was still natural, "wild" and free.

Eight years passed before Tarkas returned to his western passion. In the year 1962 he led his unit to Kuusamo in northern Finland, and *The Gold of the Wild North* was premiered the following year. The film itself had no links to its predecessor, except that it, too, was located in the mythical wild north. The central figures were the Vorna brothers, Joel (Åke Lindman), Tommi (Helge Herala), and Kai (Vili Auvinen). The Vorna brothers closely resemble the leading trio in Howard Hawks's *Rio Bravo* (1959). Joel is a father figure similar to Chance (John Wayne), Tommi is weaker and susceptible to temptations like Dude (Dean Martin), and Kai is young and inexperienced like Colorado (Ricky Nelson).

The motivation is again gold. The Vorna brothers have found pieces of gold in the river and, in the opening scene, they are riding up the river and tracing its origin. Their journey is interrupted by an armed young lady, Karin Jäärä (Tamara Lund), who looks like Calamity Jane. She declares that they have no permission to enter the lands of her father (Kalervo Nissilä). Disappointed, the brothers leave and arrive in the nearest town. In the saloon, the name Vorna is well known. Fifteen years ago, the brothers had been suspected of having committed robbery and murder. Again, the establishment, this time the saloon owner Risto (Leo Jokela) and the banker Markus (Kauko Helovirta), are behind the crime.

In order to get access to Jäärä's land, Markus tries—and has already been trying for some time—to marry Jäärä's beautiful daughter, planning to kill his new father-in-law after the "Amen." Finally, he obtains his favorable answer, but Jäärä demands 100,000 dollars as a condition for the marriage. Markus organizes the robbery of his own bank to get the money and shifts the blame to the Vorna brothers. The chase begins, and Kai is almost hanged. In the end, the brothers succeed in proving their innocence, Risto and Markus are arrested and Kai—who has fallen in love with Karin—gets his beloved. In the last frames, Joel and Tommi leave the happy couple and continue their seemingly endless ride over the distant fells.

The Gold of the Wild North combines elements of the classic Western plot with what Wright calls the "transition theme." At the same time,

Figure 3.2. Kai Vorna (Vili Auvinen) meets a "native" in *Gold of the Wild North* (1963). Courtesy of the Finnish Film Archive.

this film is probably the most classic of the Finnish Westerns. In *The Wild North*, the people of the north used modern technology, but in *The Gold of the Wild North* horses are back: the Vorna brothers ride in typical Western clothing, classically equipped, but the background is the Finnish Arctic—or, more precisely, tundra—landscape with its rocks and rapids, pines and fells. In fact, the landscape looks quite similar to that of the Anthony Mann westerns of the 1950s, such as *The Far Country* (1955).

One important Western element is also present: the natives. In other words, *The Gold of the Wild North* includes ethnic coloring, although this remains marginal. Some scenes include references to a minority named "Indians." In the saloon scene, a singer (Rose-Marie Precht) presents a vocal intermezzo entertaining her audience of miners and cowboys. She also sings about "Indians," but the men around the table are clothed not like Indians, but like native Lapps. In this short sequence, Indians and Lapps are thus identified with each other. These "Indians" are neither a threat nor an equal part of the society: in the little northern town, they are perhaps as marginalized as they are in the narrative. Their only function seems to be to give an atmosphere of frontier life.

In the next sequel of the Wild North series, *The Secret Valley of the Wild North* (1963), "Indians" play a much more important role. *The Gold of the Wild North* was a success, and Aarne Tarkas did not lose time in exploiting his ideas. The Vorna brothers are again adventuring and continuing their endless ride. Joel is once again played by Åke Lindman, but the other roles have been changed: Tommi and Kai are this time portrayed by real brothers, Tommi and Taneli Rinne.

The brothers are wandering in the northern highlands when they suddenly meet an escaped man. He tells them that the men of the secret valley are pursuing him. An arrow with a golden tip kills him before he succeeds in revealing more, but luckily he has drawn a map under his gold panning dish. The legends tell that the people of the secret valley have so much gold that they almost bathe in it. But the Vorna brothers are not the only ones who have got a hint of the valley. A bunch of greedy white men is also tracing the legend. In the valley, the Vornas meet two native girls, Inga (Elina Salo) and Pirita (Pirkko Mannola), who are engaged in some midsummer night's magic. The chief of the valley, Tapio (Tapio Rautavaara), does not want to trust any white man. He has his men take the Vornas captive and is about to condemn them to death, when his son Jouni (Harri Tirkkonen) arrives and tells him that the brothers are not ordinary white men: outside the valley they had saved his life. But at the same time, the robber gang invades the valley. In the subsequent fight, the Vornas take the side of the "Indians." Finally, the threat is repulsed, and the secret is preserved. The brothers promise that they never will reveal where the valley is, and continue their ride toward new adventures.

The Secret Valley of the Wild North is the only Finnish film where Indians play a major role. The similarities between the American and Finnish frontiers are underlined by stressing problems of ethnicity. Specifically, Indian and Lappish elements are deliberately fused. The people of the secret valley live in tepees like the American Plains Indians and have totem poles in the center of the village. In reality, the Lapps also used to live in tepeelike huts called *kota*, but the tepees in this film display far more Indian than Lappish characteristics. Besides, the men of the village are clothed just like North American Indians and run along the fells whooping like Indians and shooting arrows.

The women, on the contrary, look more like Lapps. Their costumes have traditional Lappish decorations. There is also one man who wears Lappish clothes, the shaman of the village, Juuso (Leevi Kuuranne). Juuso is very typical of the representation of Lappish shamans in Finnish film in general. The god of the valley people, too, is named after the Lappish *seita*.

The religion of the secret valley is quite similar to the authentic

Figure 3.3. Indian chief Tapio (Tapio Rautavaara) with two Lappish-looking Indian girls (Elina Salo, left, and Pirkko Mannola, right) in *Secret Valley of the Wild North* (1963). Courtesy of the Finnish Film Archive.

Lappish religion, although the totems in the village seem to refer to American Indian features. In addition to these religious characteristics, there are also some elements of the ancient Finnish pagan religion, which was different from the Lappish one. The Vorna brothers come to the valley on Midsummer Night, when Inga and Pirita are trying to make magic in order to see the reflection of their future husbands in the water. This magic, and the mythology of Midsummer Night, played an important role in the ancient Finnish religion, which was supplanted by Christianity after the first Swedish crusade to Finland in the twelfth century, but this paganism has never been entirely displaced. It has survived for centuries in Finnish folklore but has no real connection with the Lappish religion.

The names of the valley people, too, display interference between Lappish and Old Finnish elements. The names Jouni and Oula are typical Lappish names, whereas Tapio comes indisputably from the ancient Finnish religion, where Tapio was the king of the forest. Even more peculiar, however, are the girls' names. Inga does not refer to Lapps at all but to another Finnish minority, the Swedes. Originally, Inga is a variation of Ing, who was an ancient Scandinavian god. The name Pirita points towards Karelia in the east, although the name was probably also used in western Finland (Vilkuna 124, 138, 141, 245–246). It remains unclear, however, how deliberate and intentional the choice of these names is. What is certain is that they are not picked out of the dominant Finnish culture but from the margins. The name Tapio reminds the Finns of the primeval symbiosis with nature that was replaced by Western civilization after the twelfth century. The ancient Finnish religion had close contacts with the Kingdom of Tapio, with nature and its magic spirits. The other names, on the other hand, associate the valley people with the margins of Finnish identity: with the Lapps, Swedes, and Karelians. But why are these marginalities combined? To answer this question, we need to take a closer look at the logic of nationalist rhetoric in general.

We may argue that there is both an internal and an external method of constructing and strengthening national identity. The internal method is focused on inner social conflicts, which it aims to defuse. For example, during the war, Finnish films avoided presenting conflicts, and stressed the cohesion of the nation; if conflicts were represented, in the end all the problems were resolved. The external method has a different function. It sets out to master the outer reality of the community (e.g., through stereotyping images of other nationalities). This is quite close to the definition of myth proposed by Claude Lévi-Strauss. According to Lévi-Strauss, myth has a double social meaning in the communication between society and its members: it aims to solve a basic inner conflict and, at the same time, to make the world outside the society understandable by conceptualizing it (Lévi-Strauss 226–227). Both of these aspects can exist simultaneously.

Lévi-Strauss based his binary method (which has exercised a powerful influence on Western studies) on the ideas of the Swiss linguist Ferdinand de Saussure. In his book *Cours de linguistique générale*, published in 1915, Saussure argued that a concept always divides the world into two parts, objects and non-objects (Saussure 99). This principle can be interpreted from the perspective of the external function of a national identity construction. Let us take the concept *Finn*; it is a similar category of nationality like that of *Swede* or *American*. Following Saussure's ideas, the concept *Finn* divides people into *Finns* and *non-Finns*. National rhetoric does not underline the similarities between categories like *Finns* and *Americans* but drives at convincing the auditor that Finnish is something special or unique, different from all other categories. In this mode of thinking, *Swedes* and *Americans* are associated on the grounds of their *non-Finnishness*.[8] We can find this logic in a variety of cultural products. In cinema, non-Finnishness was usually characterized by type actors. They symbolized the Other and embodied exotic, strange elements. For example, Ville Salminen played roles of a Russian lieutenant in *Activists* (*Aktivistit*, 1939), a Spanish stepfather in *On Deck* (*Laivan kannella*, 1954), an American gangster in *The Adventures of Kalle-Kustaa Korkki* (*Kalle-Kustaa Korkin seikkailut*, 1949), and a Mexican officer in *Lord and Master* (*Herra ja ylhäisyys*, 1944). The same logic explains why such actors as Charles Boyer and Anthony Quinn have represented so many different nationalities or ethnic minorities in the American cinema. Charles Boyer was an Algerian in *Algiers* (1938), a Spaniard in *Confidential Agent* (1945), an Arab in *The Garden of Allah* (1936), and a Czech in *Cluny Brown* (1946). Anthony Quinn's ethnic diversity is equally impressive: on screen, Quinn has been seen as an Eskimo and a Hun, a Mongolian and an Indian, an Italian and a Romanian, a Greek and a Frenchman. In sum, Quinn represents *non-American*.

The Secret Valley of the Wild North applies this same logic. The inhabitants of the valley form the ethnic minority par excellence. The Lappish-Indian fusion is broadened by incorporating Swedish and Karelian nuances. These prototype non-Finns are presented as an element contrasted to the white men of the south, the dominant Finnish culture. The film—like its predecessor, *The Gold of the Wild North*—draws parallels with the position of Lapps in Finland and that of Indians in the United States. Both are ethnic minorities in danger of becoming assimilated by the dominant culture. In American—or, more precisely, Turnerian—thinking, the encounter of white men and Indians is needed for the rebirth of American identity. These Finnish films, however, imply that such an encounter could not ultimately be fertile. It would lead to total disaster, and the best solution is for the people of the secret valley to continue to live in secrecy.

The Secret Valley of the Wild North quite closely resembles American adventure films, especially in terms of its "secret valley" theme. In the American Western, this theme does not appear. The idea that, somewhere, there still could live North American Indians who never have encountered white men is, in a way, contradictory to Turnerian Western ideology. Usually, the secret valley theme appears in exotic adventure films located in Africa or South America. Let us think only of *Tarzan Escapes* (1936) by Richard Thorpe, *King Solomon's Mines* (1950) by Andrew Marton and Compton Bennett, or *Tarzan and the Valley of Gold* (1966) by Robert Day. The convention seems to say that there are two kinds of white men, those who are greedy to acquire the riches of the natives, and those who have no material ambitions and, finally, help the people of the valley.

Perhaps this convention implicitly deals with the colonial heritage and the exploitative history of the white man. Because such cultural criticism would have been too harsh, however, the film also offers alternative white men suitable for the audience to identify with. By these means, the consciousness of the audience members remains pure as they fight alongside those who defend the inviolability of the minority. The destroyers are other white men, not us. This is valid also for *The Secret Valley of the Wild North*. The Vorna brothers offer an opportunity for identification, a means of moving freely between the minority and majority without being guilty of the destruction of the former. The film absolves the audience of responsibility by showing an ideal ethnic community that still exists on the frontier, distant from the fussy life of the south.

Like the ideal West in the American cinema, therefore, there is an ideal North in Finnish mentality and film, "the Wild North which is a sort of unattainable happy milieu for the modern nervous citizen." Perhaps none of the American Western directors could have called the West a "happy milieu." As we have seen, there are many differences between American and Finnish Westerns. In the Turnerian conception, the frontier life and especially the following of "Indian trails" led to the regeneration of national identity through ethnic conflict. In Finnish Westerns, however, the ethnic minority could remain in its secret valley, untouched. Whereas the Indian representations of American Westerns have been shaped by how cruel and violent the encounter between "civilized men" and "savages" finally was, the Indians—and Lapps—of Finnish cinema are usually idealized. The origin of the ethnic encounter is temporally

Figure 3.4. The shaman Juuso (Leevi Kuuranne) in *Secret Valley of the Wild North* (1963), a typical representation of the Lappet shamans in Finnish film. Courtesy of the Finnish Film Archive.

more distant, and it never was particularly violent. Perhaps ethnic conflict has never been such a traumatic experience for the Finns as it has for the Americans. This may also explain why the Finnish Westerns have a resemblance to American adventure movies, which frequently deal with the ethnic conflict common to the whole Western world, the encounter with the Third World.

Notes

1. Leone's *Once Upon a Time in the West* (1968) is an exception, however, made as a compilation of American Western mythology.

2. This national conflict can be raised to a global scale. We can also read it as a reflection of the gap between the industrialized states and the Third World, especially in the later spaghetti westerns. The Cuban actor Tomas Milián, who was one of the greatest stars of the "political spaghetti," has described himself as "a symbol of poverty" for the audiences of the Third World. Tomas Milián's star image offered a strategy for winning response in Latin American countries during the late 1960s (Frayling 265).

3. During World War II, Finland was involved in three distinct wars. The Winter War (1939–40) began with a Soviet assault and ended in a Soviet victory. The Continuation War (1941–44), on the contrary, began as a Finnish offensive aiming at regaining the lost territories or even at expansion eastward. In 1944, Finland surrendered and was required to pay reparations to the Soviet Union. Finally, in the War of Lapland (1944–45), Finland succeeded in expelling the remaining German troops.

4. We can also mention Jorma Nortimo's *Lord and Master* (*Herra ja ylhäisyys*, 1944), dealing with the Mexican Revolution, which shows a stereotypical Indian character; and Armand Lohikoski's *Pete and Runt in a Chain Collision* (*Pekka ja Pätkä ketjukolarissa*, 1957), including a long Western sequence.

5. This orientation was in part expansionist. There was, for example, extensive interest in the Finns' ethnic relatives, the Finno-Ugric peoples beyond the eastern border.

6. The quest for gold has a real basis. Some gold has been—and still is—found in Lapland. Gold is one of the parallels between the Wild West and Lapland. (See the essay on *Broken Arrow* by Frank Manchel.)

7. In this genre, the main location is the Finnish province of Ostrobothnia (Pohjanmaa), located in west-central Finland on the Baltic coast.

8. I have previously tried to apply this logic to German national rhetoric (Salmi, "*Die Herrlichkeit* . . . ").

Works Cited

Bagh, Peter von. "Suomiäidin sylistä." *Filmihullu* 3 (1989): 3.

Baudry, Pierre. "L'idéologie du western italien." *Cahiers du Cinéma* 233 (1971): 55–56.

Frayling, Christopher. *Spaghetti Westerns: Cowboys and Europeans from Karl May to Sergio Leone*. London: Routledge & Kegan Paul, 1981.

Grillo, R.D. "Introduction." *"Nation" and "State" in Europe: Anthropological Perspectives*. R.D. Grillo, ed. London: Academic Press, 1980.

Kitses, Jim. *Horizons West: Anthony Mann, Budd Boetticher, Sam Peckinpah*. London: Thames & Hudson, 1969.

Laine, Kimmo. "Against Russians or Upper Classes? On the Interpretative History of the Pohjalaisia Saga." *Lähikuva* 4 (1992): 18–31, 65.

Leone, Sergio. "Leone spiega se stesso." *Bianco e nero* 9/10 (1971): 37–39.

Lévi-Strauss, Claude. *Structural Anthropology*. Garden City, N.Y.: Anchor, 1967.

Naremore, James. *Acting in the Cinema*. Berkeley and Los Angeles: University of California Press, 1988.

Nowell-Smith, Geoffrey. "Italy sotto voce." *Sight and Sound* 3 (1968): 147.

Rieupeyrout, Jean-Louis. *Le Western ou le cinéma américain par excellence*. Paris: Éditions du Cerf, 1953.

Salmi, Hannu. *"Die Herrlichkeit des deutschen Namens . . . " Die schriftstellerische und politische Tätigkeit Richard Wagners als Gestalter nationaler Identität während der staatlichen Vereinigung Deutschlands*. Turku: University of Turku, 1993.

Salmi, Hannu. "Lännenelokuvan binäärisesta analyysista." *Synteesi* 1–2 (1985).

Saussure, Ferdinand de. *Cours de linguistique générale*. Paris-Editions Payot, 1969.

Tarkas, Aarne. "Villin Pohjolan salattu laakso." *Seura* 48 (1963): 16.

Turner, Frederick Jackson. "The Significance of the Frontier in American History." *A Documentary History of the United States*. Richard D. Heffner, ed. New York: New American Library, 1976.

Wagner, Jean. "Le Western, l'Histoire et l'Actualité." *Le Western*. Henri Agel, ed. Paris: Lettres Modernes, 1961.

Vilkuna, Kustaa. *Etunimet*. Keuruu: Otava, 1976.

Wright, Will. *Sixguns and Society: A Structural Study of the Western*. Berkeley and Los Angeles: University of California Press, 1977.

Trapped in the History of Film
Racial Conflict and Allure in
The Vanishing American

> *We are shape-shifters in the national consciousness, accidental survivors, unwanted reminders of disagreeable events. Indians have to be explained and accounted for, and somehow fit into the creation myth of the most powerful, benevolent nation ever, the last best hope of man on earth. . . . We're trapped in history. No escape.*
> —Paul Chaat Smith (9)

The Vanishing American (1925) stands as a distinct and bittersweet example of the epic silent western. As a compelling—and sometimes contradictory—mixture of stereotype and insightful social commentary, it is an ambitious work aiming to portray the plight of American Indians as the culmination of an inevitable historical process of domination wrought by "progress." Casting this theme through the story of a group of Navajo and Euro-Americans whose lives become intertwined in the Southwest at the time of World War I, the film centers on a hero named Nophaie "the warrior" (played by Richard Dix). Nophaie is portrayed as a keenly intelligent man caught with one foot planted in the traditions of his people and the other caught amid early modern American culture.

While battling the discrimination and racism directed toward his people, Nophaie falls into an unrequited love affair with the kindhearted white schoolmarm, Marion (played by Lois Wilson). Seeking to gain her favor and transcend the cultural gulf that divides the couple, he enlists in the war effort and ships off to Europe, taking with him a group of his fellow Navajo. Told that they are "Americans now," they believe that participation in "the war to make the world safe for democracy" will help ensure an improved life for Indians by helping them gain acceptance as full-fledged Americans. However, on their return, they find themselves still scorned, humiliated, and exploited by the local whites, treated every bit as badly as before they left. In addition, now more acutely aware of their differential place within American society and the world at large,

Figure 4.1. Nophaie (Richard Dix) is portrayed as a compassionate and virtuous man with one foot planted in the traditions of his people, the other caught in modern American culture. Courtesy of the Museum of Modern Art/Film Stills Archive.

they are left with a realization that their traditional way of life may be doomed to historical progress, yet there may not be an equal place for them within the mainstream modern American order.

George Seitz's film begins with a quotation from the English philosopher and proponent of Social Darwinism Herbert Spencer, a statement that characterizes the patterns of history as an inevitable and ongoing conquest: "We have unmistakable proof that throughout all past time there has been a ceaseless devouring of the weak by the strong . . . a survival of the fittest." Thus Spencer's famous catch phrase, which has been popularly and erroneously credited to Charles Darwin (Hofstadter 39), is employed to set the tone for the film. These famous words, inscribed against a backdrop of dinosaurs engaged in fierce battle, frame the film in reference to the widespread public interest in Social Darwinism that had carried forth, in numerous permutations, from the late nineteenth century into the 1920s. Thus, from the start of the film, a melodrama unfolds pitting a series of changing human "races" moving across a stage of time from "darkness into dark."

So this film begins, a cinematic tableau wherein humankind's major theme is seemingly its own ceaseless domination of itself; or alternately, the ceaseless domination of one "racial" group by another. This story is moored throughout to popularized notions of "progress" and "destiny," modes of characterization that were prevalent in the cultural logic of America coincident with its rise as a world power at the turn of the nineteenth century. "Progress" had, of course, already emerged by this time as a moral metanarrative symbolic of American virtue (H. Smith 218).

In writing on the intellectual climate of the 1910s and 1920s in the United States, Richard Hofstadter has suggested that the focus on individualism of the late 1800s had been replaced in the Progressive Era with a consciousness of the individual's embeddedness within social groups functioning as a collective whole (168). There were many emergent schools of thought that treated society, and social institutions, at their core. Among them was a popular, even faddish, manifestation reworking social evolutionism as eugenics—the acquisition of particular qualities through breeding—as a base to establish a "scientific" explication of stratification and racial difference by applying notions of heredity to social theory. Within such a milieu, terms like "racial stock," "collective destiny," and "original capacity" were commonly brandished to explain inequality and legitimize conquest for an American public "thoroughly grounded in notions of racial superiority" (Hofstadter 171).

The opening sequences of *The Vanishing American* serve as a narrative prolog historicizing the main story in terms of racial conquest. Beginning with a series of fleeting images, diverse groups of people each traverse the same place, appearing and disappearing in a sequence suggestive of the passage of vast spans of time. "How many races?" the screen inquires. First we are shown arcane paleo-Indians, rough-hewn caricatures intended to represent the first inhabitants of North America. Then other fictive aboriginal denizens of the past follow: the "Basket Makers," "Slab-House People," "Cliff Dwellers," and the "Indians." And then finally the "whites" came to this land, first in the form of Coronado's advance men variously spying the Grand Canyon, battling and defeating Indians, and driving them into supplication. The "final chapter" of the conquest of the Indians opens three hundred years later, when Anglo-Americans continue the "march of destiny" across the desert lands and encounter the Navajo. At any rate, after the comings and goings of Kit Carson, the Navajo are pushed back to the reservation by the start of the twentieth century. When this time-transition montage concludes, the narrative moves at an altogether different pace in, the present (1925).

Figure 4.2. The opening sequences of *The Vanishing American* historicize in terms of racial conquest. Courtesy of the Museum of Modern Art/Film Stills Archive.

At the Indian Agency, the incompetent Mr. Amos Halliday (played by Charles Crockett) devotes himself to fiddling with file cabinets to ensure that the paperwork is well organized, symbolically manifesting the emergent and swelling federal bureaucracy charged with governing Indian affairs. At this moment his scheming, vile, and malicious assistant Henry Booker (played by Noah Beery) enters into the unfolding scene by kicking an Indian from the agency's doorway. Whereas Halliday, like the government itself, is abstract and coldly removed, Booker stands as the day-to-day reality for the Indians. Although not the ultimate seat of authority, he is instead the actualized power that bureaucracy fails to control. Booker's henchmen steal horse after horse from the Navajo and disguise their acts as taken in the best interests of the Indians by removing "diseased animals" that could threaten others. As a boy watches them take his horse, the subtitle announces, "Even in his short life, Nasja had learned that the white man must have his own way—that the Indian can only watch and endure, and dumbly wonder." Thus with few courses to counter the corrupt and bungling officials, the Navajo are left with only two options: reliance on the mercy of the merciless, or perhaps subterfuge.

Given the totality of their subjugation at the hands of the whites, neither is an attractive or particularly fruitful alternative.

Thus *The Vanishing American* is clearly sympathetic to Indians inasmuch as they are presented as oppressed peoples. They are cheated and abused by the government appointed to represent their interests. What is more, the whites who endeavor to help are themselves of limited power, in this case powerlessness is constructed as either the old (the caretaker) or female (the schoolteacher). Throughout their mistreatment the Indians maintain their composure, gaining cinematic karma through the process. But even as they are ennobled and individualized by their forbearance, their presence remains notably unreal to life on the screen. In being cast as the last practitioners of a dying way of life, the vanquished Indians are at best only ghosts of the past.

Popular images of Native Americans have tended to concentrate on two polar ends of an oppositional spectrum of the imagination—alternately conjuring an image of the innocent "noble child of nature" in stark counterpart to that of the of the "vicious savage." The construction of this duality is tied to the colonization of America and its subsequent westward expansionism. In his seminal book *Virgin Land*, Henry Nash Smith noted that by the early 1800s, and probably long before, there had arisen two prevalent, and simultaneous, notions of the West: one relatively immediate and domesticated through agricultural settlement, and the other conceived as a realm of wilderness lying beyond, inhabited by Indians and their white mountain-man counterparts (55). Similarly, William Goetzmann has linked the expansionist ideology underlying the exploration, exploitation, and repeopling of the region with the construction of a "romantic horizon" offering great latitude for the formation of largely imaginary visions of Native America (12). Thus, throughout the nineteenth century, the West was widely conceived of as a zone of wilderness ripe for exploration and economic conquest, and from within this expansionist frame of mind the region's native inhabitants were envisioned as part of a natural order to be overcome in the name of progress (Ruthven 46).

Historically, such images of Native Americans as embodiments of nature can be readily illustrated in the works of the pioneering artist-explorers, whose relationship with native peoples can be characterized as one of "author" to "subject." For example, the frontier artist George Catlin sought to collect cultural information, envisioning himself as a "historian" of the American Indian—yet his work has been widely critiqued as an inseparable mix of truth and fancy (Goetzmann 16). The famed frontier photographer Edward S. Curtis likewise sought to document, and in the process also produced a body of art that has been widely questioned and labeled an "essentializing distortion" that is part of a "tradition of using photography to mummify a so-called 'vanishing race'" (Rushing 60).[1] As products of their milieu, such works manifest an emergent mythology of the "red man" that followed from the same American political and economic interests that promoted intensified westward expansionism in the late nineteenth century, particularly after the close of the Civil War.

Despite their contrivance and questionable veracity as ethnographic records, such images usefully evidence the exploration and expansion of a Euro-American mind-set into the American West. As they were in part rendering the preconceptions that dominant American culture maintained, they were creating a record of their own activities as reinventors and shapers of culture. Indeed, although vastly different in intent, such early documentary projects shared a sentimentality later manifest in popular culture forms such as the cinema. Thus the process of depicting Native Americans, even in its beginnings prior to film, carried with it a striking similarity to the freely creative cinematic representation of Native America as allegorical fiction in treatments such as *The Vanishing American*. In all cases, cultural preconceptions have shaped both the reinvention of historical details, as well as the way they are read through the cultural expectations of their audiences. As Hofstadter suggests, "In determining whether such ideas are accepted, truth and logic are less important criteria than suitability to the intellectual needs and preconceptions of social interests" (204).

Thus the conflict between Indians and whites is rendered as the edge where one model replaces another, earlier, one—but only inasmuch as each is still drawn largely by the rules and understanding of the dominant cultural order. What of the Native peoples then, those finding themselves (or their alter egos) represented in film and who are thus caught up in this alleged changing of the vanguard? Finding themselves trapped in a moment where great change is mandated, would they meld happily into the new cultural order of America, relishing and thriving in their newfound status as American citizens? Envisioned from a perspective as yet incapable of imagining a viable yet distinctly Native American future, of necessity would they not either assimilate into the "superior" race, or else die off as a result of their loss in the Darwinian struggle for life—thereby becoming the vanished Americans prophesied throughout so many earlier strains of social evolutionism.

Whereas by the 1920s the lifeways of Native Americans had indeed been increasingly touched by modernization, so, too, it was increasingly apparent that they had not simply vanished as so frequently predicted.

Indeed, the persistence of distinct Native American identities in the West drew increasing attention from America's intelligentsia. Beginning immediately prior to the turn of the century, and developing through the 1920s, the social transformations experienced in the cities of the eastern seaboard—such as rapid population growth, escalating industrialization, and disillusionment wrought by the bitter experience of World War I— had led to a sense of alienation and an intensification of nationalist and nativist ideology (Nash 112–113). These developments provided the context for a strong regional movement in the United States and a concomitant search to locate a distinctly American identity. This period also saw the beginnings of a notable influx of easterners into the Southwest and the accompanying development of a tourism industry centered largely on the allure of the exotic and marketing of ethnicity (Rodríguez, Weigle).

The wake of World War I carried with it a diminishing of the militant strains of Social Darwinism, and the prevalent racist militarism, which had enveloped the turn of the century rise of American empire (Hofstadter 202–203). By the start of the 1920s, tourists, artists, and literati ventured into the Southwest seeking escape and adventure, as well as alternatives to the perceived spiritual decline and horrors of mass destruction that were increasingly thought of as the baggage of modernity. This period also saw film crews working in some of the remote regions of the West, using the same resources—such as the Fred Harvey Company and the railways—that the rest of the literati were using to access and market the region (Brownlow 240, 331). Just as the material conditions of the lives of Native Americans were redrawn through captivity, the reservation system, and political oversight by the federal government, so it goes that their spiritual and cultural dimensions had been circumscribed in the American popular culture by containing Indians within a field of romantic nostalgia. In this sense "spiritual" and "primitive" were linked as Native ethnicity was recast in an increasingly desirable image (Wilson 25–26).

The image of the Native American, as much imaginary as real, had long since become the penultimate "wilderness symbol." But construed in opposition to the rapid industrialization of America, rather than the national self-image of an agrarian nation, "wild" peoples and places were reinvested with newfound "aesthetic and ethical values." Thus the symbolic juxtaposition of contrary ways of life continued as a model for the American social order. However, rather than requiring annihilation of indigenous peoples as a means to achieve a uniform sense of national identity, the controlled presence of aboriginal culture was increasingly seen as useful to the interests of nationalism as representative of distinctly American traditions. From within such a climate, the seeming contradictions between Darwinian evolutionism and progressive sympathy characteristic of *The Vanishing American* could coincide, and the mixture of positive and negative stereotypes which had always shadowed Native Americans could be redrawn into closer proximity.

It was still symbolically useful to the agenda of this newly emerging nationalism to locate Native American lifeways outside the dominant American culture, rather than as distinct traditions forging headlong into the future on equal footing. But rather than symbolically (or literally) kill off the Indians in the murky confines of the past, their difference was to be maintained though other symbolic channels. Instead of positing inevitable evolutionary destruction, which was becoming harder to rationalize when faced with the persistence of Native Americans in the twentieth century, the confinement of Native Americans to other cultural and temporal orders was accomplished through containment within fields of nostalgia. So vanquished, Native American lifeways could then be transformed into a newer, but equally useful allegorical construct: just as "wilderness" as a symbolic order (disorder?) is simultaneously distanced and increasingly controlled by "civilization" through the parceling off of national parks, forests, and wilderness areas, indigenous peoples were increasingly subject to a type of paternalistic control that sought their protection as cultural attractions rather than their destruction as threats (Riley, Hinsley). As Devereaux suggests, "representation is always happening across the notional boundaries of psychological, social, or cultural specificities" (8).

Other plays on the incorporation of Indians into American society are manifest in *The Vanishing American*. Indeed, one of the themes that makes this film distinctive as a Western, and uniquely marks the time and conditions surrounding its production, is the presence of the Great War. At first, the U.S. military sought merely the help of the Navajo; they were asked to supply horses for the war effort in an era when motor transport was not yet dominant. This sudden focus placed on the issue of horses redefines the relationship between government and its wards, and simultaneously draws attention to the wrongdoings of Booker. This is a moment of great victory for the Native Americans in the film, as it leads to the firing of the corrupt official. As a result, a profound sense of order and justice seemingly emerges to mark this new world—a new world order holding a promise for the Indians as full-fledged citizens. Booker's firing is met with exuberant cheers in the film. And as the Navajo are told they are Americans now, first and foremost, the opportunity to serve their country becomes a chance to prove themselves collectively by leaving the past behind, just as it stands as a potential bridge across the cultural chasm that separates Nophaie and Marion. Eventually the Navajos attempt transcendence:

not only do they bring in their horses, but they enlist as a group and head off to serve in President Wilson's crusade.

As fate and moviemakers would have it, when the soldiers finally return to their ancestral homeland, they march in parade thinking themselves to be American war heroes. They also return from the service ever more thoroughly enculturated into the white man's ways—visibly so, for they departed wearing their traditional Navajo clothes, but return in military uniforms. Alas, it is not a hero's welcome that awaits the veterans, no warm embraces, handshakes, or slaps on the back from the hands of the other (white) Americans. Instead they remain oppressed and are mistreated and scorned as much, if not more so, than before they went off to fight. Alternately ignored and reviled, they even find their earlier moment of justice inverted, as the evil Booker has somehow returned to replace Halliday as the Indian agent! The fair Marion has also departed for the East, ostensibly to marry a returned white soldier, thereby leaving Nophaie at a loss for his life's love—the woman of whom thoughts and fancies had kept him motivated in the trenches.

Late in the film, the hero Nophaie again finds himself cast as a mediator between two worlds. Marion has unexpectedly returned from the East seeking to find Nophaie, and as they are reunited he learns she has not married the white soldier after all. But even while hope returns to Nophaie in this moment, unrest continues to grow among the rest of the Indians. Finding themselves unaccepted and scorned by the white world, the war heroes relinquish their identities as Americans and return to mythologized "Indian" ways (which are now vastly more stereotypical than their characterizations at the start of the film). Ironically, trained as warriors by their historic conquerors, the Navajo veterans emerge reborn as stereotypical warriors.

Once again wild—and paradoxically both less American and more American than ever before—they attack and lay siege to the town and its white inhabitants, trapping Nophaie and Marion with the other townspeople. The evil Booker is soon killed (by an arrow through the neck), but the onslaught does not subside. Finally Nophaie resolves the crisis: he exits the safety of the fortification to plead for an end to the violence. But before his proposal can be heard, he is mortally wounded. The film ends there, with the hero dying in the arms of his grieving beloved. In the end, the love between a red man and white woman is not allowed to redefine the future, and the promise of racial unification and equalization embodied in the moment is forever dashed; another promise lies broken in the dust[2]. No escape is offered as the film returns to the point from which it started, destined to repeat the "ceaseless devouring of the

Figure 4.3. Nophaie (Richard Dix) returns to his homeland after World War I, only to find that his arch rival, Henry Booker (Noah Beery), is now the Indian Agent. Courtesy of the Museum of Modern Art/Film Stills Archive.

weak by the strong" as we travail across the stage of time, moving from "darkness into dark."

The Vanishing American is a bitter and ironic film, suggesting many questions (and questionings) about themes marking the first decades of the twentieth century—Manifest Destiny, Euro-American political and military supremacy, racial relations, industrialization, the rise of empire, and the course of progress are all touched upon. In each regard Seitz's film maintains a self-conscious focus on Native Americans caught in the jaws of history. Thus it might be fairly characterized as a sympathetic work; yet its "sympathy" maintains and carries with it an ingrained assumption of its time, that indigenous peoples are embodiments of antiquated lifeways and, hence, are rendered as emblematic of the past, rather than as viable participants in the world of the present. As such, it embodies a larger collective enterprise that was actively reinventing the popular image of Native Americans within the dominating order of American society, and doing so through a set of lenses that looked astigmatically for examples of racial distinctiveness and stages of social evolution. Furthermore, it was a milieu that was actively capitalizing on popular notions of race through such vehicles as Western movies.

Westerns that were relatively sensitive to Native American interests were by no means unknown in the 1920s, yet they were relatively isolated as individual examples within the genre as a whole (O'Connor 18, Tuska 40). However, Kevin Brownlow contends that, contrary to popular opinion, silent films as a whole were more sympathetic to the plight of Native Americans than were later Westerns (329). Still, as an early western, *The Vanishing American* is unusual for its time in many ways: its hero is an Indian, many of the white characters are portrayed as wrongdoers, there is a love interest between Nophaie and Marion, and the film is set not just against the western cultural landscape, but also against the backdrop of World War I, standing as an emblem of modernity and ultimately serving as a thematic link between Native America, Euro-Americans, and the modern world.

As a product of its day and the circumstances governing its production, this is not a film which comfortably portrays, or even finds reason to approach, any issues from native perspectives. The lead actors are heavily made-up whites, the overall slant is extremely paternalistic, and Native Americans are portrayed as generic Indians, for the most part devoid of specific tribal identities. Still, the film's interest in racial inequality apparently created some concern within the movie industry, due to the belief that "the problem of the Indian and his betrayal by the government was more clearly etched in this picture than in any other silent film" (Brownlow 345). At any rate, whatever its shortcomings as a portrayal of history or culture, the film has much to tell as a simultaneous allegory, critique, and manifestation of early modern American social thought at a time when it was caught in the throes of rapid transformation.

Thus one might well ponder the question that, if a film like this is not about real Indians, then who is it really about? John O'Connor offers the observation that "The dominant view of the Indians has always primarily reflected what the white man thought of himself" (17). Is *The Vanishing American* then best read as Seitz's nihilistic portrait of his own people? Is the Indian a palimpsest upon whose bodies dominating tellings of history, as well as its critique, are inscribed? What then is *The Vanishing American*? Allegory of race relations? Morality play? Cliché western? Experimental cinema? In truth this film is all of these things—and none of them.

By the early twentieth century the West was no longer so wild. Native Americans, always marked, were increasingly marketed. Images of Indians have long abounded in popular culture—dime-novel Westerns

Figure 4.4. *The Vanishing American* is notable for the unrequited love affair between Nophaie and Marion (Lois Wilson), a kindhearted white schoolmarm. Courtesy of the Museum of Modern Art/Film Stills Archive.

were popular by the mid-1800s, the years prior to the turn of the century saw the rise of Wild West shows, and, as film emerged, Westerns were already a familiar genre. Indeed, not just images of Native Americans, but the people themselves (if the two constructs could still be separated) were often the subjects of display as public spectacles, such as at the

Chicago Exposition of 1893 wherein "public curiosity about other peoples, mediated by the terms of the marketplace, produced an early form of touristic consumption" (Hinsley 363). And the American Southwest increasingly became the last stand of America's ideological West: with its unique humanscape, given to accompany and populate its landscape, it came to represent in the collective mind-set what Barbara Babcock and Marta Weigle have both considered "America's Orient."

Feature films unquestionably reflect the cultural realities of their makers and serve to project these themes both inwardly and outwardly as cultural productions (Weakland 50). Over time Hollywood Indians, as images stated largely in the terms of the dominant cultural order, have come to populate our cultural landscape as mythologized icons of the romantic, the exotic, and the mystical on one hand, while also standing as emblems of the downtrodden, the impoverished, and the vanquished on the other. This is exemplified in *The Vanishing American*, as well as many notable contemporary films ranging to *Little Big Man* (1970), *Thunderheart* (1990), and *Powwow Highway* (1989). Thus Native America is an ongoing reinvention, perhaps one of mass media's most enduring and fanciful creations. In the end, the many faces of Native America, as mediated identities, must be understood in terms of the times and circumstances, as well as the motivations, of those who are representing the past (Handler and Linnekin, Clifford, Hinsley). Thus in the cinema the objectification of Native Americans becomes a path toward a form of "ownership" by the dominant culture. Furthermore, the displacement of image into new contexts of presentation creates conceptions of cultural reality with an authority that often transcends and obliterates alternative tellings such as indigenous or countercultural perspectives. Yet within this diversity, one of the crucial characteristics is the persistence with which Native America has come to symbolize simultaneously both nobility and savagery, alterity and common humanity.

Ultimately *The Vanishing American* was incapable of freeing itself from the stereotypes and preconceptions of its day; caught under the same cumulative weight through which culture delimits and shapes representation, just as it limits and constrains consciousness (Devereaux 15–16). Thus the similarities of the Indians to living, breathing people are replaced with similarities to a stereotype of an idealized savage, and their presence in this film remains largely that of a popular construction of the dominant media—yet it stands as a compelling and poignant statement just the same. To return to the quote by Paul Chaat Smith that began this chapter, Native Americans, as "shape-shifters" of the "national consciousness," are indeed "trapped in history. No escape." But perhaps this passage could also be purposefully revoiced in this manner: *Native Americans, as shapes shifted by the national unconsciousness, are forever trapped in the history of film.*[3]

Notes

1. For a relatively kind treatment of Curtis's project that historicizes the photographer's motivations within the predicament of being a white trying to understand native traditions, however imperfectly, see Kevin Brownlow, 338.

2. As Stallybrass and White have pointed out, the junctures where marginalized segments of society collide with the mainstream help reveal the makeup of our social fabric. Nowhere is this more a case in point than in interracial romantic couplings, which often engender strongly emotional, and frequently hostile, reactions. For example, in his 1925 review of the film in the *New York Times*, which is generally favorable, Mordant Hall penned this characterization: "Marion Warner is torn between affection for Captain Ramsdell and admiration for the redskin" (280).

3. As interaction between cultures has intensified throughout this century, and as members of different ethnic groups have increasingly gained awareness of their location within a shared economic and political order, the question of authority over the production and consumption of identity has become a pressing concern. Indeed, the negotiation of the image has served as both a means for the dominant culture to contain ethnic identities within the boundaries of its established working stereotypes, and for ethnic groups to lay claim to the rights of the cultural production of identity (such as the movement for indigenous groups and other minorities to produce their own films).

Works Cited

Babcock, Barbara. "Mudwomen and Whitemen." In *Discovered Country: Tourism and Survival in the American West*, 180–95. Scott Norris, ed. Albuquerque: Stone Ladder Press, 1994.

Brownlow, Kevin. *The War, the West, and the Wilderness*. New York: Alfred A. Knopf, 1979.

Clifford, James. "Objects and Selves—An Afterword." In *Objects and Others: Essays on Museums and Material Culture*, 236–46. George W. Stocking, Jr., ed. Madison: University of Wisconsin Press, 1985.

Devereaux, Leslie. "An Introductory Essay" and "Experience, Re-Presentation, and Film." In *Fields of Vision: Essays in Film Studies, Visual Anthropology, and Photography*, 1–18 and 56–73. Leslie Devereaux and Roger Hillman, eds. Berkeley: University of California Press, 1995.

Goetzmann, William H. "The West as Romantic Horizon." In *The West as Romantic Horizon*, 11–30. William H. Goetzmann and Joseph C. Porter, eds. Omaha: Center for Western Studies, Joslyn Art Museum, 1981.

Hall, Mordaunt. "The American Indian." *New York Times Film Reviews (1913–1931)*. New York: New York Times & Arno Press, 1970.

Handler, R., and J. Linnekin. "Tradition, Genuine or Spurious." *Journal of American Folklore* 97.385 (1984): 273–290.

Hinsley, Curtis M. "The World as Marketplace: Commodification of the Exotic at the World's Columbian Exposition, Chicago, 1893." In *Exhibiting Cultures: The Poetics and Politics of Museum Display*, 344–65. Ivan Karp and Steven D. Lavine, eds. Washington, D.C.: Smithsonian Institution Press, 1991.

Hofstadter, Richard. *Social Darwinism in American Thought*. 1948. New York: George Braziller, 1959.

Nash, Gerald D. *Creating the West: Historical Interpretations 1890–1990*. Albuquerque: University of New Mexico Press, 1991.

O'Connor, John E. "The White Man's Indian." *Film & History* 23.1–4 (1993): 17–26.

Riley, Michael J. "Constituting the Southwest; Contesting the Southwest; Re-Inventing the Southwest." *Journal of the Southwest* 36.3 (1994): 221–241.

Rodríguez, Sylvia. "Ethnic Reconstruction in Contemporary Taos." *Journal of the Southwest* 32.4 (1990): 541–555.

Rushing, W. Jackson. "Native American Subjects: Photography, Narrative, Local History." *Artspace* 15.1 (1990): 60–63.

Ruthven, Todd. "The Imaginary Indian in Europe." *Art in America* 60.4 (1972): 40–47.

Smith, Henry Nash. *Virgin Land: The American West as Symbol and Myth*. New York: Vintage Books, 1950.

Smith, Paul Chaat. "Ghost in the Machine." *Aperture* 139 (1995): 6–9.

Stallybrass, Peter, and Allon White. *The Politics and Poetics of Transgression*. Ithaca: Cornell University Press, 1986.

Tuska, Jon. *The American West in Film: Critical Approaches to the Western*. Westport, Conn.: Greenwood Press, 1985.

Weakland, John H. "Feature Films as Cultural Documents." In *Principles of Visual Anthropology*, 45–67. Paul Hockings, ed. New York: Mouton de Gruyter, 1995.

Weigle, Marta. "Southwest Lures: Innocents Detoured, Incensed Determined." *Journal of the Southwest* 32.4 (1990): 499–540.

Wilson, Chris. "New Mexico Architecture in the Tradition of Romantic Reaction." *Artspace* 13.1 (1988): 22–28.

The Representation of Conquest
John Ford and the Hollywood Indian, 1939–1964

> THURSDAY: *"I don't see them, not a one."*
> YORK: *"Well, they're down there sir, among the rocks."*
> —Fort Apache

Not only was John Ford canonized by the first wave of auteurist critics, but his own stubborn attachment to the central myths of Western culture in general and American culture specifically also made his work seem for decades to be commercial Hollywood's principal representation of the American experience. And because Ford worked so thoroughly within the system rather than in opposition to it, one may be hard pressed to save his oeuvre from one of the most pervasive and damning charges made against the Hollywood tradition—that it was racist and sexist at the core.

In the late 1990s the debate was again joined over Ford's Westerns; in particular, Richard Maltby explicated persistently racist elements in Ford's work, and William Darby attempted (rather vainly) to maintain the traditional view of Ford, arguing, "Though it has often been alleged (even by Ford himself) that the director's films were demeaning to Indians, such a charge is difficult to sustain when one considers the portrait of Cochise in *Fort Apache* and those of such later figures as Scar (Henry Brandon) in *The Searchers* and the tribal leaders (Victor Jory, Ricardo Montalban, Gilbert Roland) in *Cheyenne Autumn*. If anything, Ford is scrupulously fair to the Indians and their motives" (97).

Frank Manchel also attempted the difficult task Maltby and Darby reject as impossible or unnecessary: to redeem Ford's late Westerns, particularly *Sergeant Rutledge*, from simplistically general charges of racism.

I am not sure that such redemption is possible. At the same time, arguments such as Maltby's do not seem to me to account sufficiently for the variation that exists in Ford's depictions of Native Americans. Thus, without attempting to separate Ford's films from the larger project in which they are implicated, I do wish to look somewhat more carefully at development and change in the figure of the Indian in Ford's Westerns by considering those films from several perspectives.

One of the most widely discussed topics in the criticism of John Ford's films is the relationship between history and myth. A newspaper editor at the end of *The Man Who Shot Liberty Valence* (1962) has been widely quoted as speaking for Ford in saying, "When the legend becomes fact, print the legend." In a more troubling way, the John Wayne character in *Fort Apache* (1948), Kirby York, makes a similar decision in electing not to expose the errors in the developing myth of his Custer-like former commander. Both decisions have often been widely interpreted as representative of Ford's view of the necessarily difficult relationship between history and myth, as if Ford's films ought to be evaluated more as epic poetry than as history.

That antihistorical view of Ford's work, which was particularly employed by earlier critics, tended to restrict discussion of Ford's historical subjects, and no such subject was so common in his Westerns but so little discussed until recently as his treatment of Native Americans. Jon Tuska, whom Maltby also quotes, says that what such critics mean by myth is the part of the film "which they know to be a lie but which, for whatever reason, they still wish to embrace" (237).

The epic poetry argument thus deflected discussion of Ford's film away from history. For years, it was common to assume that Ford's Westerns were not "about" Indians, just as it was assumed that *The Quiet Man* was not "about" Irish politics or gender. But ten of his films—*Stagecoach* (1939), *Drums Along the Mohawk* (1939), *Fort Apache* (1948), *She Wore a Yellow Ribbon* (1949), *Wagonmaster* (1950), *Rio Grande* (1950), *The Searchers* (1956), *Sergeant Rutledge* (1960), *Two Rode Together* (1962), and *Cheyenne Autumn* (1964)—involve Native Americans as significant elements of the plot, and Ford's participation in constructing the Hollywood portrait of the Indian certainly deserves more serious scrutiny than it has received until lately.

More than most directors of Westerns, Ford did tend to base his films at least loosely on historical incidents, particularly on specific Indian wars. *Stagecoach*, the cavalry trilogy (*Fort Apache, She Wore a Yellow Ribbon, Rio Grande*), and *Sergeant Rutledge* are all loosely situated during the Apache wars of the 1870s, although *Fort Apache's* treatment of Colonel Thursday echoes the story of Custer as well. *Drums Along the*

Figure 5.1. Sal Mineo as Red Shirt and Delores Del Rio as a Spanish woman in *Cheyenne Autumn* (1964). Courtesy of the Museum of Modern Art/Film Stills Archive.

Mohawk is set in New York during the Revolutionary War and centrally features the Battle of Oriskany, although the siege of the fort in the film was fictional. The precise date of *Wagonmaster* is not clear, but it is set during the Mormon migrations.

The Searchers takes place between 1868 and 1873 and includes an event that is strongly reminiscent of Custer's massacre of Black Kettle's group of Cheyenne at Washita in Oklahoma in the fall of 1868; Ford makes his group Comanche, but like Black Kettle's Cheyenne, they are destroyed by the Seventh Cavalry. *Two Rode Together* is set sometime before Quanah Parker's surrender at Fort Sill in 1875, and *Cheyenne Autumn*, like Mari Sandoz's novel, on which it is based, treats the long trek of the Cheyenne from Oklahoma back to the Tongue River Reservation in 1878–79.

Even though Ford's Westerns begin rooted in history, the usual epic poetry argument has them ending in myth. Frank Nugent, who wrote the scripts for *Fort Apache*, *Wagonmaster*, *The Searchers*, and *Two Rode Together*, helped to perpetuate that view when he talked about the genesis of *Fort Apache*: "He gave me a list of about fifty books to read—memoirs, novels, anything about the period. Later he sent me down into the old Apache country to nose around, get the smell and the feel of the land. . . . When I got back, Ford asked me if I thought I had enough research. I said yes. 'Good,' he said, 'Now just forget everything you've read, and we'll start writing a movie'" (Anderson 77–79). At most, such a view suggests, Ford's films refer to history, but they do not seriously try to represent it.

If we consider the interaction between narrative strategy and audience response in these films, however, things look a little different. Most audiences were probably not likely to see *Drums Along the Mohawk* as accurately depicting the history of the American Revolution. That is so partly because they were used to encountering that revolution, along with the rest of white American history, in the "serious" historical arena of courses and textbooks; typical viewers could distinguish fictional from historical intent in the film because they brought a well-developed historical sense into the theater with them.[1] But the much rarer and more scattered accounts of native American life that were known to the general public during Ford's lifetime made it much more likely that his constructed vision of the Hollywood Indian would begin to assume the status of historical truth for many viewers.

If, then, as Maltby contends, the films are intentionally false, they have much for which to answer. "Those texts themselves have a history, but they also contain an idea of history, and of the West as history, which is itself 'legend' rather than 'fact'—mythology. The subject of my enquiry is mythology rather than history; to be more precise, it is the history of a mythology which masquerades as history but, like the Senator [Stoddard, in *The Man Who Shot Liberty Valance*], knows itself to be lying" (38).

Furthermore, Ford's narrative strategy often encouraged ignorant audiences to make this kind of mistake. His films regularly combine fictional white characters in the foreground with images of historical Native Americans in the background. Viewers of *Fort Apache*, for example, might have easily recognized the fact that Owen Thursday resembled George Custer without mistaking the two. But Cochise, who had no differently named alter ego in the film, occupied a very different representational space. The movie allowed (perhaps even encouraged) the substitution of its representation of Cochise for the historical person, particularly because most viewers had little specific knowledge of Cochise beyond the name. Thus, Ford's representation of Cochise assumed the status of history in a rather different way than did his representation of Thursday.

Consequently, as far as Native Americans are concerned, Ford's Westerns are probably more typified by the conflation of history and myth than by the binary opposition between them that traditional Ford criticism has invoked. In this sense, too, whether Ford's Westerns were intended to be accurate historical representations (or whether they were, as Maltby contends, intended to be inaccurate historical representations) is not the sole important consideration. If fictional representations are taken as history, they have real historical consequences (Stam 15). In this sense Ford's films function as if they were historical texts, constructing a sense of Native American life on the frontier, participating in the social and political debates of the era in which they were produced, and helping to construct much of what still stands for popular historical knowledge of Native American life.

And like historical texts, these films need to be examined and evaluated, not just for the accuracy of the information they supposedly contain, but also for the rhetorical prestructuring of the material that they present. In his essay, "Historicism, History and the Imagination," Hayden White argues; "A rhetorical analysis of historical discourse would recognize that every history worthy of the name contains not only a certain amount of information and an explanation (or interpretation) of what this information "means," but also a more or less overt message about the attitude the reader should assume before both the data reported and their formal interpretation. This message is contained in the figurative elements appearing in the discourse which serve as subliminally projected clues to the reader about the quality of the subject under study" (White 105).

The history of Native Americans in North America is undoubtedly not accurately represented in Ford's films, but beyond the question of accuracy, his films, like all historical texts, come with hermeneutic instructions on how to interpret that history. But what sort of readings of our history are being prearranged in the films?

In many ways, Ford's representations of Native Americans developed out of traditional Hollywood portrayals. Hollywood had never shown any serious respect for the importance and individuality of Native American peoples and cultures, for their own respective histories, or for the vitality of Native American life. As Maltby points out, "in the Hollywood Western, there are no 'real' 'Indians'—no Iroquois, no Lakotas, no Navajos, only Hollywood Indians with different names. With hardly an exception throughout its history, the Hollywood Western has obliterated the ethnic and cultural distinctions between the many indigenous people of North America" (35).

As a form which developed early in the century, the Western reflected national policy in this respect. The period at the end of the nineteenth

Figure 5.2. A faceless and violent Indian death in *Stagecoach* (1939). Courtesy of the Museum of Modern Art/Film Stills Archive.

century had been characterized specifically by a national policy of detribalization. One major expression of this policy was the establishment of Indian schools placed under the centralized control of the Bureau of Indian Affairs. By the end of the century, nearly half of all Native American children had spent at least some time in these schools, where their individual tribal identity could be partially effaced and English could begin to supplant their indigenous languages (Berkhofer 170–72). In film particularly, Native American roles were largely restricted to the Western genre and limited to a relatively brief portion of the American past by the genre's strict time limitations. The vast array of Native American cultures was flattened out into screen constructions that were principally amalgamated from the Plains tribes, as if all Indians were from those cultures alone (Churchill 232–39).

For much of Hollywood, this tendency also meant that white actors played Indian roles. Ford undermined that practice in some measure, casting Native Americans in indigenous parts, at least so long as those parts were not major speaking roles. Ford never was able to overcome studio traditions for larger parts, however, and even in *Cheyenne Autumn*, where he made an overt commitment to tell the Native American side of the story, he was forced to use non-Indian actors for major Cheyenne characters, most notably Sal Mineo, Ricardo Montalban, and Gilbert Roland.[2]

Maltby makes a good deal of the dominance of this pattern, noting that it is more complex than the device of disguise in literature because it tends to depend on a simultaneous double awareness in which the audience must accept the fiction, yet see through the disguise in order "to maintain the security of their viewing position and identification" (48). He goes on to point out that things get more complex when the non-Indian actor is black, as in Woody Strode's impersonation of Stone Calf in *Two Rode Together*.

Ford did make some distinctions between Native groups beyond those that were common at the time; the Indians in *Drums Along the Mohawk*, for example, are always shown on foot, rather than mounted, as were their Plains counterparts. But Ford made no effort to cast authentic members of the tribes he represented. Chief Big Tree, an Iroquois, who played Gilbert Martin's friend Blue Back in *Drums Along the Mohawk*, also appeared as the drunken Christian Apache chief, Pony That Walks, in *She Wore a Yellow Ribbon*. And Ford's main group of Native actors for all of his Westerns was drawn from the Navajos he befriended near Monument Valley. This same sort of casual substitution allowed Ford to transform Black Kettle's Cheyennes into Comanches in *The Searchers*.

If Hollywood has denied the cultural diversity of the Native American experience, as did the Bureau of Indian Affairs through the Indian schools, also like those schools it has disregarded their languages. Indians in Westerns traditionally spoke a peculiarly stylized form of pidgin characterized by assorted grunts and broken syntax. White characters occasionally were presented as knowing indigenous languages, but because the stories always were told in English and from the point of view of white characters, their language was usually presented as competent and proficient. The apparent contrast invariably made white characters appear to be more capable than their Indian counterparts.

Again, Ford tended to preserve this stereotypic pattern, particularly in the earlier films, though in *Fort Apache* he also made his Cochise proficient in Spanish. In one sense, *Cheyenne Autumn* was a significant exception; in that film he allowed Cheyenne characters to make extended untranslated speeches, sometimes even without inventing a dramatic reason to provide an English translation. Because his actors were mainly Navajo, however, the language was not authentic.[3]

In the earlier Westerns as well, Ford tends to appropriate the Hollywood habit of suggesting Indian communication through simulated bird and animal cries, as if all Native Americans—once they were hidden by darkness or the landscape—expressed themselves as a part of the animal order. Interestingly, this pattern, too, is finally reversed in *Cheyenne Autumn*. A very important element of the reversal is marked by the fact that the motley group of Dodge City vigilantes ventures into the country in hopes of encountering the Cheyenne, accompanied by the frenzied whoops and cries usually uttered by Hollywood Indians during their attacks. The inversion of the pattern underscores the dehumanizing qualities of the normal Hollywood pattern.

Along with traditional Hollywood, Ford's early films reinforce the traditional Western pattern of ascribing the most extreme violence and brutality to Indians much more often than to white characters. The mutilated troopers tied to the wagon wheels in *Fort Apache*, the torture and killing of Rynders in *She Wore a Yellow Ribbon*, the murder of Chris Hubble in *Sergeant Rutledge*—all these deaths are unanswered in kind in their respective films and present the Indians in the films as more cruel and bloodthirsty than the white settlers. This traditional pattern, too, begins to break down in some measure in *The Searchers* and *Cheyenne Autumn*, where, increasingly, Ford attributes violence to whites and begins to suggest reasons for Indian rage against whites, as well as the opposite.

Like other Westerns, too, all of Ford's plots, with the exception of *Cheyenne Autumn*, construct Indians as a savage presence set in opposition to the advance of American civilization, particularly as that civilization is embodied in white families. Consequently, Ford's traditional Westerns prominently feature white women and children who are jeopardized by an Indian presence, their jeopardy automatically justifying the military actions of the cavalry. On the other hand, Ford seldom shows Native American women and children similarly jeopardized, or any other images that would explain and justify Indian violence toward whites.[4] This iconography, perhaps as much as any other in the traditional western, serves to justify what Maltby calls "a racist discourse in which racism was offered and enacted as a theory of history" (37).

But this pattern, too, begins to break down in some measure in *The Searchers*. The massacre of the Comanche camp is expressed particularly in the death of Look, Martin's Comanche "wife." In the final attack on Scar's village, Ford shows Comanche men firing at the attacking rangers even as they attempt to shield and save their own children. The pattern is more dramatically reversed in *Cheyenne Autumn* when Ford finally dwells much more heavily on the endangered Indian family, showing white culture primarily as a threatening military presence, the sort of representation reserved for Indians in the earlier films. In both these later cases as well, Ford includes scenes of taking scalps and, in both cases, the scalpers are white—Ethan Edwards in *The Searchers* and the trail driver in *Cheyenne Autumn*.

Linked to the differential associations with vulnerability and threat is the significant discrepancy that the Western maintains in the valuation of white and Native American lives. Through the star system and a variety of other narrative and nonnarrative devices, viewers of Westerns are normally encouraged to grieve over white deaths and generally to rejoice in Indian deaths. White funerals are shown; Indian funerals almost never are. Indians fall from their running horses and are forgotten.

Again, Ford's early films conform to the pattern, and, even in the later films when the pattern begins to break down, discrepancies in the relative value of lives are apparent. While Look's death is treated with pathos and sympathy in *The Searchers*, it is a thinkable and viewable death because Look was at best a likably comic stereotype, and thus the camera can reveal Look's body to the audience.

Martha's death, which drives Ethan mad, is not shown. Ethan expressly forbids Marty to look at Martha's body, and his prohibition stands, in effect, for the audience as well. The denial of her body corresponds to Ethan's denial of his desire for her, of course, and the film allows us to see that fact. But the film also transforms Ethan's potential sexual guilt into actual sexual transgression and projects that transgression onto the Indian raiders; the fact that her death is unwatchable both signifies and constructs the unthinkable horror of her murder and supposed violation. Those implications, raised in Ethan's mind, are allowed to remain unchallenged in the minds of the audience.

In *Cheyenne Autumn*, such traditional patterns are partially subverted, but not entirely replaced. The Cheyenne in Sandoz's novel were accompanied on their trek, at least initially, by a middle-aged Quaker spinster. But, as Ford said, in Hollywood "you couldn't do that—you had to have a young beautiful girl" (Bogdanovich 104). Hollywood convention demanded a plot that would eventually unite the ideal white couple, and Carroll Baker became the Quaker woman and simultaneously the love interest of the male lead, Richard Widmark.

In consequence, the film does not simply represent the horror of U.S. artillery rounds dropping among Cheyenne families; given the centrality of the Carroll Baker character in the narrative, those rounds must particularly threaten her and the white resolution at the end of the film for which she is required; clearly the studio saw the threat to Cheyenne lives as insufficient to sustain audience interest without the additional threat posed to a photogenic star.

The particular conventions of the genre, then, equate progress in the West with the destruction of indigenous cultures, and studio imperatives did not see an honest contemplation of that destruction as marketable. The result is a doubly Eurocentric narrative, where both the action and the emotional tone of the narrative are defined by white characters and white consciousness. Ford's films all conform to that pattern, even to some measure *Cheyenne Autumn*, where he said that he wanted to present the Indian side of the story.

Other supporting narrative devices in the Western, Ford's included, preserve the same values. Music, which is typically used to guide emotional responses in the audience, maintains this Eurocentric emphasis in the positive emotional resonance Westerns give to folk songs, military tunes, and traditional hymns. Indian music, when it is suggested, is as limited as Indian speech and almost invariably associated with war, stereotypically invoking a sense of threat and suspense.

And finally, when overt narration is employed in Western films, the narrative voice is a white voice. Here again, Ford's films are no exception. Captain York, of course, is one belated narrator of *Fort Apache*, followed by an anonymous off-screen voice that valorizes the ordinary soldiers of the cavalry as the instruments of Manifest Destiny. The male narrator at the beginning of *She Wore a Yellow Ribbon* maintains the same stance. The musical narration in the title song of *Wagonmaster* focuses on the white settlement of the West. The same sort of song in *The Searchers* sentimentalizes Ethan Edwards much more than the plot does, softening his racism by emphasizing the values of the white family and home. Even *Cheyenne Autumn* is narrated by a white character, the anguished liberal Captain Archer.

Ward Churchill's disparaging comment applies to Ford's film as well as to other Westerns: "To date there has not been one attempt to put out a commercial film which deals with native reality through native eyes" (236). Perhaps Churchill's most telling point is one he borrows from Oneida comedian Charlie Hill—that the cumulative effect of such tale-telling made the killing of Indians into the American childhood game of cowboys and Indians, a game whose import we can perhaps better understand if we imagine our children playing at Nazis and Jews instead. That is to say, then, that the historical inaccuracies and biases of the traditional Western, including Ford's, have had important cultural consequences.

In a filmed interview, Ford once said, "My sympathy was always with the Indians." In some ways that may have been the case. But the shaping power of studio decisions and generic conventions regularly and reliably turned the principal sympathies of his audiences toward his white characters. The Western was at root an expression of white culture justi-fying its expansion, and Ford largely participated in that expression, some-times by choice, at others by default. On the other hand, as I have already suggested, Ford (in conjunction with his collaborators) did struggle in some measure to modify the terms of this terrible white discourse on Native Americans, and the nature of that struggle deserves some further consideration.

It is probably true, as Ford indicated, that he felt profoundly sympa-thetic with Native Americans and that such sympathy grew out of his Irish background. At the same time, he accepted the myth of Manifest Destiny with fervor: "Perhaps it's my Irish atavism, my sense of reality, of the beauty of clans, in contrast to the modern world, the masses, the collective irresponsibility. Who better than an Irishman could understand the Indians, while still being stirred by the tales of the U.S. Cavalry? We were on both sides of the epic" (Gallagher 341). With the frontier con-flict so doubly coded for Ford, it would not be surprising to see his atti-tudes shift over time in response to changing political climates.

I have already suggested that there is some development in Ford's treatment of Native Americans. In *Stagecoach*, Geronimo and his band are presented as little more than an ominous external threat to the mot-ley social group traveling together. *Drums Along the Mohawk* does only a little to expand on that minimal treatment; the Mohawks, in league with the British, pose the principal physical threat to the colonists, but the film provides no explanation of their lives beyond the raids to indicate why they have forged an alliance with one group of whites to fight an-other. Likewise, the "good" Indian, Blue Back, is not explained either, and the audience is left merely with the formulation that there were good Indians who sided with the colonists and bad ones who resisted.[5]

But if the early treatment of Native Americans in Ford's Westerns had been perfunctory and negative, the films from the end of the 1940s brought something of a change. As Darby argues (97), in *Fort Apache* Cochise is presented as a highly individualized and principled leader who is dedicated to prevent the degradation of his people at the hands of the corrupt Indian agent, Meacham, and the plot places him in direct oppo-sition to the ambitious and foolish Colonel Thursday.

Some of the patterns of *Fort Apache* remain in *She Wore a Yellow Ribbon*; the Indians are being stirred up and corrupted by an unscrupu-lous agent, but they are presented as more angry and militant in the sec-ond film, and their leader, Pony That Walks, is doubly debilitated by whiskey and white religion—a figure who entirely lacks the charisma of Cochise in the previous film.

Figure 5.3. The Euro-centered narration of *Cheyenne Autumn* focuses on Deborah Wright (Carroll Baker). Courtesy of the Museum of Modern Art/Film Stills Archive.

In *Wagonmaster*, the band of Navajos encountered by the Mormon train are endowed with considerable dignity and restraint. The Indians are basically friendly (which is to say that they accept the presence of white settlers in their land without rancor or resistance), and they invite the Mormon group to join them in a dance that parallels the dance the settlers had held earlier. Although the Mormon women are obviously beset by sexual fears of the Navajos and remain apart from the dancers, the violence which erupts is white violence: one of the Clegg sons attacks a Navajo woman. Yet the Indian group, perhaps improbably, do not insist on exacting their own justice; they accept the whipping ordered by the Mormon leader as sufficient punishment, proving to be at least as civil and humane as the group of settlers, and far less predatory than the Cleggs.

Ford's portrait of Indians turns increasingly negative again in *Rio Grande*. Natchez and his band return to being the faceless, ill-defined threat of *Stagecoach*, and there will be no portrait of an Indian leader comparable to *Fort Apache*'s Cochise until *Cheyenne Autumn*. On the other hand, Ford does make his white society and white heroes increasingly racist and bloodthirsty in *The Searchers*, *Sergeant Rutledge*, *Two Rode Together*, and *Cheyenne Autumn*.

It is probable that these changes are reflective of changes in Ford, revealing in some measure a harsh attitude toward cultural enemies in the climate of 1939, just before World War II, followed by the decay of an initially generous postwar optimism into cynical Cold War pessimism.[6] The portrait of an increasingly racist American society provided by films of the 1950s and 1960s, of course, develops in the context of a growing general awareness of an American tradition of racism—an awareness that was engendered by the developing civil-rights movement. It is difficult not to think that all of these changes would have had significant impact on Ford's delicately balanced ambivalence about the role of Native Americans in the history of the West.

Undoubtedly Ford's collaborators affected the portraits drawn in these pictures as well. James Warner Bellah, who wrote the short stories on which the calvary trilogy was based, was a political conservative whose fiction was described by Dan Ford as heavy on rape and racism (214). The script of *Fort Apache* (along with *Wagonmaster*, *The Searchers*, and *Two Rode Together*), however, was written by Ford and Frank Nugent, a liberal half-Irish, half-Jewish son of an immigrant family. On the other hand, Bellah collaborated on the script of *She Wore a Yellow Ribbon*, along with Lawrence Stallings, a graduate of Annapolis and an injured Marine veteran of World War I. *Rio Grande* was adapted from Bellah's story by James McGuinness, a conservative friend of Ford and John Wayne (Ford 214–233). All these collaborators doubtless affected the ways in which Native Americans were presented in the films they wrote, but Ford did, of course, ultimately have the opportunity to choose his scriptwriters, and thus those choices may also have been influenced by the political drifts of the times.

But the impact of the written script on the final shape of any Ford film is itself problematic. Nugent said that the films were always Ford's far more than his scriptwriters'. He said that Ford complimented his work on *Wagonmaster* by saying, "I liked your script. In fact, I actually shot a few pages of it" (Gallagher 465). The result of Ford's improvisation is that important mannerisms and motifs come out again and again in Ford's Westerns.

One of the most persistent of those patterns in Ford's treatment of Native Americans is his repeated suggestion of certain kinds of physical violence that he refuses to show. Fictionally, the evidence of these acts of violence is typically supposed to be kept from the delicate perceptions of white women characters in the film, but, in fact, Ford does not choose to reveal to the audience the bodies of those who are supposed to have died so horrifically either.

In *Fort Apache*, Colonel Thursday is appalled that his daughter should have had to see the bodies of the dead soldiers that she and Michael

O'Rourke encountered on their unauthorized ride into the desert, but the bodies are not shown to the audience. I have already discussed the handling of Ethan's discovery of Martha's body in *The Searchers*. Ford treats the discovery of Lucy's body similarly; the discovery is not shown, only narrated later. A similar treatment is accorded the apparently mutilated body of Chris Hubble in *Sergeant Rutledge*.

In all of these cases, the suggestion that these scenes are too horrible to be shown is very powerful; in effect, Ford invokes the conscious and unconscious fears of the audience to describe the nature of the Indian threat. And this operation of white racial fear is itself explored overtly on several occasions in Ford's westerns.

One such occasion occurs in *Drums Along the Mohawk* on the evening when Gilbert and Lana first arrive at his frontier cabin. Lana sits before the fireplace as Gil has gone out to stable the mare. She hears a noise from behind her and she turns toward the door. The following reverse angle shot reveals an Indian carrying a rifle standing in the doorway, accompanied on the soundtrack by a clap of thunder. Lana screams in terror, and ends up a few shots later in the scene cowering on the floor against the wall as Blue Back's shadow falls over her.

The audience discovers belatedly, along with Lana, that Blue Back is Gil's friend, and that he is there to deliver half a deer for their larder; but Ford withholds prior information about Blue Back's identity and intent from the audience in order to evoke the same sort of fears in the audience that Lana experiences.

Ford handles a scene early in *Sergeant Rutledge* in a similar manner. Mary Cantrell has been left alone at an isolated railway station at night, and she discovers the stationmaster dead with an arrow in his chest. She runs out of the station and directly into the grasp of a black man who turns out to be Rutledge. At that point she does not know who he is, and although the audience has already seen Rutledge in the story's frame, they do not know exactly what to expect from him at this moment either.

In a cutaway shot back to the courtroom, Mary describes Rutledge's appearance: "It was as though he'd sprung up at me out of the earth." Ford underscores the import of her remark by having it modified slightly by the racist prosecutor, who intones: "And that man who sprang at you from the darkness like something from a nightmare, is he here in this court?" These images of terror may have less connection with the facts of history than with the nature of the white American mind, but particularly in *Sergeant Rutledge*, Ford suggests that they may have significant historical consequences all the same.

In both of these sequences, Ford reveals the power of irrational racial and sexual fear by representing it in a character on screen, by simultaneously making the audience experience the same fear themselves, and finally by revealing that fear to be grossly mistaken. In both cases, Ford shows how graphically and powerfully racist fears fill in the undefined spaces in an ambiguous situation, creating a sense of danger where there may be none, creating a perceived enemy out of a potential friend.

There is a definite drift in Ford's films in this regard; from the simple realization that Lana is embarrassingly—but rather innocently—wrong in *Drums Along the Mohawk*, Ford's films lead to the darker and darker sense that such fears, expressed so strongly by the families of the missing children in *Two Rode Together* and so irrationally by the residents of Dodge City in *Cheyenne Autumn*, were the source of much of the worst violence on the frontier. Increasingly, Ford suggests that his white society does not really see his Indians, but rather, out of its fear and inadequacy, that society projects images of violent savages upon Native Americans, whom they can then feel justified in killing.

One might make a final observation about Ford's portrayal of Native Americans by returning again to the scene of Mary Cantrell's first encounter with Sergeant Rutledge. The scene is particularly interesting for the way in which it conflates racial fears of blacks and Native Americans—in flight from one feared ethnic minority, Mary encounters another. And Maltby points out that if Woody Strode is not a raping, murdering savage as Rutledge, he is indeed the raping, murdering savage as Stone Calf in *Two Rode Together* (45).

Some of this conflation may be at work in all Westerns, where the presence of Native Americans on the frontier provides a symbolic space for a restating and reworking of racial fears after the issue of Southern slavery had been settled by the Civil War, as well as a socially acceptable cinematic signifier for racism when blackface performers became unacceptable: "The violent controversy generated by *The Birth of a Nation* inhibited Hollywood's use of blackface as a dramatic, rather than a comic, device. In this arena of malleable signifiers, the threat of the sexual Other migrated elsewhere, among other places, to its dormant position in the Western, where it is several times disguised" (Maltby 48).

The Western's period of greatest vitality came in the late 1940s and 1950s, at about the time that returning black war veterans began a renewed drive to gain their civil rights. Maltby's argument may well suggest a connection, inasmuch as he suggests that the Western developed a vision that validated and justified racial separation.

But Maltby's account finally ignores, it seems to me, the changes in Ford's later representations of Native Americans. In his essay on

Sergeant Rutledge, Frank Manchel carefully explores ways in which the national debate over race may have been changing Ford's thinking. Still, I am less sure than Manchel that those changes were sufficient to justify the films and the Western form.

Perhaps Maltby is right to argue that "only so long as the Indian remained disguised as an empty signifier could the Western's narrative function in its contained generic self-consciousness. Contesting the Westerner's claim to the ascription of self, Other and national identity simply made the story of the heroic repression of savagery untellable" (49). But Maltby does not consider how Ford's later films helped strip away the disguise, eventually helping to make the tale of heroic repression untellable.

In this sense, Ford's later Westerns helped to kill the very form he is usually credited with bringing to prominence. That may be a good thing, for Ford never could quite rescue his own work from the racist social discourse in which it was enmeshed. But, if we are never able in Westerns to see Native Americans as they saw themselves, Ford's late films can at least serve to remind us that there are real Indians down there somewhere, hidden among the rocks of our imagined history.

Notes

1. John O'Connor has also provided a detailed account of studio efforts to downplay or change the historical elements of the novel and to foreground the personal drama of Gil and Lana Martin (played by Henry Fonda and Claudette Colbert) in an excellent essay on the film in *American History/American Film*. (See also his essay "The White Man's Indian" elsewhere in this volume.)

2. Interestingly, Ford did use perhaps the most famous Native American actor of his day, Will Rogers, in other films, albeit not to signify the Native American experience. Peter Rollins discusses these films in an essay on *Steamboat 'Round the Bend* in *American History/American Film* and in a documentary film, *Will Rogers' 1920's: A Cowboy's Guide to the Times* (Churchill Films 1976).

3. There is a very funny scene in Tony Hillerman's novel *Sacred Clowns* in which one of his characters, Jim Chee, goes to a drive-in screening of *Cheyenne Autumn* attended by a large Navajo audience. The Navajo, who understand the often irreverent and dramatically irrelevant dialog, treat these portions of the film as an elaborate joke played on the white establishment which denies them genuine images of themselves (140–144).

4. Frank Manchel and Robert Baird both explore this idea with regard to other films and other directors in their essays in this volume.

5. In fact, the last shot we see of Blue Back is a curiously ambiguous one. After the climactic battle at the fort, the colonists are gathered in the church and someone inquires about the fate of Caldwell, the Tory agent who had been leading the Mohawks against the colonists. By way of answer, Blue Back appears in

the pulpit wearing Caldwell's eyepatch, implying that he has killed the Tory. But in the context of traditional Hollywood iconography about the eighteenth century, eyepatches like Caldwell's normally signify evil intent (often piracy), and Blue Back takes on a more menacing appearance than he had since his initial frightening appearance to Lana. Andrew Sinclair is quite wrong to see the eye patch as a joking reference to Ford's own; at this point in his life, Ford was not yet wearing one.

6. Richard Slotkin, in *Gunfighter Nation*, argues that *Rio Grande* is particularly reflective of the impending Korean crisis (347–365); I make a similar argument in "Printing the Legend in the Age of MX: Reconsidering Ford's Military Trilogy."

7. Although he would probably find the connection arbitrary or strained, I am indebted to Leland Poague for his argument on the centrality of the issue of sight in Ford's Westerns.

Works Cited

Anderson, Lindsay. *About John Ford*. London: Plexus, 1981.

Berkhofer, Robert F. *The White Man's Indian*. New York: Random House, 1977.

Bogdanovich, Peter. *John Ford*. Berkeley: University of California Press, 1978.

Churchill, Ward. "Fantasies of the Master Race: Categories of Stereotyping of American Indians in Film." In *Fantasies of the Master Race*, 231–41. M. Annette Jaimes, ed. Monroe, Maine: Common Courage Press, 1992.

Darby, William. *John Ford's Westerns: A Thematic Analysis with a Filmography*. Jefferson, N.C.: McFarland, 1996.

Ford, Dan. *Pappy: The Life of John Ford*. Englewood Cliffs, N.J.: Prentice-Hall, 1979.

Gallagher, Tag. *John Ford: The Man and His Films*. Berkeley: University of California Press, 1986.

Hillerman, Tony. *Sacred Clowns*. New York: HarperCollins, 1993.

Maltby, Richard. "A Better Sense of History: John Ford and the Indians." In *The Book of Westerns*, 34–49. Ian Cameron and Douglas Pye, eds. New York: Continuum, 1996.

Manchel, Frank. "Losing and Finding Sergeant Rutledge." Forthcoming in *Historical Journal of Film, Radio and Television*.

Nolley, Kenneth. "Printing the Legend in the Age of MX: Reconsidering Ford's Military Trilogy." *Literature/Film Quarterly* 14.2 (1986): 82–88.

O'Connor, John E. "A Reaffirmation of American Ideals." In *American History/American Film*. 97–119. John E. O'Connor and Martin A. Jackson, eds. New York: Continuum, 1988.

Poague, Leland. "'All I Can See is the Flags': *Fort Apache* and the Visibility of History." *Cinema Journal* 27.2 (1988): 8–26.

Rollins, Peter. *Will Rogers: A Bio-bibliography*. Westport, Conn.: Greenwood Press, 1983.

Sandoz, Mari. *Cheyenne Autumn*. New York: McGraw-Hill, 1953.

Sinclair, Andrew. *John Ford*. New York: Dial Press, 1979.

Slotkin, Richard. *Gunfighter Nation*. New York: Atheneum, 1992.

Stam, Robert. "From Stereotype to Discourse: Methodological Reflections on Racism in the Media." *CineAction* 32 (1994): 10–29.

Tuska, Jon. *The American West in Film: Critical Approaches to the Western*. Westport, Conn.: Greenwood Press, 1985.

White, Hayden. *Tropics of Discourse*. Baltimore: The Johns Hopkins University Press, 1978.

Cultural Confusion
Broken Arrow (1950)

For many people, Hollywood's depiction of Native Americans in the Western film provides a moral gauge not only for the history of our nation but also for the film industry.[1] Nowhere is this more evident than in the movies about the taming of the wilderness, where our modern mythmakers recount the fate of Native Americans, lumped all together, who stood in the way of Manifest Destiny.

Central to any revisionist approach is an awareness that the conflicts between Euro-Americans and Native Americans over the settling of the West began during the days of Columbus and not in the 1800s. For more than four hundred years, the two vastly different cultures engaged in a violent conflict that was predicated on radically different perceptions of the earth both wanted. As Haffner and Lusitania's television series *The Real West* points out, Native Americans never conceived of land in terms of ownership. They viewed it as "part of their family." Euro-Americans, on the other hand, "saw the continent as empty; by their perception, there were no cities or towns, no fences—the Indians were just another obstacle to be overcome in obtaining the land." This immense cultural disjuncture between whites and Indians established a formidable conceptual chasm that exists to the present.

Film scholars take different approaches to the theme of Native Americans in film. Their initial historical research highlighted how Hollywood stereotyped, distorted, misrepresented, and patronized the American Indian. Often obscured were the roots of the conceptual conflict between the two cultures. Almost never did anyone raise the issue of why whites insisted on viewing the West as a wilderness that needed taming, or why it was to the white man's advantage to depict Native Americans as romanticized opponents who fiercely fought against our mass migration westward.[2]

At the end of the 1960s, a new generation of scholars avoided value judgments on the positive or negative depiction of American Indians and downplayed the film industry's historical, cultural, and political distortions. Their approach was to scrutinize the filmmakers responsible for the production of the formulaic conventions that embody the ethics and immorality of mainstream America (Aleiss, "Hollywood's Ideal" 54). Fair enough, but such scholarship sometimes minimizes the possibilities that integration, assimilation, and brotherhood were Euro-American ideas that euphemistically relieved whites of making legitimate concessions to Native American desires, rights, and values.

This essay examines one film, *Broken Arrow* (1950), to illustrate the critical differences between perception and reality. It explores the relationship between movies and society in an historical context. One useful way to make the comparison is suggested by Pierre Sorlin.[3] He identifies four criteria in selecting a film for historical analysis: "the originality of the film, its relationship to current events, its favourable reception by the public and the fact of its being produced and distributed during a time of crisis"(19). That is, by taking a commercial film that meets his criteria, one can recognize how it may serve to influence public opinion at a particular period in history and gauge how it holds up over time.

Few Westerns illustrate Sorlin's prerequisites more completely than Twentieth Century-Fox's production *Broken Arrow*.[4] Made in 1949 and released a year later, it came during crises both in America and in Hollywood. As the nation struggled with the problems of the Cold War, the resurgence of the Red Scare, urban blight, and social injustice, the film industry reeled from the breakup of the studio system, the advent of television, costly labor strikes, divisive blacklisting practices, and the "invasion" of foreign films into America's movie theaters. Hollywood resorted to many new approaches to break out of its box-office slump, including ones that would not antagonize audiences confused by conflicting demands for cultural diversity (Native Americans should be recognized for their ethnic heritage) versus assimilation (African Americans should be integrated into white society).

The relationship of *Broken Arrow* to these issues, especially in its groundbreaking efforts to promote tolerance and racial equality, is discussed in the major commentaries on the film. It is worth noting that, when the film appeared, almost a quarter of all Hollywood movies made up to that time had been Westerns,[5] and that the film *Broken Arrow* was one of the first movie Westerns to be adapted into a television series.[6] By the start of the 1960s, at least twenty Western shows were shown each week in prime time on television.[7]

Knowing about *Broken Arrow*'s popularity with audiences and critics permits us to turn to the issues of content and reception. One important caveat is needed. I do not find historical inaccuracies irrelevant in films, especially ones that claim to be true accounts of events or personalities. Although we need to understand that some errors are less pertinent than others, what could be more foolish than to ignore how the creators of *Patton, Malcolm X, JFK,* or *Schindler's List* treated the accepted accounts of the events depicted in their biographical interpretations? If such works are truly influencing our national memories—and I think they are—then we need to appreciate what perspective is being presented and why.

Consider the book–film issue in *Broken Arrow.* Elliot Arnold's 1947 novel *Blood Brother* covers the years from 1855, when Euro-Americans settled in Arizona, to 1874, the year Cochise died.[8] The issue, for me, is not that the filmmakers—studio head Darryl F. Zanuck, producer Julian Blaustein, director Delmer Daves, and screenwriter Michael Blankfort—omitted half the novel and focused basically on the relationship between Tom Jeffords and Cochise. What is important is how that relationship is treated, and what historical inaccuracies do to the film's approach.

Far more vital for this essay is the fact that the filmmakers and their marketing experts made a concerted effort to depict accurately the life- style of the Apaches and the thinking of Euro-Americans during the post–Civil War era in the Arizona territory (Aleiss, "Hollywood's Ideal" 29). Our concern, therefore, is with what this film tells us about the Chiricahua Apache culture. How does Daves treat Cochise, Geronimo, Euro-American settlers, the prospects for peace between the two cultures, and the role of the U.S. government and the military during the Indian Wars?

Because other commentators have pointed to the movie's many flaws—for example, Native Americans speaking English, a romanticized Indian culture, and whites taking Indian roles—this essay explores several key scenes dealing with Indian/white relations and the issue of peace between the Chiricahua Apache and the U.S. government. The intent is to compare what the film states and shows with omitted historical realities.

Broken Arrow begins with a long take of a parched Arizona landscape; the voice-over narrator, Tom Jeffords (James Stewart), tells us:

> This is the story of the land, of the people who lived on it in the year 1870, and of a man whose name was Cochise. He was an Indian, leader of the Chiricahua Apache tribe. I was involved in the story, and what I have to tell happened exactly as you will see it. The only change will be that when the Apaches speak, they will speak in our language. What took place is part of the history of Arizona. And it began for me here, where you see me riding. Since getting out of the

Figure 6.1. Tom Jeffords (James Stewart), the ex-Civil War trooper, parlays with Chiricahua Apache chief Cochise (Jeff Chandler) in an effort to bring peace to the Arizona territory in 1870.

> Union army, I've been prospecting for gold off and on. One day I got a message that a new colonel had come to Tucson and wanted to see me.

Let's stop to consider both image and narration. The focus on the "land" is perfect: the history of white/Native American relations is tied to land ownership. But two interesting omissions result from the choice of the date, 1870. First, it allows the filmmakers to skip over the inconvenient fact that the Chiricahua Apaches had been fighting for more than sixty years with Spaniards, Mexicans, and Euro-Americans.[9] Equally important, this introduction makes Jeffords's traveling alone, at this point in American history, somewhat artificial, mainly because government policies encouraging the slaughter of the buffalo, allowing unlawful prospectors to mine for gold and silver on Indian reservations, and giving away "free" land to white settlers had started the nation's greatest westward migration. Second, in claiming that Cochise was "the" leader of the Chiricahua Apaches, *Broken Arrow* suggests that the tribal government functions in much the same way the U.S. government operates. One leader can speak for the entire group. Cochise could not and did not. A council representing each of the tribes in the nation had to decide what the collected tribes would do.[10]

In suggesting the reason Jeffords has come to Arizona—"prospecting for gold"—we are given very important information about the motivations of the whites. It is crucial to how we see the film to realize that Jeffords does not mention that he is prospecting in the "off limits" area of the lower Salt and Middle Gila river basins belonging to the Chiricahua Apaches, that there have been a number of frontier gold strikes since 1849, or that a treaty had been signed in 1867, tricking Native Americans on the Southern Plains into relinquishing important buffalo grazing lands and coming under the protection of the U.S. government.[11] It was largely due to the failure of Washington to honor its treaty obligations and to protect the "new" territorial rights of the Indians that the scope and the intensity of the Apache Wars increased.

It is also not trivial that Jeffords mentions that a "new colonel" had arrived in Tucson. The comments raise important questions about the military's intentions, and why Tucson, the territorial center then attracting hordes of prospectors and located along the route of the newly completed transcontinental railroad, is selected for the film's major white settlement.[12] We should not overlook the fact that it is at this stage in American Indian warfare that General Philip Sheridan, commander of the military forces in the West, issued his infamous comment, "The only good Indian I ever saw was a dead one." As for Tucson, it is not enough that this was the setting in the novel, or that this is where Jeffords worked. Just who is opposing the Chiricahua Apaches?

Jeffords's voice-over narration tells us, "The story started when I saw some buzzards circling in the sky. Buzzard is a smart bird. Something . . . or somebody was getting ready to die. I figured it was a hurt deer, or a rabbit, or a snake. Not a rabbit, not a deer. His kind was more dangerous than a snake. He was an Apache. For ten years we'd been in a savage war with his people, a bloody no-give, no-take war." Compare that statement with the acts of omission already noted, and you can see the Euro-American perspective being developed. By arguing that the hostilities are only a decade old, and that neither side is more reprehensible than the other, Daves's narrative confuses and obscures the major issues between the two cultures.

As the film story begins, we learn that the Apache is a fourteen-year-old Chiricahua boy who is on his "novice time," the period when adolescents go on treks alone to learn how to survive and how to become men. The importance of this idea is that it establishes the Apaches as a warrior nation. Jeffords gives the boy some water, and though the youngster tries to kill him and is wounded in the struggle, the white man stays to tend to the youngster's wounds. Days later, when they are about to part as friends, Jeffords learns that the Apache's family must be worried about him, their only surviving child, his brother and sister having been killed at Big Creek. A voice-over narration tells us that Jeffords is stunned by the news that Indian mothers cry for their children. "Whites," he tells us, "had always considered Apaches like wild animals."

At this point, a band of five Apache warriors find the missing youth. Though they want to kill Jeffords, they do not because the boy intercedes for him. The voice-over narrator tells us that he learned something else that day, that Apaches were men of honor. The plot now moves into one of the major themes of the movie: the parallel misconceptions that whites and Indians have about each other. For example, Daves stresses that the boy's father is upset that his son has become a "tame Apache." (In a later scene, a white father will justify his hatred of the Apaches because of the death of his wife and the near-killing of his son.) The Indians are curious that Jeffords did not kill the boy, inasmuch as white men pay money for Indian scalps, and say, "It is the way of all whites." Jeffords replies that it is not his way. He explains that he is not like other white men; he does not kill for scalps, and neither do the Apaches.

Again, it is interesting what the film states about the Indian Wars. The scalp issue is an extraordinary reference, inasmuch as it reminds us not only that during much of the eighteenth and early nineteenth century, the Mexican government encouraged people to scalp Indians, but also that the intense hatred that Cochise and Geronimo had for Mexicans could be traced back to an 1850 Mexican raid on an Apache village, where Geronimo's mother, wife, and three children were killed and scalped.[13]

The most outrageous distortion, however, occurs when Jeffords explains to the Apaches that he is looking for gold and silver. Daves has the Indians puzzled about the white man's words. They do not understand about gold and silver. Keep in mind that this is 1870, and for more than twenty years the U.S. government had been following a deceptive policy, making treaties with Native Americans to clear the way for further westward migration and protecting prospectors who had illegally established claims on Indian lands. At the core of much of the trouble between the whites and the Indians was the way in which they understood the significance of treaties. As Hyatt and Terkin's television program *Time Machine: Savagery and the American Indian* observes, Native Americans initially were willing to sign treaties and share: "Their understanding of what they were signing was different from the Euro-Americans. They felt the agreements were about sharing an open landscape; the Euro-Americans thought of it as owning continually and fixing boundaries of property." But as the land became more lucrative to the goals of new administrations, Euro-Americans "used treaties as short-term devices that could be altered or ignored. Indians, on the other hand, were appalled at the speed with which treaties were torn up and new negotiations required." The cultural confusion created by Daves's perspective so early in the movie is the result of the filmmakers' failure to establish that the war between whites and Indians is a war in which the former are concerned with material acquisitions and the latter are fighting for their very survival.

The remainder of the film reinforces the approach taken in these opening moments of the movie. From time to time, we are given tidbits about the Chiricahua Apache culture, but rarely any crucial information about the essential meaning of the struggle between the two cultures. In almost every instance where the reasons for the hatred and distrust between Indians and whites are raised, the explanations are simplistic, misleading, and meaningless. Equally disturbing are the images of the Indians and whites themselves.

There are many examples of cultural confusion in *Broken Arrow*. A case in point is Jeffords's first encounter with whites and his defense of the Chiricahua Apaches. Aligned against him is a fictitious Col. Bernall (played by Raymond Bramley), who has just been given the command of Fort Grant, with orders to clean out Cochise and his Apaches from the Pinaleño Mountains area. Like the screen Jeffords, he knows nothing about Indian culture or warfare, and, as will soon become apparent, he is totally inept at his job.

The dialog, again, is useful for suggesting the film's cultural confusion. On the one hand, most of the men stationed on the frontier were ill equipped to deal with the Indian problem, but it is false to suggest that the military benefited mainly from the help of white scouts like Jeffords. It was not until the recruitment and use of Indian scouts, approved by Congress in 1866, that men like Sherman, Sheridan, and Custer were able to undertake successful campaigns against the Plains Indians and especially against Geronimo. The irony of *Broken Arrow* is that it takes place in 1870, the year that Indian scouts began depending on their military status for economic and social survival (primarily because the buffalo were being annihilated). The reservations had become death traps, and this was their last "legal" chance to practice their warrior lifestyles.[14]

Another disturbing bit of dialog takes place during Jeffords's initial defense of Cochise against the hatred of the whites. He reminds his antagonists that Cochise did not start this war: "A snooty little lieutenant

Figure 6.2. Because Tom Jeffords often faces death in his search for peace with Cochise's people, *Broken Arrow* misleads its audience into believing that the military achieved its objectives because of white scouts. Courtesy of the Museum of Modern Art/Film Stills Archive.

fresh out of the East started it. He flew a flag of truce, which Cochise honored. And then he hanged Cochise's brother and five others under the flag." The reference to an 1861 incident with an inexperienced, young Lt. George Bascom is fascinating. Not only does it omit the fact that Cochise hanged hostages in a futile attempt to free his family and that no one is sure which hangings took place first, but also director Daves conveniently overlooks the fact that Cochise had been at war with Euro-Americans soon after the government annexed all the land from the Rio Grande to the Pacific Ocean following the Mexican-American War.

Audiences learn a lot about *Broken Arrow*'s understanding of history and the Chiricahua Apaches while witnessing Jeffords' experiences in Cochise's camp. Instead of seeing a weak, hungry, and ravaged tribe, viewers see an idyllic setting, where many strong, healthy Native Americans live peacefully and comfortably with their families. Instead of a tired and weary Cochise, eager for peace because he understands that the whites are too numerous and too strong for his people to overcome, audiences see the Noble Savage, all wise and all knowing.

When the two men first talk in Cochise's *wickiup*, Jeffords convinces Cochise that there is a distinction between the U.S. Mail and military dispatches. This is another major distortion in the film. Although it is true that the screen Jeffords believes what he is saying, we need to remember that much of the government duplicity against the Indians was based not on military dispatches but on the news sent back East by prospectors, settlers, pioneers, buffalo hunters, and railroad men complaining about the Indians' obstructing progress and murdering whites. Public opinion generated by civilians and propagandists, not the military, decided the nature and course of the Indian Wars.

We turn now to the actual peace negotiations themselves. The central figure is Gen. Oliver O. Howard, who, we are told in *Broken Arrow,* has been sent by President Grant to negotiate a peace with Cochise. The reason for Gen. Howard's peace mission, never explained in the film, is that on April 30, 1871, five hundred peaceful Aravaipa Apaches, who had settled near Camp Grant for the protection promised by the U.S. government, were massacred by vigilantes and enemy Indian scouts. Their boasting of the killing created such a revulsion among Easterners that a new government policy was instituted to protect Grant's political image (*How the West was Lost*).[15]

Knowing that, notice how the dialog between Howard and Jeffords produces a different reaction from the liberal intentions of the filmmakers. Howard tells Cochise's friend that President Grant wants peace. Jeffords replies, "To be changed later." "No," is the answer. "Any treaty I make will stand. I have President Grant's absolute word on that." Jeffords asks what Howard means by a "fair" peace. Howard replies, "Suppose you tell me." To which Jeffords says, "Equality. The Apaches are a free people. They have a right to stay free on their own land." (Clearly, this was not the only issue. It was a question of land and culture, both of which were, and would be decimated by the treaty and reservation life.) But there is more. Howard responds, somewhat irritated, "You mean the whole Southwest?" (Why not? It's their land!) Cochise's friend never raises that issue. Instead, he says, "No. Even Cochise wouldn't ask for that now. [The operative word is "now."] He's a realist about that. But a clear territory that's Apache. Ruled by Apaches. No soldiers on it. That's what I mean." Howard agrees in principle, and Jeffords goes out to set up a meeting between them and Cochise.[16]

Finally, *Broken Arrow* comes to the actual peace treaty itself. Because Cochise cannot decide this matter by himself, he convenes the leaders of the Apache nation.[17] They deliberate for four days in private; then Howard and Jeffords are brought before them to answer questions. Just three inquiries are raised: (1) Can the Apaches still war against the Mexicans? The answer is no. (2) What if the "Chief of the Whites" dies—will the treaty still be kept? The answer: "His word is a bond on the chief who follows him." (3) What will happen if white men break the treaty, enter the restricted territory, and kill Apaches? The answer is that the military will take care of things.

The final affront is that the primary troublemaker at the peace council is Geronimo, shown as Cochise's contemporary and chief antagonist, when in reality the relationship was one of deference and respect. The trouble begins when the white men leave, and Geronimo, yet unnamed, addresses the peace council: "I trust none of it." He points out that in the short time they have been discussing peace they have lost the right to raid Mexico,[18] and their territory has grown smaller.

The insult to history is compounded when Cochise agrees to try the peace, while Geronimo and a handful of supporters are forced to leave the territory. Then, the prescient Indian warrior announces to the gathering that, from now on, he will be known by his Mexican name, "Geronimo." Keep in mind that this was the name he adopted in 1850, twenty years earlier, when he took revenge for the massacre of his family. For the remainder of *Broken Arrow*, one of the greatest Apache leaders is shown as a renegade who refuses to accept peace for foolish reasons, when in fact he honored Cochise's word and lived on the reservation until Cochise died on June 8, 1874.

Moreover, the film ends with no mention that Jeffords became the only Indian agent for Cochise's tribe and that the conditions on the "Chiricahua" reservation were deplorable: lack of food and supplies, widespread disease, malnutrition, and constant humiliation. In the end, Washington betrayed the Apaches, and there was nothing that Jeffords or Howard could do to stop the racist policies of conquest.

Figure 6.3. General Oliver O. Howard (Basil Ruysdael) offers Tom Jeffords a peace proposal to be presented to Cochise. Courtesy of the Museum of Modern Art/Film Stills Archive.

Many film historians who have discussed *Broken Arrow* point to its groundbreaking role in Hollywood's treatment of the American Indian. This essay suggests that there is yet another perspective. *Broken Arrow* did more than reflect the mood of the times. It portrayed Indian/white relations in the old West not as they were, but as Euro-Americans wanted them to be. The film's treatment of the Chiricahua Apache culture minimizes the importance of land to their lives; ignores the diseases, devastation, and disruption brought by Euro-Americans to Native American society; and legitimates the treaty signed between Cochise and the U.S. government. Its characterization of the relationship between Cochise and Jeffords grossly distorts the experiences of both men, misrepresents their motives for peace, and callously ignores the consequences of their tragic treaty.

White men do not come off much better. Whatever the misconceptions that Euro-Americans had of the American continent and its inhabitants, the pioneers and settlers who trekked westward took serious risks, fought against great hardships, and showed enormous courage in pursuing Manifest Destiny. They were probably too possessed by their dreams of

Figure 6.4. Cochise, General Howard, and Tom Jeffords offer the peace proposal to the leaders of the Apache nation. The only voice opposing them is that of Geronimo, who prophetically tells his people not to trust the whites. Courtesy of the Museum of Modern Art/Film Stills Archive.

wealth and rebirth to be charitable or reasonable when it came to the grievances of Native Americans. But to present them as primarily weak, revengeful, and simple-minded is absurd. In a metaphor about a "wilderness" filled with so much hatred, hostility, loneliness, and death, why does anyone want to stay, let alone die to own it?

The image of the military is also disturbing. They were not simply of two types: incompetent troopers or Bible-thumping good Samaritans. The men who rode against the Chiricahua Apaches were tough, no-nonsense combatants who enforced Sheridan's policy of "total war," which resulted in the destruction of the enemy's property and the annihilation of his family. They achieved their mission by crushing Native Americans with ruthless methods and uncompromising strategies. Although there might have been naive or idealistic officers who deluded themselves that their civilian leaders could be trusted, few military men of the West ever advocated a policy other than violence as a solution to the Indian problem.

If *Broken Arrow* is remembered by many as a well-intentioned film, it may be because they are willing to say that in 1950 people did not know any better, that this was a significant step forward compared to what had come earlier. Reasonable people will have no difficulty in accepting Angela Maria Aleiss's position that the film reflects the controversial policies of "termination" that Congress pursued in the 1950s, which effectively jettisoned any federal responsibility for Indian lands, treaties, and individuals. But there is a need to go beyond recognizing the policy to commenting on its consequences. One need only read Vine Deloria's *Custer Died for Your Sins* to see how calamitous the termination policies were for both Native Americans and Washington. By distorting and misrepresenting the reasons for the cultural clash between the two parties, *Broken Arrow* sowed more seeds of distrust against the film industry and further undermined our trust in our institutions.

Furthermore, as film historians, we make a serious error when we discount the importance of historical inaccuracies in films purporting to tell the truth about the past. Movies are not just escapism, and when they offer simplistic, emotional solutions to complex problems, they muddy not only the problem but also create cultural confusion. From this perspective, there is an ironic truth in Twentieth Century-Fox's extolling *Broken Arrow* as an accurate rendition of "the American traditions of justice, tolerance, and dignity for all men."

Notes

1. I am grateful to the valuable reactions to an earlier draft of this paper by Nick Danigelis, Littleton Long, and Denise Youngblood of the University of Vermont. In addition, I owe a debt of gratitude to Martha Day for her generous help in securing research materials.

2. For a good introduction to George Washington's designs on Native American property, see Reginald Horsman, "American Indian Policy in the Old Northwest, 1783–1812."

3. Frank Manchel, *Film Study: An Analytical Bibliography*.

4. *Broken Arrow* was produced by Julian Blaustein for Twentieth Century-Fox in 1949. It premiered on July 17, 1950. Directed by Delmer Daves, the story is set in the Arizona territory in 1870. The plot, narrated by Tom Jeffords, an ex-Union officer whose admiration for the Chiricahua Apaches alienates him from his white associates in Tucson, follows his attempts to mediate between Cochise and the U.S. government and bring about an honorable peace. His efforts also lead to Jeffords's falling in love and marrying an Indian woman. The film stars James Stewart as Tom Jeffords, Jeff Chandler as Cochise, Debra Paget as Sonseeahray, Will Geer as Slade, Basil Ruysdael as General Howard, Arthur Hunnicutt as Milt, Raymond Bramley as Colonel Bernall, Jay Silverheels as

Geronimo, and Billy Wilkerson as Juan. The screenplay by Michael Blankfort is based on the novel *Blood Brother* by Elliott Arnold. Ernest Palmer is the cinematographer. Made in Technicolor, the film runs ninety-three minutes.

5. Howard Suber, in his commentary on the laserdisk version of *High Noon* (Voyager Special edition).

6. The series ran on ABC television from September 23, 1958, to September 20, 1960. John Lupton played Tom Jeffords; Michael Ansara played Cochise. Particularly significant is the fact that Jeffords is an Indian agent working with Cochise to keep the peace. In the film version, we never learn that he has become an Indian agent. For more information see Terrace 94.

7. *The Real West*. In the show's 1994 opening monolog, Jack Perkins points out that there were twenty Westerns aired in prime time every week in the early 1960s.

8. For the most detailed analysis of the novel, see Angela Maria Aleiss, *Hollywood's Ideal of Postwar Assimilation* and *From Adversaries to Allies*.

9. *The Real West*. Those readers who would like to know more about the historical sources used in *The Real West*, should consult the writings of the series major consultants, including Paul Andrew Hutton (University of New Mexico) and Brian W. Dippie (University of Victoria, British Columbia).

10. The filmmakers overlooked that the Apaches were not a tribe but a nation, with many bands living in areas from Oklahoma to New Mexico and Arizona to northern Mexico. For more information, see *How the West Was Lost*.

11. By 1867, the U.S. government had created the Department of the Missouri—Southern Plains. It had also signed the Medicine Lodge Treaties of 1867, which allegedly were fashioned to bring a peaceful solution to the Indian Wars. On the surface, the treaty was hailed as a humane effort: Indians got a safe reservation in Oklahoma, and they were protected by the military. In practice, the deceitful pact compelled the Indians to leave their buffalo grounds and live under white rule. Moreover, the U.S. government abandoned its responsibilities within a year. Almost none of the supplies promised to the Indians ever reached the reservation. Gen. Philip Sheridan, who commanded the bulk of the western frontier during the timeframe of *Broken Arrow*, balked at any attempts to air reasonable Indian protests about broken promises. Thus the Cheyenne, Arapaho, Comanche, and Kiowa, who had once again put their trust in a white man's treaty, were disillusioned. Sheridan, on the other hand, never put any faith in Indian treaties. Like his commanding officer, William Tecumseh Sherman, he insisted on a policy of "total war" against Native Americans. To help him implement such a policy, he secured the services of his Civil War friend, George Armstrong Custer. Together, these three military officers—Sherman, Sheridan, and Custer—would search for any excuse to attack the Indians. For more information, see *General Sheridan & the Indians*.

12. Talks about forging a transcontinental railroad began as a result of the Mexican War and the land annexation of 1848 and later years. Actual construction began in 1862, and the railroad was completed on May 10, 1869. It ran right

through the Arizona territory. Every company that participated in the construction of the railroad received a square plot of ten acres of "public land" for every mile of track laid. In 1864, Congress doubled the land grant. To encourage business for the railroad, the companies sold their land cheaply. Moreover, railroad crews slaughtered the buffalo herds for meat. For more information, see *The Real West*.

13. According to one source, the policy started in 1839. For more information, see *How the West Was Lost*.

14. For more information, see *Indians and the Army*. It is useful to reflect on reservation life. According to one source, "reservations were like prisons." Traditional culture was destroyed; disease, despair, and poverty were widespread. Native Americans had lost their autonomy. Moreover, "A new culture was imposed by missionaries, Indian agents, and teachers." See *The Final Clash—Wounded Knee*.

15. *How the West Was Lost*.

16. The irony of this discussion is that the reservation proved devastating for the Apaches, and that later Gen. Howard, who lived to see Washington break its promises, not only follows orders but is also the officer assigned to pursue the Nez Perce and capture Chief Looking Glass and Chief Joseph. This is the same Chief Joseph who said, "No man's business to divide [the land]; only the one who created it has the right to dispose of it. The government treaties are based on hollow words." For more information, see *The Real West*.

17. The event took place at Dragoon Mountains in November 1872.

18. The fact is that the Apaches continued their Mexican forays. Cochise and his people never had signed a peace treaty with Mexico. Although he kept his word, Cochise never interfered with other Apaches who continued the raids. For more information, see Edwin R. Sweeney, *Cochise: Chiricahua Chief*, 366.

Works Cited

Aleiss, Angela Maria. "From Adversaries to Allies: The American Indian in American Films, 1930–1950." Ph. D. Dissertation, Columbia University, 1991.

———. "Hollywood's Ideal of Postwar Assimilation: Indian/White Attitudes in *Broken Arrow*." MFA Thesis, Columbia University, 1985.

Deloria, Vine, Jr. *Custer Died for Your Sins*. New York: Avon Books, 1969.

Horsman, Reginald. "American Indian Policy in the Old Northwest, 1783–1812," In *Promises to Keep: A Portrayal of Nonwhites in the United States*, ed. Bruce A. Glasrud and Alan M. Smith, 97–112. Chicago: Rand McNally, 1972.

How the West Was Lost. Discovery Channel documentary series, 1993.

Manchel, Frank. *Film Study: An Analytical Bibliography*, Vol. 1. Rutherford, N.J.: Fairleigh Dickinson University Press, 1990.

The Real West. Arts & Entertainment Network documentary series, 1993.

Sweeney, Edwin R. *Cochise: Chiricahua Chief*. Norman: University of Oklahoma Press, 1991.

Terrace, Vincent. *Fifty Years of Television: A Guide to Series and Plots, 1937–1988.* Cranbury, N.J.: Cornwall Books, 1991.

Time Machine. Arts & Entertainment Network documentary series, 1991–1992.

The Hollywood Indian versus Native Americans
Tell Them Willie Boy Is Here (1969)

Students of American film have long noted the fascinating connections between Hollywood portrayals of major social issues and the conflicting tensions in the American society that produced them (O'Connor and Jackson; Rollins, *Hollywood as Historian*; Slotkin). An ostensible film biography of Emiliano Zapata, famed leader of the Mexican Revolution of 1910, tells us nothing about Zapata's agrarian radicalism, his anarchist-communist notions of taking land from the rich and distributing it among the poor according to their needs. Instead, it focuses on his opposition to dictatorship. In *Viva Zapata!* (Twentieth Century-Fox, 1952), historian Paul Vanderwood persuasively argues, we see director Elia Kazan, himself an active anticommunist, transform Zapata from a radical Mexican revolutionary into an American "cold warrior," one totally opposed to communism (183–201). Through the Hollywood lens, Zapata is inverted and perverted into something he was not.

Yet, if Mexicans and Mexico are subject to Hollywood stereotype and distortion through ignorance, profit-seeking, and some racism (Greenfield and Cortés, Cortés), the portrayal of Indians springs from a deeper source of misunderstanding. That source Herman Melville calls the "metaphysics of Indian-hating," an attitude born in the American notion of its special mission to "civilize" this land and its peoples, ruthlessly and remorselessly, so as to usher in a new and better age (172–81).

As Roy Harvey Pearce explains, the role of the civilizing mission, according to Melville, led to the idea of the tragic role of both Indian-hater and Indian, inextricably linked in the conquest of the wilderness. To Pearce, Indian-hating "functioned not so much as an argument but as an assumption; not so much as a step in a logical chain leading to action, as the very foundation of logic itself. Even those who were genuinely concerned with the welfare of the Indian acted on this assumption" (33).

Telling or retelling an episode in Indian-white relations, a narrative usually undertaken by a member of the dominant culture with access to printing presses and cameras, risked expression of the assumption in the very way the teller told the tale. Not questioning the assumption of Indian-hating has meant that much of what we think we know about Indian-white history is one-sided; frustrated seekers trying to correct the record, especially about the Hollywood Indian, have generally failed to see that no correction is possible unless an alternative, Indian version, is given credibility and expression. When films supporting the Indian voice are made, such as *Powwow Highway* (1989) and *Geronimo* (1993), the booking line in theaters is short and typically the audience few in numbers. Credibility in Indian films is further confounded by the Western genre, to which most Indian stories belong, and its traditional cavalier disregard for accuracy (Tuska 147).

Abraham Lincoln Polonsky's *Tell Them Willie Boy Is Here* (1969) reveals the interplay of all these elements. Our analysis suggests the ways in which *Willie Boy* mirrors American social concerns in the late 1960s and how it masks an Indian version that our ethnographic fieldwork has brought forward. The film is based on a 1909 incident in Banning, California, in which an allegedly drunken and lust-crazed Paiute, Willie Boy, stole a rifle and shot to death the sleeping father of a young woman whom he then abducted and raped. Willie Boy and the girl ran away on foot, to be pursued by two mounted posses neither of which could catch them. When she began to slow his flight, Willie Boy murdered her and ran off across the desert. A week later he encountered another posse at Bullion, later renamed Ruby Mountain. In the ensuing shootout, down to his last bullet, Willie Boy committed suicide.

When yet another posse returned to the skirmish site, its members decided to burn Willie Boy's bloated, decomposing body. Most of the posses had Indian trackers from the Morongo Reservation in Banning to help them. Willie Boy's behavior and the burning of his corpse were interpreted at the time by one sympathetic journalist as expressions of his Paiute culture. Pearce reminds us, nevertheless, that even the best intentioned accepted the Indian-hating assumption—in this case, that Willie Boy had tried to accept white ways, to assimilate but, tragically, and under the influence of the white man's alcohol, the power of his tribal culture caused him to abandon white example and to revert to "savagery."

In 1960, journalist Harry Lawton wrote a novel of the episode, which

Figure 7.1. Film treatment: Indian possemen with Willie Boy's body. Courtesy of the Museum of Modern Art/Film Stills Archive.

he called the "last great manhunt in the Western tradition," and praised the various posses and possemen (x). Scriptwriter and sometime director Polonsky bought the film rights and wrote the screenplay for *Willie Boy*, reversing Lawton's posse praise and using the incident instead to make his own commentary on America of the late 1960s and the Vietnam War.

Polonsky crafted his tale around four main characters, and we have charted his story development through three script versions (early, first, and final) and compared that product with the final filmed version. Willie Boy, played by Robert Blake, was to embody Paiute athleticism and inscrutability. The young woman, whom Polonsky named Lola, Katherine Ross portrayed in "man-tan" and straight black wig. Her white opposite Polonsky dubbed Elizabeth Arnold or Liz, an Eastern-born, highly educated, and snobbish woman holding both a degree in anthropology from the Smithsonian and an M.D. from Johns Hopkins; she works in this forsaken corner of the West as the Indian agent at Malki (known to non-Indians as Morongo) Reservation in Banning. Susan Clark played her as Polonsky had written her: a single woman in favor of a single sexual standard and the vote for women. In reality, Clara True, Indian agent at Malki during the episode, remained single, pressed a frontal campaign against liquor and for Christianity, and opposed women's suffrage (Sandos and Burgess 22, 66–67). Part of his "Amazonian contingent," Commissioner of Indian Affairs Francis E. Leupp described her (Lake Mohonk Conference 25, 30).

Polonsky compressed all four posses and over twenty deputies into one man, named him Coop, and chose Robert Redford for the role. Coop is the undersheriff of Banning and the son of a famous Indian-fighter who had been killed by a mixed blood sometime before the story begins (Sandos and Burgess 54–71).

Polonsky made no attempt to portray period Indian costumes, opting instead for the street dress of the late 1960s and beginning the film with Willie Boy jumping off a modern freight train. Polonsky's use of the anachronisms underscores the allegorical and timeless nature of the tale he chooses to tell (O'Connor 64), even though Susan Clark's voice-over before the title tells the audience that what is about to be shown is true and happened on the deserts of Southern California in 1909.

Liquor initiates the tale but, in Polonsky's version, Willie Boy buys a bottle from a bootlegger or "blind pigger" during the fiesta at Malki and arranges to meet Lola in the orchard at midnight. Meanwhile, Liz discovers the bootleggers and insists that Coop arrest them. Later, after several more drinks, Willie Boy goes into a poolroom in town where he clubs a white drummer with his pool cue after the man insults him. Coop, instead of following after Willie Boy, tells the drummer to come in the next morning to swear out a complaint. Coop then turns the "blind piggers" loose with an admonition not to return and heads out to Malki. Coop seeks an assignation with Liz, which she is reluctant to accept, not because she is not attracted to him but because the physical attraction is the core of their involvement.

Coop's love scene with Liz in her house is intercut with Willie Boy's love scene with Lola in the orchard. Liz is naked under a sheet on the bed; the Indians are naked on the ground. The dialog between Liz and Coop revolves around their exclusively physical mutual attraction, lack of mutual respect, and Coop's unwillingness to make any commitment to her. Willie Boy and Lola talk of their love, her father's opposition to it, and Lola's dream of becoming a teacher like Liz and of Willie Boy's becoming a farmer in Nevada. Polonsky gives Lola the assimilationist lines, whereas Willie Boy speaks uncompromisingly of his Indianness. Lola's father, armed with a rifle and accompanied by her two brothers, finds the couple *in flagrante delicto* and, in a struggle for the weapon, the clearly naked Willie Boy kills the old man while Lola covers herself with the white dress she wore for their meeting. The two then start running.

Coop and Willie Boy are brothers symbolically, one representing the light and the other the dark side of the same character. Willie Boy is cunning, impetuous and violent; Blake, who had earlier portrayed the well-intentioned although bumbling Indian sidekick, Little Beaver, in the *Red Ryder* television series, here plays Willie Boy as a screen rebel in the tradition of James Dean and Marlon Brando. Willie Boy's Indianness, however, is incidental to his role as Coop's Doppelgänger. Coop is equally cunning and violent, but Redford plays him as a reluctant, rather than confident hero, one who must be spurred to action. The women are mere temptresses: Lola is the cause of Willie Boy's troubles, and Liz distracts Coop from doing his job that night and then shames him into pursuing Willie Boy to the end. Liz compares Coop to his famous father and finds Coop lacking because he "cannot even kill an Indian."

Liz wants Coop to bring Lola back because Willie Boy has engaged in "marriage by capture." Liz claims, "It's the Paiute way and always was," but Liz believes that Lola "didn't want to go with him, she doesn't want to be a desert squaw." This appeal, coupled with the shame and the wounding of an old friend of Coop's father who led the posse while Coop was away, all combine to prompt Coop to ride.

Because Willie Boy and Coop are "brothers" and in conflict, the clash can only be resolved by death; Coop must recognize Willie Boy as his brother and touch him. In the closing episode Coop sprawls beside a drinking hole for water and sees Willie Boy's handprint in the mud. Coop places his own hand inside it; they match. At Ruby Mountain Coop "surprises" a crouching Willie Boy, whose back is to the lawman, his rifle cradled across his knees. Willie Boy stands, turns, and raises the rifle menacingly. Coop shoots and kills him, then checks the rifle. Willie Boy had no more bullets. Willie Boy forced Coop to kill him; Willie Boy dies

Figure 7.2. Liz Arnold (Susan Clark) and Coop (Robert Redford): a lack of mutual respect. Courtesy of the Museum of Modern Art/Film Stills Archive.

Indian and Coop lives, having killed his alter ego, standing alone in the twilight of a frontier that has gone.

Coop slings Willie Boy's body over his shoulder and carries him down to the base of the mountain where waiting Indian deputies build a fire to cremate the corpse. Coop washes Willie Boy's blood from his hands with desert sand. When the sheriff arrives and denounces the burning, claiming that "people'll want to see something," Coop utters the last words spoken: "Tell them we're fresh out of souvenirs." Polonsky's word choice again was deliberate. He told an interviewer, "The past is not now. It's just a souvenir and we should not be bound by souvenirs" (Sherman and Rubin 36).

Willie Boy mirrors the discontent and angst many Americans, especially the young, felt about the country and its mission at the depths of disillusionment over the Vietnam conflict. A year before *Willie Boy's* release, during the 1968 Tet offensive, Americans had confronted televised images of Viet Cong sappers inside the American embassy compound in Saigon. Popularly regarded as being the first television war, these images of battle in the streets of a supposedly secure Saigon and in other cities combined to shake to its core American confidence in its civilizing mission in Vietnam (FitzGerald 519). For those who missed the televised violence of the Tet offensive, television coverage of the riots surrounding the Democratic National Convention in Chicago that summer forced Americans to confront the divisions over the war at home (Rollins, "Television's Vietnam" 114–35, "Introduction" 1–10).

Polonsky wanted to comment on that mission. His intended message, as he told an interviewer, was that "civilization is the process of despoiling, of spoilation of people, which in the past we considered a victory, but we now suspect is a moral defeat for all" (Sherman and Rubin 25). The American destruction of Vietnam parallels American destruction of Indian nations at home. Polonsky uses his film to comment on relations between the oppositely attracted sexes to show how civilization has gone awry. Willie Boy and Lola are the embodiment of true heterosexual love, avatars of a lost past. They are seeking a new life of freedom together away from the domination of both the Indian family and white society. They represent marriage and family. Coop and Liz, alternatively, reflect the dark side of the 1960s' sexual revolution. They want individual freedom without mutual responsibility; marriage and family have no place in their conversation.

To underscore the significance of the Indian version of love, in his final (draft) screenplay Polonsky wanted the scene of confrontation with Lola's father to begin with a gnarled hand entering the frame, grabbing Lola by her hair, flinging her back. The clash would end with her father sprawled on the ground as "the wild doves flutter fearfully in the almond trees, and Willie and Lola, naked and ghost-like, turn to each other like Adam and Eve on that fateful night in Eden." Even though the doves did not make the final print, the scene is crucially important to his story.

Polonsky's imagery suggests a myth beyond that of the American frontier. The Indian as "noble savage" teaches "civilized" whites the meaning of love. But the Indian fails; he is no longer prelapsarian because he, and she, commit Original Sin and are driven from the Orchard/Garden. Coop and the deputies are God's own angels pursuing Willie Boy and Lola somewhere east of Eden. Because Willie Boy and Lola are to die, their lesson must die too. It is too late—we cannot learn, we cannot return to the Garden. Polonsky's point conflicted sharply with the 1960s counterculture, which at 1969's Woodstock Festival had claimed that it was possible to return to the garden, a wish elaborately articulated in Charles Reich's *Greening of America* (217–64, Weiner and Stillman).

Polonsky expands his biblical imagery to embrace the New Testament at the end of the film when Coop, having brought Willie Boy's body back to burn, washes his bloody hands with the dirt of the West. Coop

Figure 7.3. Coop with the body of Willie Boy (Robert Blake). The American West or Saigon/Hue during the Tet Offensive, 1968? Courtesy of the Museum of Modern Art/Film Stills Archive.

replays Pontius Pilate's washing his hands of the death of Jesus of Nazareth, meaning that Willie Boy has become a Christ figure, the ultimate innocent destroyed by a corrupt world. What was good has been killed and is gone. Only the fire remains.

Polonsky's pessimistic message bothered some American viewers and critics at the time. *New Yorker* film critic Pauline Kael thought that blaming American society for what it did to Indians, and by extension to the Vietnamese, as Polonsky had done in *Willie Boy*, left viewers with only one way out of their collective guilt—Kael's "genosuicide." Kael rejected "genosuicide" outright, claiming that the only people who could accept the film and its collective guilt are "the kind who want to believe that the corollary of 'Black is Beautiful' is 'White is Ugly'"(50).

Although *Willie Boy* undoubtedly mirrored deep reservations about America's mission at home and abroad, disturbing some Americans, it simultaneously masked the story of the Native Americans it ostensibly told. Katherine Ross drew criticism for her portrayal of the Indian girl because, despite her intentions "not to make her [Lola] another Hollywood Indian" (Friar and Friar 255), she was, as Polonsky had written her, just that. Ross was what Hollywood thought a young Indian girl should look like and behave.

Using Indians as foils for his own commentary on American culture was business as usual for Polonsky and Hollywood, and we do not suggest that there was intentional insult or affront. Polonsky filmed on the Morongo Reservation, providing then much-needed employment for Indians as extras; he incorporated bits on Cahuilla dances and games into the film, and treated Indians respectfully. Indian-hating simply renders telling the tale from an Indian perspective impossible unless the assumption is questioned, and there was no impetus for Polonsky to do so.

Willie Boy, the girl, and their respective families, however, were not Cahuilla and not from Morongo. Once one moves past the stereotype of "Indian" and recognizes individual tribes and people, then the opportunity arises to question the Indian-hating assumption and the traditional, white story. From our research into the incident, described in *The Hunt for Willie Boy*, we wish to raise only a few points. Our sources are both the traditional written documents familiar to historians and also our ethnographic fieldwork among the Indian families affected by the real Willie Boy in 1909. Together, these sources provide an ethnohistorical viewpoint of the incident and permit a retelling from an Indian perspective. We can illustrate the kind of story that lies beyond the lens.

According to Bureau of Indian Affairs records, Willie Boy was a Paiute-Chemehuevi. He had a Paiute father; from descendants of Willie Boy's family, we learned that Willie Boy had been reared by his mother and her people, meaning that, culturally, Willie Boy had grown up a Chemehuevi. Indeed, Willie Boy's mother was a famous Chemehuevi basketmaker. Thus, at the outset, any attempt to portray Willie Boy as following old Paiute customs was simply wrongheaded, displaying ignorance of the culture in which he lived. Neither the Chemehuevi nor the Paiutes in California had any type of bride-capture or bride-kidnap tradition, meaning that whatever whites thought had happened would have been a tragedy from the Chemehuevi perspective, a breaking of tribal taboo, rather than an observance of some "savage" custom.

We further learned that Willie Boy belonged to a special cult called the Runners, select young men used as messengers, youths able to run great distances across the desert with little water while carrying a chief's staff. Runners, through their traditional songs, knew where to find water in the desert and how to continue vigorously and undaunted across what would look to whites like a wasteland. Thus Chemehuevi culture helps to explain Willie Boy's feat in outrunning mounted white men pursuing him across the desert. Runners were not likely to abuse alcohol, and the story of Willie Boy's alleged drunkenness appeared only toward the end of the manhunt. The story, perhaps not surprisingly, arose within the white community. A deputy sheriff, who also worked for the Bureau of Indian Affairs, claimed that a white youth had bought some whiskey and beer in "wet" San Bernardino County the night before the confrontation between Willie Boy and the old man. This white youth brought alcohol back to the Gilman Ranch in "dry" Riverside County and hid it in the bunkhouse. After the manhunt began, this same boy believed that Willie Boy must have found the alcohol and consumed it. Willie Boy's previous reputation among whites as hard-working and non-drinking disappeared in the face of this allegation, an allegation that did not say anyone saw Willie Boy drinking, only that alcohol had been proximate to him. Indian-hating, rather than an eyewitness, saw Willie Boy drinking whiskey.

From our oral interviews with descendants of the girl's family we learned that her name was Carlota, that she was sixteen, not fourteen, and that she was capable of starting a family according to Chemehuevi culture. Most important we learned that from the Chemehuevi perspective this was a family story involving a violation of tribal taboo. At the time of the incident, Chemehuevi culture forbade marriage between cousins regardless of the degree of blood relation. Such strict exogamy made marriage among the Chemehuevi difficult and prompted intermarriage with other tribes. Willie Boy and Carlota were distantly related but mutually attracted. They had run away together before and members of both families pursued, captured, separated, and returned them to Twentynine Palms. Carlota's family had moved to Banning to work the fruit harvest, and Willie Boy followed. He precipitated the events that began the night of September 26, 1909. Their story, whatever whites may have thought, was one of challenging sexual taboo, family, and tribal values for love. The Willie Boy episode has more in common with Shakespeare's *Romeo and Juliet* than with Nicholas Ray's *Rebel Without a Cause*.

We have reduced a Chemehuevi oral telling of the story to print to bring it into dialogue with white texts as a basis for considering a new story and film approach.

> Whenever my mother would tell this story she always began by saying, "Love is hard."
> Willie Boy lived with his mother in the desert. She was a wonderful basketmaker, and her sign was the rattlesnake. She made her baskets without fear that the snake would strike her. Willie Boy was a

very good hunter because he could run faster than many animals. He needed a wife, but there were no young women nearby. He was young and strong, so he went across the desert looking for a wife. One day he saw his cousin, Carlota, and he wanted her. She looked back at him openly, and they both ran away together. Family [members] followed and found them. Willie Boy and Carlota were separated. He was not to look at her again. Both their hearts were still restless. He wanted Carlota but her father was a man of power. One night Willie Boy got a rifle and came to see her father. They argued, and Willie Boy got mad. Willie Boy killed her father, then he and Carlota ran away again.

This time whites chased them, along with some of the People [Chemehuevi]. Willie Boy hid his wife in a wash, gave her his coat and his waterskin, and went for food. He ran in the old way, for he was like the wind, and no one could catch him then. He came back with food but could not find his wife. He searched everywhere, but she had died. He found the men chasing him and shot their horses with his rifle so that they would have to run like he did. They could not. He was so much faster that he quickly ran off.

In his running he came again to his mother, but she now turned away. He ran further, far out into the desert, away from all his family. None of the People saw him again, and we later heard that he had died (113).

This Indian version differs radically from the account told in *Willie Boy*. An Indian perspective exposes the blinders of the Indian-hating assumption and provides material for a very different type of Indian film. The Chemehuevi version of the story begins, like many Indian tales, within the context of family and culture, stressing both the qualities of the individual and the individual's relationship within Native society. Conflict that disrupts tribal norms is given a cultural context, and when whites are involved, the Indian version contradicts the standard white telling.

Developing a more inclusive version of the story, one in which the Chemehuevi voice can be heard, requires much research. It yields a story, however, with rich cinematic possibilities at once more interesting than the prevailing white-told story and more resonant with the past Indians shared with whites.

When a filmmaker appeals to history to make more credible his or her art, then the way that history is used may elicit critical analysis from historians. Polonsky, the writer and director, told his story without regard for the accuracy of the historical information he portrayed. The discrepancy between the historical Clara True and her film counterpart, Elizabeth Arnold, for example, has been noted.

Figure 7.4. Willie Boy on the train to Banning. Can Hollywood discard its confrontational mask? Courtesy of the Museum of Modern Art/Film Stills Archive.

A similar fictional recreation is followed for Indians. Polonsky told interviewers, regarding the Indian girl he chose to call Lola, that "of course, you know, in history no one knows who Lola is, as a person. She's a name from history, that's all" (Sherman and Rubin 26). By disregarding or ignoring historical reality and creating fictional characters that suited his story, Polonsky objectified real Indians and used them as foils in his morality play.

Geronimo is an improvement, a recent film dealing with an historical Indian figure that attempts to provide an Indian perspective. The complex story of this man and his opposition to the U.S. army has been compressed to a brief part of his career, focusing on the events leading to his surrender and final relocation of his band. The film attempts to respect Geronimo's Apache culture by depicting fragments of the visions that motivated him. Alas, the fleeting glimpses of Geronimo's visions do not enable the average filmgoer to understand the reasons for his decisions. In this film, attention to telling the historical tale resulted in an insufficient expression of Indian cultural context.

In contrast to this approach, a film like *Powwow Highway* presents a complex and compelling story told from an Indian perspective. Although it makes no attempt to tell a historical tale, it delves deeply into Cheyenne culture to create contemporary figures who are at once believable and completely Indian. The "traditions of the warrior and the trickster are . . . the key to survival and identity of the two central characters" (Hilger 263).

Combining the two approaches of *Geronimo* and *Powwow Highway*, a template can surely be created for portraying more accurately and authentically a historical episode from the Indian–white past. We have tried to demonstrate that the challenge to Hollywood filmmakers can no longer be ignored. With a bit of awareness about the pitfalls of Indian-hating and a willingness to invest modestly in research, Hollywood can discard the conventional mask with which it has fitted Native Americans and craft instead a commercial film that truly mirrors an American society with Indians in it.

Works Cited

Cortés, Carlos. "To View a Neighbor: The Hollywood Textbook on Mexico. In *Images of Mexico in the United States*, 91–118. John H. Coatsworth and Carlos Rico, eds. San Diego: Center for U.S.-Mexican Studies, 1989.

FitzGerald, Frances. *Fire in the Lake: The Vietnamese and the Americans in Vietnam*. New York: Vintage, 1972.

Friar, Ralph, and Natasha A. Friar. *The Only Good Indian . . . The Hollywood Gospel*. New York: Drama Specialists, 1972.

Greenfield, Gerald Michael, and Carlos E. Cortés. "Harmony and Conflict of Intercultural Images: The Treatment of Mexico in U.S. Feature Films and K–12 Textbooks." *Mexican Studies/Estudios Mexicanos* 7 (1991): 283–301.

Hilger, Michael. *From Savage to Nobleman: Images of Native Americans in Film.* Lanham, Md.: Scarecrow Press, 1995.

Kael, Pauline. "Americana: *Tell Them Willie Boy Is Here.*" *The New Yorker*, December 27, 1969: 47–50.

Lake Mohonk Conference of the Friends of the Indian and Other Dependent Peoples. *Report of the Twenty-sixth Annual Meeting of the Lake Mohonk Conference of the Friends of the Indian and Other Dependent Peoples.* Lake Mohonk, N.Y.: Lake Mohonk Conference of the Friends of the Indian and Other Dependent Peoples, 1908.

Lawton, Harry. *Willie Boy: A Desert Manhunt.* Balboa Island, Calif.: Paisano Press, 1960.

Melville, Herman. *The Confidence Man: His Masquerade.* 1857. New York: Grove Press, 1949.

O'Connor, John E. *The Hollywood Indian: Stereotypes of Native Americans in Film.* Paterson, N.J.: New Jersey State Museum, 1980.

O'Connor, John E., and Martin A. Jackson, eds. *American History/American Film: Interpreting the Hollywood Image.* New York: Ungar, 1979.

Pearce, Roy Harvey. "The Metaphysics of Indian-Hating." *Ethnohistory* 4.1 (1957): 27–40.

Polonsky, Abraham Lincoln. Willie Boy, a film treatment. Early Draft. First screenplay no. 00889. Final screenplay no. 02023. Harry Lawton papers, University of California, Riverside.

Reich, Charles. *The Greening of America.* New York: Random, 1970.

Rollins, Peter C. "Introduction: The Gulf War and Television." *Film & History* 22 (1992): 1–10.

———. "Television's Vietnam: The Impact of Visual Images." *Journal of American Culture* 4 (1981): 114–35.

Rollins, Peter C., ed. *Hollywood as Historian: American Film in a Cultural Context.* Lexington, Ky: University Press of Kentucky, 1983.

Sandos, James A., and Larry E. Burgess. *The Hunt for Willie Boy: Indian-Hating and Popular Culture.* Norman: University of Oklahoma Press, 1994.

Sherman, Eric, and Martin Rubin. *The Director's Event: Interviews with Five American Film-Makers.* New York: Atheneum, 1970.

Slotkin, Richard. *Gunfighter Nation: The Myth of the Frontier in Twentieth-Century America.* New York: Maxwell Macmillan, 1992.

Tuska, Jon. *The American West in Film: Critical Approaches to the Western.* Lincoln: University of Nebraska Press, 1988.

Vanderwood, Paul J. "An American Cold Warrior: *Viva Zapata!* (1952)." In *American History/American Film: Interpreting the Hollywood Image*, 183–201. John O'Connor and Martin A. Jackson, eds. New York: Ungar, 1979.

Weiner, Rex, and Deanne Stillman. *Woodstock Census: The Nationwide Survey of the Sixties Generation.* New York: Viking, 1979.

Native Americans in a Revisionist Western
Little Big Man (1970)

Arthur Penn's *Little Big Man* inverts the common mythologies of the American frontier usually presented in the Western film genre. The film is recognizably a Western. Like others, it is set in the post–Civil War period during the great westward expansion that took place between 1865 and 1890, on the first leg of the journey west, on the Great Plains. Few Westerns are complete without a conflict between Indians and whites, and *Little Big Man* is no exception. Although the film uses established generic conventions, within the form it does something very innovative: it reconsiders the impact of westward expansion on Native Americans. Instead of savages threatening heroic pioneers, the Indians are victims of malevolent treatment by the United States Army, which, using a highly developed technology against innocent and peaceful natives, took the land and food sources and destroyed the indigenous culture. Whereas most traditional Westerns do not develop individual Indian characters or their customs, *Little Big Man* presents the Cheyenne as living together in harmony, a flourishing tribe with a defined culture. Whereas classic Westerns portray the whites as representatives of civilization and the Indians as barbarians, this one suggests the opposite. Whereas the westward expansion is usually represented as producing unmixed benefit, this film suggests that the land was conquered through the use of brutal force that decimated people and nature.

To convey this revisionist view, the narrative structure combines elements from two literary traditions: the picaresque (the roguish hero encounters a series of adventures) and the initiation archetype (the hero attains mature insight through experiences that shape him). Like youthful hero figures of other texts, Jack Crabb is initially innocent and ignorant, but through his exposure to both white and Cheyenne cultures he develops and learns and is able to choose between them. This structure of initiation and transformation is repeated in the contemporary Western *Dances With Wolves*. Both films offer a revisionist treatment of the subject matter, and both challenge generic expectations. But whereas *Dances with Wolves* is a serious and dramatic rendition, *Little Big Man* is a comic and ironic narrative that demythologizes famous legendary figures, the Western hero, and the Indians. The fusion of cinematic elements—the generic reversals, the tone, the complex narrative structure, the convincing representation of Native Americans—makes it unique.

Between the seventeenth and nineteenth centuries Americans learned two contradictory myths about Indians. One, deriving from the Puritan fear of the uncontrolled wilderness and its inhabitants, depicted Native Americans as bloodthirsty savages. The other, which flourished in the writings of the eighteenth-century European Romantics, presented Indians as noble savages living in an unspoiled wilderness, spiritually pure, uncorrupted by civilization and at one with nature. In nineteenth-century America, Henry Wadsworth Longfellow's celebrated narrative poem *The Song of Hiawatha* (1855) perpetuated this idealized view. James Fenimore Cooper's popular novels incorporated both portraits. In *The Pioneers, The Last of the Mohicans, The Prairie, The Pathfinder*, and *The Deerslayer*—all five collected in *The Leather Stocking Tales*, published between 1823 and 1841—Indians were wild, uncivilized, and ferocious, but they were also brave, dignified, proud, and wise teachers.

The visual arts of the period transformed these literary stereotypes into powerful images that eventually became the basic iconography of the Hollywood Western film. Nineteenth-century artist George Catlin painted romanticized scenes of Indians within landscapes reminiscent of the garden of Eden, concentrating on dramatic portrayals of buffalo hunts, exotic tribal dances and ceremonies, and heroic portraiture of the natives—all in vivid hues. Swiss watercolorist Karl Bodmer painted striking panoramic views of the frontier and remarkable scenes of wild natives in the fierce buffalo and scalp dances, pictures that illustrated his conceptions of a savage new world. These representations of the Plains Indians, widely distributed through lithographs and aquatints, established the image of Indians on horseback wearing primitive ceremonial costumes, thereby molding that conception of them in the popular imagination. In contrast to this fabrication of the Indian as an untamed yet noble people, artists Frederic Remington and Charles M. Russell introduced the cowboy-as-epic hero, a character type whose role was to repress the threat-

Figure 8.1. Little Big Man (Dustin Hoffman) and Chief Old Lodge Skins (Chief Dan George) are juxtaposed in identical attire, a sign of their kinship. Courtesy of the Museum of Modern Art/Film Stills Archive.

ening Indians and win the West. The cowboy dominated the scene until the early twentieth century, when Edward Curtis posed Native Americans before his camera, recording a romanticized vision of noble Indians and their vanishing way of life, and championed their cause.[1]

Paintings, photographs, dime novels, illustrated magazines, and Buffalo Bill's Wild West Show reinforced this dual conception of Indians.

Shaped by the marketplace, these popular media depicted Native Americans both as scantily dressed men with feathers in their hair, bareback on horses, brandishing spears as they attacked innocent whites, and also as calm, wise elders, in full-feathered headdress, models of stoic restraint. These stereotypes became the basis for movie images.

Although some silent films, such as D.W. Griffith's *Massacre* (1912) and James Cruze's *Covered Wagon* (1923), conveyed a tolerant view of Indians, the classic Hollywood Western of the 1930s and 1940s reinforced those images and stereotypes that had evolved during the previous century and that relied almost entirely on the figure of the bloodthirsty warrior whose hostile actions and threatening presence impeded the great westward expansion. This conception of American history shifted slightly in the 1950s when a variation arose in the genre. Several directors made B-Westerns that showed the white man's poor treatment of Native Americans: for example, greedy white traders swindling them in Stuart Gilmore's *The Half-Breed* (1952) or hateful cavalry officers provoking them into battle in Sam Fuller's *Run of the Arrow* (1956). Anthony Mann's *Devil's Doorway* (1950), Delmer Daves's *Broken Arrow* (1950), and Robert Aldrich's *Apache* (1954) introduced a different characterization of Indians. Native Americans (albeit played by white actors) are central characters who are honorable and brave, yet targets of racism. The struggle between an admirable Indian and greedy, bigoted whites creates the conflict at the basis of the narrative (Fenin and Everson 282).

In the early 1960s, several major releases brought this more sympathetic view of Native Americans to mainstream audiences. After his success in *Jailhouse Rock* (Richard Thorp, 1957), rock & roll star Elvis Presley played a character who is the blameless object of prejudice just because he is a "half-breed," the mixed-race son of a white father and Indian mother, in Don Siegel's *Flaming Star* (1960). Then John Ford, a major filmmaker largely responsible for the accepted stereotypical view of the savage Indian, directed *Cheyenne Autumn* (1964). Ford modified the negative portrayal of the Native American in his previous Westerns by depicting the heroism of the Cheyenne people as they attempted to trek on foot, under terrible conditions, a thousand miles back to their homeland. The film reveals the dignity of the Indians in the face of the United States government's harsh and unfair military policy toward them.[2]

By the late 1960s, films like Martin Ritt's *Hombre* (1967) and Sydney Pollack's *The Scalphunters* (1968) expanded this sympathetic attitude toward Native Americans. During that period the escalating war in Vietnam, along with the emerging civil rights, feminist, ecology, and American Indian movements, dominated the public discourse and affected the content of many films.[3] A growing antiestablishment mood reflected the disappointment felt by many Americans, especially the young, whose dreams and ideals were dashed by the assassinations of John F. Kennedy, Martin Luther King, Jr., Robert Kennedy, and Malcolm X. Films first signaled a shift in cultural values when offbeat protagonists and counterculture themes emerged in *Bonnie and Clyde* (1967), *The Graduate* (1968), and *Butch Cassidy and the Sundance Kid* and *Easy Rider* (both 1969). *Little Big Man* was also produced during the political and social turmoil of this era, and reflected the consciousness of the movements of the time, the social attitudes they generated, and an overall reevaluation of America's morality and values. The film criticizes America's historical military aggression against the Indians by graphically dramatizing an overwhelming military force employed against a technologically primitive people. Viewers at the time may have connected the portrayed genocide of the Indians to America's attack on the Vietnamese people.

Changes in the American film industry made it possible to express the disillusionment and growing cynicism of a good part of the population. The breakdown of the studio system and the increasing prestige and influence of European art films encouraged independent film production and production of movies targeted to specific markets, especially, and for the first time successfully, the youth market. In addition, the elimination of the Production Code in 1968 permitted the depiction of graphic violence and sex on the big screen.[4] The films produced as a result of these factors dared to offer nontraditional themes in nontraditional cinematic formats. By the end of the decade, mainstream films had begun to reflect the themes and experiences of the counterculture.

Little Big Man was adapted from Thomas Berger's novel of the same title during a six-year period by Calder Willingham in collaboration with Arthur Penn (Crowdus and Porton 12), and was released in the winter of 1970.[5] The differences between Berger's book, written in 1964, and Willingham's final script illustrate the shift in social attitudes that had occurred during those years. Willingham transformed Jack Crabb, Berger's ambiguous and not entirely agreeable protagonist, into a reliable narrator and a congenial hero with whose point of view the audience identifies. The screenwriter also recast the novel's ambiguous and not entirely sympathetic Indians into amiable and moral—and victimized—characters for whom the audience has great empathy. Both the book and the film treat the narrative with humor and irony, and that lightheartedness is one aspect that makes the movie noteworthy. It ribs and needles Christian fundamentalists, legendary heroes, clergymen, hucksters, hippies, gays, oddballs, strong-minded women, and, in passing, Jews, shopkeepers,

Figure 8.2. During the massacre at the Washita River, Sunshine (Amy Eccles) is fleeing from the cavalry officer. Courtesy of the Museum of Modern Art/Film Stills Archive.

and many others, devising a parody very few Westerns, and certainly none with an underlying serious message, had ever attempted.

The film introduces a narrative structure that Westerns of the 1990s subsequently adopted: the story unfolds through the eyes of a white man who, moving and living among Native peoples, gradually becomes disillusioned with his own culture, and, deeply changed by his experiences, casts off his Euro-American identity. Jack, like Lt. John Dunbar in *Dances With Wolves* (both descendants of James Fenimore Cooper's Natty Bumppo), learns the ways and language of the natives, dons their garb, is given an Indian name, and is initiated into the tribal community. This initiation archetype relates *Little Big Man* structurally—but not in tone— to *Dances With Wolves* (1990), and also to *Black Robe* (1991), *Thunderheart* (1992), *The Last of the Mohicans* (1992), and *White Fang 2: Myth of the White Wolf* (1994).

Little Big Man presents the story of Jack Crabb, who is, as he says, "the sole white survivor of the Battle of the Little Big Horn, popularly known as Custer's Last Stand." His seriocomic adventures cover nearly a hundred years of American history during which time he meets the legendary frontier heroes George Armstrong Custer and Wild Bill Hickok.

Jack alternates between two divergent societies—Indian and white—and, having lived in two worlds, he is able to compare, contrast, and evaluate each of them. The film's depiction of the virtues and customs of the Cheyenne conveys regret for the destruction of a culture in the name of progress, propelling the narrative into a protest against the historical treatment of Native Americans and racial intolerance in general.

The film opens with Jack Crabb (Dustin Hoffman), now 121 years old and in a Veterans Administration hospital, talking into an interviewer's tape recorder. He tells his story (which begins in the 1850s), relates the "facts" of his life, and periodically comments on these events in a voice-over. His experiences unfold in a flashback: a Cheyenne brave brings ten-year-old Jack to his tribe after the Pawnee kill the boy's family in a raid. Adopted by the Cheyenne Chief, Old Lodge Skins (Chief Dan George), Jack lives with them until his late teens and learns their tribal customs, language, and philosophy of life and moral order. The tribe gives him the name Little Big Man because, although he is physically small, he gains stature by saving the life of a fellow brave, Younger Bear (Cal Bellini).

During a skirmish between the Cheyenne and the U.S. Cavalry, a soldier captures Little Big Man and places him in the home of a Baptist minister, the Reverend Pendrake (Thayer David) and his wife (Faye Dunaway). From them, Jack receives a white man's education and Christian moral training. He becomes aware of their hypocrisy and leaves them, utterly disillusioned, when he discovers Mrs. Pendrake in a tryst with her lover. Jack tries various frontier occupations, each of which requires him to change his identity and acquire new skills. His enterprises bring him into contact with important and curious characters, including Custer and Hickok. However, once again disillusioned by the failure of his undertakings, he moves West with his Swedish wife, Olga (Kelly Jean Peters). On the way, Indians attack the stagecoach and kidnap her. Jack sets out to find her, but his former brothers capture him and return him to the tribe. Wanting to continue his search for Olga, he leaves the Indian village and attaches himself to Custer's Seventh Cavalry. After he sees the regiment slaughter an entire encampment of Indian women and children, he deserts and returns once again to the Cheyenne. A happy period with an Indian wife (Amy Eccles) follows, but ends when, during another massacre led and encouraged by Custer (Richard Mulligan), he sees his wife and newborn son killed.

At this point Jack longs to assassinate Custer but is unable to do so and, ashamed of his weakness, turns to drink. Alone, disheveled, and on the verge of suicide, he catches sight of Custer's regiment on the move and decides he must "look the devil in the eye and send him to Hell where he belongs." At the Little Big Horn, Custer asks Jack, now his scout, whether to attack or retreat. Jack knows that thousands of Indians from many tribes have assembled there to battle the white man, sees the opportunity to send Custer to his certain death, and challenges him to attack. Thinking Jack is trying to outwit him (and he is), Custer, thinking he will outwit Jack, leads his troops into the ravine of the Little Big Horn. In the famous battle of June 25, 1876, Custer and his entire regiment are, of course, annihilated. Jack, however, is saved by his old rival, Younger Bear, who returns him to the decimated Cheyenne tribe. Old Lodge Skins foresees the end of the Cheyenne and readies himself for his own death. When his preparations fail, the Chief, stoical and good-humored, recognizes life's inevitable ironies and comments: "Sometimes the magic works; sometimes it doesn't." The flashback ends with this scene, and the film concludes with a return to the hospital where Crabb dismisses the interviewer who, like the viewer, has been surprised and humbled by this narrative.

Little Big Man combines the two literary forms of the picaresque and the initiation archetype.[6] It shares the satirical tone and episodic plot of the picaresque tradition. It also shares the character development and dramatic structure of the initiation archetypal pattern: the hero's formation and growth, his journey from ignorance and innocence to wisdom and maturity. Jack Crabb attains maturity and insight through his contact with the two societies, white and Cheyenne.

Jack's journey opens his eyes to contrasting values. The whites of frontier society are goal-oriented, hypocritical, and exploitative. While Jack is with them, he moves through stages in which he searches for identity, tries to fit into a social mold, and learns that to succeed he must take advantage of others. In contrast, the Indian way of life emphasizes harmony. Individuals grow older, some are killed—often by whites—but new families are formed, and the tribe moves across the land according to the naturally changing seasons. The Cheyenne express their feelings honestly and accept differences: they tolerate their fellows, including the Contrary who does everything backwards and the *heemaneh* who, although male, lives as a woman.

By portraying the Cheyenne as natural, unaffected, honest, generous, and accepting, the film asserts that life among the whites is the opposite: artificial, deceitful, fraudulent, greedy, and intolerant. In contrast to the Indian recognition of a center to life, a moral and spiritual essence around which all things revolve and which gives meaning and balance to existence, whites "do not know where the center of the earth is," as the old chief says. The Cheyenne consider the cycles of time, seasons, and days to be part of the great circle of life. This concept is important in many Indian cultures and is used in the film as a strong visual and thematic element: tepees are built on a circular plan, the Indian camp is circular in arrangement, and many artifacts are based on a circular design. At one point, Little Big Man convinces his grandfather to escape an attack only by persuading him that he must flee to the river, which, he reminds the old man, "is part of the great circle of the waters of the earth." The harmonious, cyclical nature of the Cheyenne ways, embodied in the motif of the circle, contrasts visually to the activities of the whites, which are either rigidly linear (regiments of marching soldiers) or destructively chaotic (the massacres).

Through the portrayal of the Cheyenne Indians, *Little Big Man* evokes a romanticized image of the "pure life" and condemns the forces that caused that way of life to vanish—racial intolerance, unbridled greed, environmental plunder. For example, one sequence shows the Cheyenne tribe moving across the plains where, undisturbed by the presence of the Indians, buffalo graze placidly. The Indians share the earth, only killing the buffalo when their own survival is at stake. This sequence contrasts to a later scene of white buffalo hunters stacking huge piles of skins, visually emphasizing the rapacious character of those who kill the buffalo not for sustenance but for financial gain.

The moral emptiness of white American society is a primary theme of the film, developed narratively and visually through the motif of the massacre. This motif explodes the myth that the westward expansion was entirely heroic and unsullied, and exposes the historical realities of the nineteenth-century genocide of Native Americans. Three separate scenes of slaughter by the cavalry construct and constitute the motif. The film shows the first attack only in its aftermath: the camera quickly tilts down from an Indian corpse to a saddlebag marked with the letters "US," an allusion to the guilt of our country in this and other attacks on Native peoples. Jack finds himself in the middle of the second assault, but associated this time with the American soldiers. The editing by Dede Allen fragments the scene, thereby intensifying the commotion and the viewer's identification with Jack's fear, helplessness, and confusion. The third assault (actually carried out by Custer and the Seventh Cavalry in November 1868) takes place at the Washita River. In this long sequence punctuated by graphic violence, the camera, protagonist, victims, and the viewer are together in the very midst of the horror, enclosed by chaos and death, surrounded by fleeing people and falling bodies, screams of terror and cries of pain. Little Big Man escapes the immediate area and watches, powerless to save his wife Sunshine, who, carrying their newborn baby and running desperately, is shot again and again by a ruthless soldier. For movie audiences of the time, enmeshed in the controversy over American military intervention in Vietnam, these images made strong reference to the just-published newspaper accounts of the criminal massacre of women and children at My Lai, carried out months before by Army Lt. William L. Calley, Jr., and some of his troops.[7] The suppressed information emerged in shocking headlines in November 1969 as shooting on the film was being completed.[8]

Unlike most Westerns preceding it, *Little Big Man* criticizes all of white society. The film is clearly critical of the American soldiers; the once-heroic cavalry that could always be counted on to ride to the rescue of beleaguered white settlers has become a band of barbaric, invading butchers, bent on the destruction of an innocent people. Although it does not go so far as to situate the narrative point of view in a Cheyenne hero, Chief Old Lodge Skins does convey the film's moral position.[9] Characterized as a visionary, able to see deeply and clearly even when later blinded, he becomes the personification of the noble Indian. The camera work glorifies him in low-angle shots against the sky. His acting—facial expressions and delivery of philosophical and nearly poetic lines—contributes to his image as a sage and upright man.[10] In one scene Little Big Man and Old Lodge Skins wear identical clothing of buckskin garments, intricate ornaments, and maroon cloth strips in their braids. The matching clothing is the symbol of Little Big Man's attainment of his grandfather's wisdom: he has completed his development and is now a full-fledged member of the Cheyenne. One day he will assume his grandfather's place as tribal spokesman by setting the record straight. Jack Crabb's retelling of the Cheyenne story, taped in the Veterans Administration hospital, preserves the legacy of Old Lodge Skins and his people. The audience identifies with Jack and with the growing affinity and empathy for the Cheyenne that led him to criticize American colonialism and imperialism. Spectators join him in that critical stance.

Native American culture is presented more authentically than in many movie Westerns. In an interview published in *Cineaste*, Arthur Penn explains that he consulted with historian Alvin Josephy on costuming and other details (Crowdus and Porton 12). The film was shot on location in Montana and Canada, and Penn cast Native Americans in major and minor parts. All of this enhances the representation of the texture of Indian life. Yet the film is not an accurate ethnographic or anthropological document, and Penn implies that he did not intend it to be. Contemporary critics acknowledge that *Little Big Man* depicts Native Americans sympathetically, but point out that the film relies on a white protagonist.[11]

The point of view belongs to Jack Crabb, whose experiences organize the narrative and convey much of the ideology.

Although *Little Big Man* offers many details of Indian life not usually included in Hollywood Westerns, the Cheyenne in the film do not fully represent an authentic Indian culture. Rather, they reflect the fashions and mores of the Sixties counterculture, whose practices included a return to the land, experimentation with drugs and alternative lifestyles, communal living, sexual freedom, and a search for peace and harmony—all of which superficially resemble Native ways. These practices contrasted markedly with the violence and greed of the dominant society.

The film retains the novel's parodic tone at the expense of actual facts about tribal roles. Many of the characters, therefore, are sketched as predominately comical and outrageous. For example, Little Horse (Robert Little Star) is introduced as a *heemaneh*. The film draws him as an affected, homosexual stereotype: he takes on such contemporary mannerisms as fluttering his eyelashes, dancing flirtatiously, and lisping coy lines of dialogue. The *heemaneh* or *berdache*, according to Walter L. Williams, is a sexually ambiguous role taken on by some men in many native tribes that combines the behavior, dress, social and sexual habits of both women and men (2). In the days when Natives shared in these roles, the *heemanehs* might wear dresses but also carry weapons; they would serve food and care for children but also ride with hunting parties. The *heemaneh* might marry another man but would remain highly respected for his bravery, spiritual, intellectual, and artistic contributions. Among the tribes, including the Cheyenne, *berdaches* had a clearly recognized and accepted social status as well as special ceremonial and religious roles. Jack reports in his voice-over commentary that the tribe admires and respects Little Horse, but the film—disregarding his spiritual and shaman qualities—encourages the spectator to ridicule him.

The choice of comedy over factual information results in a similar limitation in the characterization of the Contrary. Younger Bear becomes a Contrary for a time, and in the film he is depicted as a lunatic, a nut—at best, an odd character. However, according to George Bird Grinnell, one of the first ethnographers to provide a detailed description of Cheyenne culture, Contraries or *Hohnuhk'e* acted by opposites and did not choose the role but were called to it by dreams or visions (2: 79). Contraries accepted enormous hardship and responsibility, and their role was powerful in the tribe. Furthermore, Contraries were considered spiritually pure because their "closer contact with the Sacred Powers" gave them "a purity of thought and action that was usually denied to man" (Bancroft-Hunt 15). This is hardly the impression one gets of Younger Bear who, behaving as he does in the film, comes across as angry, crazy, and bizarre, acting outrageously for no explained reason. Once again the film evokes the outlandish, drug-induced behavior associated with the Sixties.

Like the portrayal of the *heemaneh* and the Contrary, the depiction of the Cheyenne women suggests a Sixties stereotype with a comic twist. They personify the "natural" women of the era who engaged in communal living and practiced sexual freedom. The film introduces Sunshine as a strong woman, courageously giving birth in hiding while soldiers slaughter her people in a nearby encampment. Later Sunshine goes off alone like a wild creature to deliver her second child when actually, according to Grinnell, Cheyenne women were always accompanied and assisted at childbirth by their mother, or another woman invited by the mother (2: 145). Subsequently Sunshine is portrayed as a coy child-wife, unhampered by puritanical constraints about monogamy and fidelity: she insists on sharing her husband with each of her three sisters, who are, in turn, more than willing collaborators. A scene of communal lovemaking in the tepee mirrors the image of a hippie commune and reflects the free-love, open-marriage ethos associated with the Sixties. In reality Cheyenne women were constrained by strictly maintained rules of chastity; even courtship was conducted over a period of years and under stern guidelines (1: 127). Once again an authentic representation of the complex and highly developed Cheyenne culture is made subordinate to the comic tone of the film.

Even though *Little Big Man* pokes fun at the Indians and at the counterculture, the film indicates the serious losses experienced in the 1960s. Jack Crabb's grief over the tragic fate of the Native Americans becomes emblematic of the nation's lament over the assassinations; the extinction of cultures, species, and habitats; and the pollution and devastation of the environment. These became subjects of the decade's discourse. American youth recognized that the Indian way of life—deeply spiritual and ecologically sound—was a model that modern society had ignored. They took up these causes in the political and social arena, noting the harmony of Native American ways, as they searched for meaning and purpose in their own lives. Jack tells his story to preserve the Cheyenne heritage and also to offer lessons for America in 1970.[12] Indeed *Little Big Man* struck such a deep chord in young audiences that it became the second highest domestic box-office hit of that year.

Instead of taking the usual stance of Westerns that show white civilization taming the West and bettering the country through expansion, *Little Big Man* criticizes the frivolity and avarice that destroys a benevolent native culture for profit and power. By inverting the ideology of the genre,

Figure 8.3. In *Dances With Wolves,* John Dunbar (Kevin Costner) walks before the Sioux encampment with the captive white woman raised by the tribe and known as Stands With A Fist (Mary McDonnell). Courtesy of the Museum of Modern Art/Film Stills Archive.

the film explicitly demythologizes westward expansion, thus providing a more authentic view of the history of the American West.

In spite of its reliance on comedy and its ethnographic shortcomings, *Little Big Man* seriously contributes to a more sensitive representation of Native Americans. Old Lodge Skins emerges as a true hero of the film, and the culture of his people appears in a positive light. In the conflict between whites and Indians, the cavalry members are depicted as the real savages—brutal, corrupt, and insanely violent. The Cheyenne, on the other hand, call themselves the "Human Beings," and, because the film endows them with the best qualities of humankind, the viewer sympathizes with them.[13]

Little Big Man is important not only because of its revisionist view of American frontier history and its more authentic and sensitive representation of Native Americans, but also because the film introduces a narrative structure that subsequent Westerns adopted. For the first time in a Hollywood Western, the consciousness of a white protagonist is raised by his exposure to an indigenous culture, and he chooses to become part of the tribe. Jack Crabb comes to recognize the valuable qualities of the Native culture and thereby gains the wisdom and insight that allow him to become the Cheyenne Indian named Little Big Man. The spectator, who identifies with the protagonist, changes along with him and adopts his ideological stance toward the Indians. This narrative structure marked a step forward in the evolution of the Western and blazed the trail that Lt. John Dunbar was to follow twenty years later in *Dances With Wolves*.

The next major development in the representation of the Hollywood Indian depends largely on the contributions of Native American screenwriters, directors, and producers like Loretta Todd and Mohawk Michael Doxtater (*Forgotten Warriors*), Miwok Greg Sarris (HBO miniseries *Grand Avenue*), Cherokee Valerie Red-Horse (CBS special *My Indian Summer*), and Makah Sandra Sunrising Osawa (*The Eighth Fire*), among others. These artists are in a position to bring Native American voices, stories, and viewpoints to the media mainstream from which they have been historically excluded.[14]

Notes

1. According to William H. Goetzmann and William N. Goetzmann in *The West of the Imagination*, ethnographers were aware that Curtis had manipulated the subject matter by resorting to photographic trickery and posing Indians near modern tepees (233).

2. Mari Sandoz wrote the book *Cheyenne Autumn* from the Cheyenne's point of view; Ford's film shifts the perspective to a white character, Captain Thomas Archer (Richard Widmark), and also distorts the truth about the Army's treatment of the Cheyenne during their long march (Engelhardt 18).

3. The reemergence of Edward Curtis's photographs during the late 1960s and early 1970s "when communes and 'going native' became fashionable" (Goetzmann and Goetzmann 233) proved the popularity of the American Indian Movement. Influenced by the photographs, the youth culture adopted long hair and Native American attire. Because of their association with nature, Native Americans often inspired those who felt alienated from modern industrial society.

4. Between 1965 and 1968 the TV nightly news brought the Vietnam War into American living rooms, but violence in the movies was censored.

5. *Soldier Blue* by Ralph Nelson, *A Man Called Horse* by Elliot Silverstein, and *Little Big Man* were released in 1970. In all three films the central (white) characters are enriched by exposure to Indian culture, a transformation reflecting the influence of the American Indian Movement on Hollywood.

6. In contrast to the film, Berger's novel relies entirely on the picaresque tradition. A rascal throughout the book, Jack Crabb develops no insight from his many predicaments and adventures.

7. "Vietnam was a war which produced an unprecedented amount of press coverage with comparatively little censorship. This led . . . to a remarkable series of revelations about atrocities . . . which culminated in the trial of Lieutenant Calley for the massacre at My Lai [and] fueled the vociferous protest movement in America" (Huxley 97–99).

8. Lt. William L. Calley, Jr., who led the massacre, said in 1972: "We thought we would go to Vietnam and be Audie Murphies. Kick in the door . . . kill. . . . We were just playing games here. Cowboys, the Vietnamese called us" ("The Media and Images of War: Perception Versus Reality" 4). Journalist Seymour Hersch published the first story after being "leaked" an ongoing U.S. Army investigator's report.

9. Jack Crabb/Little Big Man and Old Lodge Skins are the only major characters treated with respect rather than as subjects of parody.

10. In 1970 Chief Dan George became the first Native American nominated for an Academy Award as Best Supporting Actor. He won both the National Society of Film Critics and New York Film Critics awards in that category.

11. Alan Lovell points out that none of the 1950s Westerns provided a meaningful description of Indian life and culture or paid serious attention to their history; all of them cast white actors as Indians (172). Engelhardt also discusses the ideological implications of spectator identification with the white protagonist's point of view, which, he asserts, "makes the intruder exchange places . . . with the intruded upon" (15).

12. In Elliott Erwitt's short film on the making of *Little Big Man*, Arthur Penn says, "History is the rumor we tend to believe." He discusses his view of the importance of reinterpreting and learning from our history.

13. The Cheyenne's name for themselves in their language is *tsis tsis tas*, "the people" (Grinnell 1: 11).

14. Native American novelists, poets, historians, and environmentalists in the United States and Canada are bringing attention to Indian history, conditions of life, and point of view. Discussion of their work can be found in the growing number of journals on Native American studies including *Aboriginal Voices*: *The Magazine of Evolving Native American Arts & Culture* (Toronto), *Indian Cinema Entertainment* (San Francisco), and *Native Peoples* (Phoenix), among others.

Works Cited

Arthur Penn Films "Little Big Man." Dir. Elliott Erwitt. Elliott Erwitt Productions for Time Life Films, 1970.

Bancroft-Hunt, Norman. *The Indians of the Great Plains*. Norman: University of Oklahoma Press, 1992.

Crowdus, Gary, and Richard Porton. "The Importance of a Singular, Guiding Vision: An Interview with Arthur Penn." *Cineaste* 20.2 (1994): 4–16.

Englehardt, Tom. "Racism in the Media." *Bulletin of Concerned Asian Scholars* (1971): 1–18.

Fenin, George N., and William K. Everson. *The Western: From Silents to Cinerama*. New York: Orion, 1962.

Goetzmann, William H., and William N. Goetzmann. *The West of the Imagination*. New York: Norton, 1986.

Grinnell, George Bird. *The Cheyenne Indians: Their History and Ways of Life*. Two vols. New York: Cooper Square, 1962.

Huxley, David. "Naked Aggression: American Comic Books and the Vietnam War." In *Tell Me Lies About Vietnam*, 88–110. Alf Louvre and Jeffrey Walsh, eds. Philadelphia: Open University Press, 1988. 88–110.

Lovell, Alan. "The Western." In *Movies and Methods* Vol. 1: 164–75. Bill Nichols, ed. Berkeley: University of California Press, 1976.

Smith, Daniel. "The Media and Images of War: Perception Versus Reality." *The Defense Monitor* 23.4 April 1994: 4.

Williams, Walter L. *The Spirit and the Flesh: Sexual Diversity among Native Americans*. Boston: Beacon, 1986.

Driving the Red Road
Powwow Highway (1989)

*"Clutch your chest. Fall off that horse," they directed. That was it. Death
was the extent of Indian acting in the movie theater.*
—*Louise Erdrich,* Love Medicine

The most popular video store in Stillwater, Oklahoma, files Jonathan
Wacks's 1989 film *Powwow Highway* under Comedy, in between *Porky's
2* and *Prelude to a Kiss*. Ask for *Powwow Highway* in Stillwater's second
most popular video store and you will be directed to the Action-Adven-
ture section, where the videotape rests alongside *A Prayer for the Dying*
on the right and *The Power of the Ninjitsu* on the left. It's equally at
home, and equally not at home, as a Western, a picaresque or "road"
movie, a buddy film, a cult film[1], and, as Ted Jojola describes it, a "sleeper
B-film" (15). To some extent, the makers of *Powwow Highway* rework
and refute the stereotypical image of the Hollywood Indian simply by
taking advantage of multiple film genres and conventions.

This trickster-like shifting from genre to genre distinguishes the film
from various other 1980s attempts to reinvent the Hollywood Indian:
Michael Wadleigh's *Wolfen* (1981) links Native American construction
workers in Manhattan to the city's highly intelligent, stealthy, nocturnal
wolf population, whereas Brian De Palma's *Body Double* (1984) features
an underhanded Hollywood actor who disguises himself as an Indian when
he brutally kills a female neighbor and stalks a voyeuristic acquaintance.
The honorable, shape-shifting Indians of *Wolfen* and the malevolent masquerade "Indian" of *Body Double* are perhaps one or two removes from
the conventional image of Hollywood Indians in all their extravagant
mortality, an image that Louise Erdrich's character Nector Kashpaw understands, from personal experience, as basically an official, cinematic
version of "the only good Indian is a dead Indian." But in both films these

changes take place within the confines of a single, clearly defined genre: the horror movie and the suspense picture or thriller, respectively. *Powwow Highway*, however, demonstrates something that should be axiomatic but instead comes off as radically inventive: Native Americans on film can inhabit a variety of genres and evoke a variety of responses in the same film—indeed, in the same scene of the same film.

In *Powwow Highway*, Cayuga actor Gary Farmer, as Northern Cheyenne character Philbert Bono, simultaneously plays two parts: from a western literary-cinematic perspective he is the comic hero, the protagonist of the narrative, and from a traditional Cheyenne point of view he is a young man mounting a quest to acquire power and status as a warrior. The movie distinguishes between these two perspectives, of course, but does not isolate them from each other; in other words, each perspective itself is a cultural hybrid, distinctly "Cheyenne" or "western" but at the same time "westernized" or "Native Americanized." Early in the movie, for example, Philbert makes CB radio contact with a man who goes by the handle Light Cloud. As they discuss the status of Indian-white history, Light Cloud remarks that no one listens to history anymore and gently corrects Philbert's innocent assumption that he is learning American history by watching reruns of *Bonanza*. Later, stopping at a remote convenience store for hamburgers and coffee, Philbert touches the coathanger antenna of an old, malfunctioning black-and-white television set; the picture clears up just long enough for him to receive an inspirational, subversive vision from early Hollywood. Glimpsing a scene from a silent movie (and a cowboy movie at that), he sees William S. Hart, in full cowboy regalia, use horsepower to pull down a jailhouse wall. Later, Philbert will do the same thing with his automotive horse (his wheezing, 1964 Buick LeSabre), pulling down the wall of his friend Bonnie Red Bow's Santa Fe prison cell. Finally, *Powwow Highway* ends with a conventional chase scene in which Santa Fe patrol cars crash and burn while various characters deliver high-anxiety punchlines and Philbert's "fine pony," the exhausted, 1964 Buick which he has named Protector the War Pony, "throws" him and explodes into flames. Here the film teases viewers by shifting, however briefly, toward another Western genre, tragedy. Philbert is not at first huddled with the survivors of the wreck, and some of them begin to mourn and eulogize him; he appears to have gone down with his metallic pony. But then Philbert emerges from the underbrush, holding up the "last token" of his Cheyenne quest, a lone door handle; this door handle, a survivor as well as a sign, completes Philbert's vision quest and reaffirms the film's comic sensibility. And with this concluding image of cultural adaptability, coupled with the emotional power of seeing this physically large and spiritually growing figure return, smiling and surviving, the film comes full circle.

Powwow Highway typically operates by grafting an American Indian—predominantly Cheyenne—point of view or sensibility onto what is essentially a conventional Hollywood formula (or, more accurately, a mélange of conventional Hollywood genre formulas). In Paul Coates's metaphor, revisionist genre movies "tune in to the wavelength of an existing genre and then overlay it with different signals" (ix). This particular film tunes in to the wavelengths of a variety of genres and overlays them with each other, and all of these signals come through on a Native American citizens'-band radio. Both literally and figuratively tuning in the CB, the television, and the expectations of Hollywood-schooled American audiences, *Powwow Highway* delights viewers who find, perhaps for the first time, a narrative that allies them with various Native American points of view while also acknowledging various non-Native ways of seeing, primarily in the formal demands of generic storylines. For some viewers, the film's comic spirit happily sweetens and offsets myriad political, social, and cultural problems faced by the Cheyenne and, implicitly, by Native Americans in general. *Powwow Highway* begins with images of contemporary poverty on the reservation, but such images dissolve or brighten as the movie continues and comedy (Philbert's "innocent" faith, combined with the visual and physical humor associated, in Western comic traditions, with the fat man) prevails over slender Buddy Red Bow's passionate politics even as both learn to work together toward essentially the same immediate political end. In other words, the film attempts to have it both ways, placating viewers wary or weary of "white guilt" and documenting realistic, legitimate political and cultural struggles of Native peoples.

To some critics, including Toby Langen (a student of Lushootseed speakers on Puget Sound) and Kathryn Shanley (an Assiniboine Indian who teaches in Cornell University's American Indian Program), the film therefore raises troubling questions. Writes Langen: "I have seen *Powwow Highway* over a dozen times, mostly in the company of students in my classes. Perhaps because of the classroom venue, I find myself doing two things at once: enjoying the film and disapproving of it" (23). During the course of a transcribed conversation with Shanley about the movie, Langen describes this disjunction in another way: "I felt that the whole theme of the love interest between Red Bow and the woman was irrelevant, that it took away from the direction in which they had been trying to develop his character, which was to get back in touch with some practices and a different way of thinking, to expand his set of values beyond the political. Also, at the point where Philbert pulls down the jailhouse

Figure 9.1. Buddy Red Bow (A Martinez) and Philbert Bono (Gary Farmer) embark on their metaphysical voyage. Courtesy of the Museum of Modern Art/Film Stills Archive.

wall, I got to feeling 'This movie is no longer what it started out to be; now we're in a Western'" (27). Thus, critics like Ted Jojola (Isleta Pueblo) are only partly right when they fault the film for its generic stasis: "The same, predictable script which froze solid sometime in the '70s. The storyline, of the Vietnam Veteran who goes through a cultural reawakening on his return back home, had become rather staid in mainstream cinema" (9). Actually, the movie refuses to home in on any one prevailing "Hollywood Indian" image or narrative; it often does not "respond" directly to a single cluster of images but rather presents versions of Native American experience in a world in which it is both unsurprising and unsettling that all sorts of crossovers and adaptations happen. *Powwow Highway* does invoke "staid" plots such as the one Jojola describes, but it does not single out that one generic storyline. In fact, the movie is as much Philbert Bono's story as Buddy Red Bow's. Philbert clearly respects Buddy's demonstrated warrior status deeply, but he himself is not once characterized as a Vietnam veteran.

Neither does the movie rehearse older, pre–Vietnam War stereotypes about Indians. In her recent book *West of Everything* (1992), Jane Tompkins provides a good general description of Hollywood Indians in their most familiar habitat, the western: "The ones I saw functioned as props, bits of local color, textural effects. As people they had no existence. Quite often they filled the role of villains, predictably, driving the engine of the plot, threatening the wagon train, the stagecoach, the cavalry detachment—a particularly dangerous form of local wildlife. But there were no Indian characters, no individuals with a personal history and a point of view" (8). Emptied out and rendered two-dimensional, these Indians say little or nothing about themselves but reveal a great deal about the filmmakers who produced these cartoon figures and the audiences who consumed them. Further, Tompkins points out, when Indians "do appear [in any particularized way] they are even more unreal. At least women in Westerns are not played by men. At least horses are not played by dogs, or cattle by goats. Faked scenery is more convincing than fake Indians are . . . when there are thousands of Native Americans alive, why should Jeff Chandler play Cochise?" (9).

Of course, Hollywood directors like John Ford made a practice of casting "actual" Indians as extras, providing much-needed income for Southwestern tribes like the Navajo. But when casting *The Searchers* (1956), he turned to a white actor, Henry Brandon, to play the more visible and complex role of the Comanche war chief Scar. As Tompkins again notes, "An Indian in a Western who is supposed to be a real person has to be played by a white man" (9). Casting can be difficult to negotiate; budgets, actors' availability, and studio politics are but three sometimes overlapping negotiating points that influence who ultimately plays whom. And obviously, actors do not necessarily have to share significant life experiences or circumstances with their characters in order to portray them successfully. Acting involves imagination and adaptation—to cite but one example, Welsh actor Anthony Hopkins plays American President Richard M. Nixon—and extraordinarily versatile performers like Hopkins, Robert De Niro, and Katharine Hepburn simply refuse to be typecast.[2] However, Tompkins is commenting on a pattern that, for several decades, has almost entirely prohibited Native American actors from playing complex Native American roles. Moreover, this particular pattern correlates with various others delineated throughout this book; taken together, they clearly help make sense of Tompkins's claims about the Hollywood Indian.

In his definitive study *The White Man's Indian* (1977), Robert Berkhofer agrees. Discussing the long Hollywood shelf life of venerable stereotypes, he writes, "Whites and Asians frequently acted the leading Indian parts, and those Native Americans hired for background action had to play any tribe because all Indians looked alike to movie and television directors. Because of the ignorance of writers, directors, and actors, the Indian was usually as stereotyped in a film supposedly sympathetic to the Native American cause as in one openly hostile to his plight" (103).

1960s and 1970s films fare no better, according to Berkhofer: "All they usually did was to reverse the traditional imagery by making the Indian good and the White bad" (103). This Indian also functions as a surrogate or "substitute for the oppressed Black or hippie White youth alienated from modern mainstream American society" (103). Rearranging rather than dismantling this simplistic binary opposition between races and cultures, most "revisionist" 1960s and 1970s movies about Indians ironically perpetuate stereotypes of the very figures they seek to present as countercultural. Vine Deloria (Standing Rock Sioux) goes further still, arguing that these predictable images of the Indian really provide "a fairly accurate map of the fragmented personality that possesses the American white man" (xi). As Deloria sees it, "the image of the Indian in contemporary American society . . . has nothing to do with Indians, of course, but it is not supposed to represent the contemporary Indian since he is a pale imitation of the real Indians of the American imagination" (xiii). It is no surprise that 1960s and 1970s movies ostensibly about Indians continue the practice of giving leading roles to established white actors, including the British actor Richard Harris in *A Man Called Horse* and the American actor Dustin Hoffman in *Little Big Man* (both 1970). Rather than center on Indian characters in their "Indian" movies, these filmmakers choose to place whites—an English gentleman and a white American, respectively—at the hearts of these stories. Rather than trouble to envision, let alone to celebrate, the multicultural nature of American society, including American movie audiences, these filmmakers cater exclusively to white moviegoers, reassuring them that Richard Harris's Medicine Pole vow is somehow more screenworthy than any Native's ceremonial experience.

Given the staying power of the conventional Hollywood western and its "Hollywood Indians," Berkhofer suggests, "Only when the countercultural use of the Indian comes to dominate the mass media and modern literature in all its forms can we say that the classic Western has finally ended as one of the chief expressions of the basic American experience in the White imagination. Until then, the whole history of White settlement of the continent may be portrayed as one gigantic Western with the Indians 'biting the dust' through the advance of civilization over savagery, both noble and ignoble. The modern novel or movie, like the Puritan history and captivity narrative, merely captures this larger story in microcosm" (103–104). Given the power of these binaries and the muscular, explanatory logic of Manifest Destiny (including Frederick Jackson Turner's remarkably tenacious "frontier thesis"), Hollywood, since its inception, has needed to do little more than reiterate an already deeply entrenched and comfortably mythic narrative.

It still does so in the 1980s and 1990s, in obvious ways (*Dances With Wolves, Pocahontas, The Indian in the Cupboard*) and in more covert forms, too: in a contemporary West Coast thriller such as De Palma's *Body Double*, "the Indian" is once again played by a white actor, Gregg Henry, and "the Indian" is very definitely a bad guy, albeit a disguise worn by Henry's character Sam Bouchard. He stalks his female neighbor, steals her purse, murders her with a power drill, and then harasses both the male protagonist of the movie, the struggling Hollywood actor and not-so-struggling voyeur Jake Scully, and Melanie Griffith's character, porno actress Holly Body. But as De Palma's title suggests, bodies in this film are routinely doubled; most, if not all, of the characters are actors playing roles (so that Gregg Henry is actually a white actor playing a white actor playing an "Indian"), identities are difficult to pin down, and the distinctions between "real life" and "make believe" are blurred; as a result, the movie furnishes a built-in excuse for its own indulgence in stereotypes.

Powwow Highway works differently. Beginning with an amber-tinted vision of a lone, traditional Indian man riding a horse and brandishing a hand-crafted weapon, then cutting to the sunless poverty of a day in Lame Deer, Montana, on the contemporary Northern Cheyenne reservation, the movie solidly grounds itself in two different versions of Indian Country and thus announces that it will proceed from a Northern Cheyenne point of view. As Rodney Simard (Cherokee) asserts, "The value of *Powwow Highway* is that it is an organic, effective film and, more importantly, that it attempts to present Indian material from an Indian perspective, something that few of the products of Hollywood (and other points) have ever even attempted" (20). That is not to say that it avoids presenting predictable images of contemporary Indians, even images that sometimes border on the stereotypes found in more conventional Hollywood movies. After the exterior reservation shots, for instance, the camera enters a reservation bar and invites viewers to a potential display of the drunken Indian stereotype. Here, a variety of Indians wearing blue jeans and western shirts drink beer and play pool; here, too, a large man named Philbert Bono (played by Gary Farmer) sits down at the bar and is quickly entranced by the television, on which a used-car salesman (a white man wearing an Indian headdress) makes his pitch: "How, folks. This old cowboy's on the warpath with heap big savings. All our choicest stock. Come on down off the rez or the ranch and pick out your pony today." (It's worth noting that the four-wheeled "ponies" he's selling are Mustangs and Pintos.) As Marshall Toman and Carole Gerster observe, the TV pitchman speaks "the broken English spoken by Hollywood movie

Indians. . . . The ad depicts Native Americans as easily exploitable" (33). For the first—but not the last—time, the movie lets such an image speak for itself, and for the first—but not the last—time, Philbert responds with a smile of interest and enthusiasm rather than with anger or bitterness. In fact, despite its condescension, this sales pitch inspires him to go out and buy a car—not from the "old cowboy" but from a junkyard owner named Fidel. "I want to buy one of your fine ponies," Philbert tells Fidel, and, placing some money, some food stamps, some marijuana, and a flask on the table, he quickly closes the deal. After a brief struggle, he starts the engine, tosses an old plastic Blessed Virgin Mary dashboard statuette out the window, and gets his physical and metaphysical travels underway.[3]

Already, in the first five or ten minutes of the opening sequence, *Powwow Highway* subtly distinguishes Northern Cheyenne culture from mainstream capitalist and Christian outlooks without overtly denigrating anybody. Gently easing viewers into an alliance with Philbert, the film begins not by magically synthesizing white and Indian cultures into a seamless, happy, organic whole but by suggesting that cultural intersections are occasional, specific, unpredictable, and more complicated than Hollywood has led audiences to believe. A western religious icon can be symbolically tossed out the window, but Philbert is in a position to do so because he has listened to, rather than spurned, the white salesman in headdress. At the same time, Philbert himself may appear a bit ridiculous to some viewers, in that he regards a rusting, crumbling, and altogether wobbly junkyard car as a worthy "fine pony." The white "cowboy" is a stereotypical used-car salesman, but maybe Philbert is a stereotypical and gullible Indian. By both acknowledging and avoiding the simplistic, ready-at-hand racial stereotypes of many of its cinematic predecessors, *Powwow Highway* offers Philbert's unfazed, smiling, and somewhat improvisatory attitude as a sort of proposal: clearly this man's behavior is somewhat mysterious and even (to some) a bit absurd, but maybe his adaptability will repay close attention. Maybe it makes sense. In any event, Philbert seems, from the beginning of the movie, to have unspoken and quite possibly good reasons for doing what he does, and, in his mysteriously purposeful behavior, he does not in any way resemble the emotionless, poker-faced, one-dimensional, "wooden" Indians of countless Hollywood films.

Philbert's benign adaptability is not, however, the only attitude associated with Native Americans in *Powwow Highway*. In the scene immediately following his purchase of the "fine pony," a group of Northern Cheyenne listen, in council chambers, to another sales pitch, this one delivered by the corrupt corporate tool Sandy Youngblood, an Indian who works for a white-owned mining company. Youngblood assures the Indian citizens that the company has their best interests in mind, a claim totally rejected by Buddy Red Bow, a young Indian man leaning against one of the chamber walls. Red Bow retorts that 75 percent of the people live below the poverty line, and argues that "this ain't the American dream we're living—this here's the Third World." The specific conflict here is not between "cowboys" and "Indians" but rather between two young Indian men representing opposing interests. As writers and readers of contemporary American Indian fiction are well aware, these conflicts within a Native culture can be particularly dangerous and destructive; in novels such as Leslie Marmon Silko's *Ceremony* (1977), for instance, the Laguna Pueblo Indians' worst enemies are other Indians. The witchery, also referred to as the destroyers, is Native in origin and predominantly Native in its contemporary manifestation. In *Powwow Highway*, however, the dramatic conflict between Buddy Red Bow and Sandy Youngblood, combined with the dramatic differences between Red Bow and Philbert Bono, provide movie audiences with something rarely seen in any ten or twenty Hollywood movies about Indians: a real diversity of Native American characters, characterizations, and conflicts.[4]

Comparing the movie version of *Powwow Highway* to the 1979 novel by David Seals (Huron), Rodney Simard contends that in the movie, "complexity of character is diminished, edging uncomfortably close to stereotypes, and the broad political canvas of the novel [Seals was a member of AIM] has been reduced to a simple polarity" (21). Important characteristics of the villains have been lost in translation from novel to film, and the "bad guy" has been simplified; in fact, as Simard argues, he (or, more accurately, it) has itself been stereotyped "into a familiar force: a materialistic and exploitative white corporation that can, by means of a simple trick, rob the Indians of their possessions" (22). Does this reductive characterization of the corporation suggest that the film oversimplifies the issues at stake and the characters who oppose the mine? Probably so: the issue of Native American identity here, specifically Buddy Red Bow's identity as a politically savvy, resisting Indian, is gradually deflected and overwhelmed by the plot of the film as director Jonathan Wacks transforms it into a generic action-adventure-rescue mission movie. In other words, the predictable force of the popular, generic movie plot washes away the more complicated political entanglements of the novel; the movie retains a "Native American" point of view, but that point of view competes with the plot and character simplifications required by various non-Native genres. Enlisting as well the powerful, accessible music of the highly successful rock band U2 and the well-known guitarist and songwriter Robbie

Robertson (Mohawk), Wacks clearly makes a market-driven play for a relatively young, Hollywood- and TV- and MTV-bred American audience.

In so doing, Wacks updates—but also emulates—the "Indian" films of the 1960s and 1970s, as described by Berkhofer; his production of *Powwow Highway* reflects both the strengths and the weaknesses of those earlier movies. Perhaps unwittingly, it measures the distance between primarily Native subjects and predominantly non-Native audiences, as well as the tensions between American commercial interests and Native American acts of cultural recovery. Thus, in both the novel and the film, Buddy goes to Santa Fe to help his sister Bonnie, who has been arrested on trumped-up drug possession charges, even though Buddy has been out of touch with his sister for ten years. As it turns out, the mining company, in collusion with the local and federal law enforcement officials in Santa Fe, has framed her to decoy him, hoping that they can pry him away from the reservation and get the company's proposal passed in his absence. But the film reduces Bonnie's character to a mostly silent, passive Indian "Princess" (Simard 21) and correspondingly reduces the characters of Buddy's fellow tribe members by presenting him as "the sole savior of his people, who, without his wayward but paternalistic presence, will yet once again sell away their lifeblood because of their childlike trust" (Simard 22). Again, the film risks stereotyping in the interests of recognizable, accessible, generic plot devices.

Stronger than the movie's political narrative and rescue mission plot, however, is its complex interweaving of Buddy's story—his temporary appropriation of tribal funds and his trek to his sister, imprisoned in Santa Fe—and Philbert's story—his patient, gradual, and highly improvisatory quest for medicine and power. "Can I count on you?" asks Buddy, thinking strictly of the exigencies of the here and now, to which Philbert responds both more traditionally and more spacily: "We are Cheyenne." The movie at this point becomes a road movie, as these two very unlike characters and their parallel, but very different, purposes begin to share the same journey; in fact, at about this point *Powwow Highway* threatens to become a buddy-movie, in which two same-sex characters gradually acquire respect and affection for each other, finally overcoming their differences to bond near the film's conclusion. True to form, Buddy and Philbert embrace in the closing moments; their hug marks the emotional climax of the buddy movie plot. But while Buddy's character as a political, resisting Indian is implicitly undercut by the demands of genre screenwriting, Philbert finds himself explicitly mocked by other characters in the film. In other words, the film builds sympathy for Buddy by muting who he fundamentally is in the novel, and it builds sympathy for Philbert by muting the abilities of other

Powwow Highway Indians to sympathize with his journey toward traditional ways. The movie invites alliances between main characters and
audiences by making trade-offs, revealing that combining Native American points of view and established Hollywood genres can be an imperfect
process. The conflicts between Philbert and other Northern Cheyenne
are, at times, painful and powerful: "The time has come for me to gather
medicine," he informs his Aunt Harriet as she watches television in her
small reservation house. Unfortunately for Philbert, his relative responds
with absolute derision, laughing in his face and scornfully telling him, "I
get sick of being asked for good old Indian wisdom. I ain't got none—so
get the hell out of here." As much as the political issues divide corporate
Indians from reservation Indians and, a little later, AIM veterans from
anti-AIM goons, Philbert's story isolates him because he is faithfully pursuing something like a traditional Northern Cheyenne path. The movie
clearly and deftly illuminates this tribal ambivalence (if not outright an-
tagonism) toward Philbert, as it also exposes the irony of the situation: a
turn toward Native tradition can be as divisive as a loss of tradition.

Some of the most intense conflicts, in fact, are between Philbert and
Buddy. After talking with Light Cloud on the CB, for example, Philbert
decides to turn East and visit Sweet Butte, part of the Black Hills in
South Dakota and, as Light Cloud points out, "the most sacred place in
America—maybe the world." Here, in a memorable scene, Philbert climbs
the mountain, begins to unwrap a large Hershey chocolate bar, and then
changes his mind; all around him he sees colorful gifts left on the
mountaintop by other Indians, and he gently places his chocolate bar
among them, looks out over the spectacular countryside, and then, in a
magnificent comic release, tumbles end over end down the mountain,
shouting ecstatically. Meanwhile, Buddy awakens from a long sleep, gradually realizes that they're not headed south on Interstate 25 anymore, and
is furious with Philbert. But Philbert manhandles Buddy and informs
him, "We are gathering power." The two men extend the South Dakota
leg of their journey further still, going to the Pine Ridge Christmas powwow before resuming their journey to Santa Fe. In other words, the parallel yet different stories of Philbert and Buddy require their car to
head—literally and physically—in different directions. But, at the same
time, the two stories are coming together, as Philbert perceives when he
joins their quests in the first-person plural pronoun: "*We* are gathering
power." Defining himself and Buddy first and foremost as Northern Cheyenne, despite Buddy's protests, Philbert asserts that their tribal kinship is
more important than their divergent individual purposes. This emphasis
on shared kinship turns out to be crucial.

Figure 9.2. Philbert Bono makes his humble offering in a holy place. Courtesy of the Museum of Modern Art/Film Stills Archive.

This gradual interweaving of their stories assumes a particular pattern: again and again, Buddy Red Bow first resists any and all turns toward traditional Northern Cheyenne culture and then participates. Wearing his Purple Heart medal at the Pine Ridge Christmas powwow, Buddy at first remains on the sidelines. He is saved from a gang fight, in fact, by his Vietnam veteran comrade Jimmy (played by Graham Greene, in a cameo), who then shakily urges Buddy to dance. But Buddy persists in rejecting the significance of "a few lousy beads and some feathers"; in this decision, the man who resists white corporate politics also resists Native traditional ceremonies and their contemporary adaptations. But eventually, urged on by Philbert, who happily eats and drums and tells him that he should be proud of his warrior's blood medal, Buddy dances, prominently displaying the Purple Heart. A little later, Philbert stops the car, wades into an icy river, and sings a traditional song; Buddy first reacts with impatience, and then joins him in the water and song. Further on down the road, Philbert tells a traditional story of Wihio, the trickster; Buddy calls such tales "fairy stories," and Philbert protests that these are "stories of our ancestors—how the Old Ones dealt with problems." Clearly the conflict is between Buddy's argument that the old stories are inadequate for dealing with new problems generated by white America's hunger—the industrial smokestacks of a huge Wyoming energy plant in the background throughout this scene seem to support Buddy's point—and Philbert's counterargument that "the problems never change, nor the people." What Buddy later calls "the old legends and all that mystical horseshit" will, in his view, "only make things worse." He asks Philbert not to continue his "blissed-out" behavior when it comes time to free Bonnie from prison. But Philbert explicitly links the trickster to contemporary politics, too, promising that "he will play a little trick on the white man." As Buddy moves closer and closer to Philbert's spiritual and traditional journey, so too does Philbert begin to support and participate in Buddy's political plans.

The mixings of old ways and new—Philbert's belief that the old and the new are in fact inseparable in a living, continually adapting and surviving tradition—prevail in the end, as Philbert borrows the old William S. Hart Hollywood cowboy-movie idea of literally pulling down the jail's wall by force in order to liberate the "captive woman," but offers up a prayer in Cheyenne before he hits the gas pedal. Perhaps more surprisingly, we are allowed to share Buddy's warrior vision: having accidentally pried the car's driver-side door window loose from its moorings, he holds onto it firmly and faces the oncoming lawmen. At this moment he shape-shifts; he sees himself—and we see him—in full traditional warrior's dress as he yells and flings the glass directly at (and into) the windshield of a fast-approaching Santa Fe patrol car. The transformation of Buddy shows us the transformation in Buddy, and both transformations are remarkable.

Powwow Highway suggests, finally, that the collaboration of Philbert and Buddy, and thus the combination of venerable traditions and new adaptations, makes a variety of desired political and spiritual results possible. In other words, the movie demonstrates that Buddy and Philbert's successes are directly linked to their distinctly Cheyenne dreams and visions and improvisations; "Cheyenne" is a vital, flexible, highly imaginative and adaptable and surviving identity. *Powwow Highway* also encourages alliances between these two main characters and viewers, inviting audiences to participate vicariously and to sympathize, in different ways and (sometimes) for different reasons, with both Philbert and Buddy. They break laws and subvert numerous mainstream American world views, but the movie persuades viewers that they are right to do so. The tensions and conflicts between Indian characters are, in the end, more productive than counter-productive, more complex than simplistic. Sometimes these tensions and conflicts threaten to erupt into stereotypes, and sometimes political contexts and secondary characters are stereotyped, but the resolution of Philbert and Buddy's differences does not rehearse stale Hollywood Indian formulas. The trick here is that, generically, the film invokes a number of well-worn Hollywood chase-scene and buddy movie clichés. Still, as *Powwow Highway* itself both maintains and breaks with established Hollywood conventions and traditions, this tension between stereotypes and reinventions—between Hollywood genres and Native traditions—enriches the movie.

Part Western, part picaresque road film, part buddy movie, part comedy, part action (or adventure), and part repository of American popular-culture images and allusions, *Powwow Highway* Americanizes Native Americans and Native Americanizes the movies, while at the same time respecting the sacred traditions of both the Hollywood Western and the Cheyenne Indians. In the context of the Hollywood Indian, the Western, and all the Nector Kashpaws who have for over ninety years now been directed to clutch their chests, fall off their horses, and then get the hell out of the picture, *Powwow Highway* is still one of the only American movies to offer a significant redefinition of a long-standing cinematic and cultural stereotype. The film is not perfect. Its dalliance in hackneyed non-Native genres and its occasional willingness to invoke, rather than reject, stereotypes merit close critical scrutiny. But clearly *Powwow Highway* does many things well, and just as clearly it raises the happy possibility that the plunge of the brave—abasement, loss of status, stereotyping, submersion, death—need no longer be "the extent of Indian acting in the movie theater."

Notes

1. The cult film differs in several important ways from the various other film genres I mention here. As J.P. Telotte and others have amply demonstrated, there is much scholarly disagreement over what a cult film is and whether a particular film qualifies as one. But, Telotte observes, one major consideration is clearly "the relationship these works establish with their audience and the sort of responses they typically evoke" (2). For a film like *Powwow Highway*, though, the potential cult audience may be either Native American or mainstream American or both— and any "cultishness" the film acquires may differ depending on audience demographics. Screening a scene from the film with fifty Pawnee high school students, I was struck by the "cult" qualities of their response: they anticipated lines of dialog and particular shots, and they publicly shared their inside knowledge of the film. In a related sense, one which comprehends the differences between Pawnees and Cheyenne as well as the differences between Native Americans and non-Natives, Timothy Corrigan argues that the cult moviegoer is a sort of tourist; cult "films are all stranger than paradise," he contends, "and it is the ability of these audiences to make a paradise out of that strangeness that marks them as cinematic tourists" (Telotte, 27). *Powwow Highway* would thus seem to qualify

as a potential cult film for both Native and non-Native audiences. To my knowledge, though, it has not yet acquired another important characteristic of the cult film, discussed by Bruce Kawin: repeatability (Telotte, 23). Until *Powwow Highway* is screened and rescreened at midnight shows, until lines from the film are more frequently repeated by more moviegoers in more contexts, the film can only partially be considered a cult film.

2. For further discussion of casting, see Giannetti 275–279.

3. In an earlier, similarly problematic road film, Dennis Hopper's *Easy Rider* (1969), Peter Fonda's character Captain America makes a similar gesture, throwing away his wristwatch before hitting the road. As David Laderman writes, "Captain America chucks his watch before they take off on their motorcycles, signaling an urge to move beyond social and narrative conventions" (47).

4. Regarding these discussions and conflicts within Native American communities, it is vitally important to keep in mind that "spiritual" and "traditional" and "political" and "pragmatic" and other such categories are not mutually exclusive. Most often they intersect in highly complicated ways, as is well demonstrated in (for example) Vine Deloria, *God Is Red: A Native View of Religion* (Golden, Colo.: Fulcrum, 1994). The writings of Deloria are an excellent place to begin studying Native spirituality and political philosophies. Also important is Paula Gunn Allen, *The Sacred Hoop: Recovering the Feminine in American Indian Tradition* (Boston: Beacon, 1986). Illuminating accounts of contemporary Native political struggles can be found in Peter Matthiessen's *In the Spirit of Crazy Horse* (New York: Viking, 1983) and *Indian Country* (New York: Penguin, 1984) and in Peter Nabokov's anthology *Native American Testimony* (New York: Penguin, 1991); the latter covers the years 1492–1992, providing first-hand Native statements about the varieties of Native political and religious experiences. See also Frederick Turner, *Beyond Geography: The Western Spirit Against the Wilderness* (New Brunswick N.J.: Rutgers University Press, 1994). And of course, these issues figure again and again in most contemporary novels, poems, and plays written by Native Americans; good (and frequently discussed) starting points include Leslie Marmon Silko's novels *Ceremony* (New York: Penguin, 1977) and *Almanac of the Dead* (New York: Simon & Schuster, 1991).

Works Cited

Berkhofer, Robert F. *The White Man's Indian: Images of the American Indian from Columbus to the Present*. New York: Random House, 1977.

Coates, Paul. *Film at the Intersection of High and Mass Culture*. New York: Cambridge University Press, 1994.

Deloria, Vine. "American Fantasy." In *The Pretend Indians: Images of Native Americans in the Movies* ix–xvi. Gretchen M. Bataille and Charles L.P. Silet, eds. Ames: Iowa State University Press, 1980.

Giannetti, Louis. *Understanding Movies*. Englewood Cliffs, N.J.: Prentice Hall, 1996.

Jojola, Ted. "Absurd Reality: Hollywood Goes to the Indians." *Film & History* 23 (1993): 7–16.

Laderman, David. "The Road Film and American Culture." *Journal of Film and Video* 48.1–2 (1996): 41–57.

Langen, Toby, and Kathryn Shanley. "Culture Isn't Buckskin Shoes: A Conversation Around *Powwow Highway*." *Studies in American Indian Literatures* 3.3 (1991): 23–29.

Simard, Rodney. "Easin' on Down the *Powwow Highway*(s)." *Studies in American Indian Literatures* 3.3 (1991): 19–23.

Telotte, J.P., ed. *The Cult Film Experience: Beyond All Reason*. Austin: University of Texas Press, 1991.

Toman, Marshall, and Carole Gerster. "*Powwow Highway* in an Ethnic Film and Literature Course." *Studies in American Indian Literatures* 3.3 (1991): 29–38.

Tompkins, Jane. *West of Everything: The Inner Life of Westerns*. New York: Oxford University Press, 1992.

"Going Indian"
Dances With Wolves (1990)

*While lying there listening to the Indians, I amused myself with trying
to guess at their subject by their gestures, or some proper name introduced. . . . It was a purely wild and primitive American sound, as much
as the barking of a chickaree, and I could not understand a syllable of it.
. . . I felt that I stood, or rather lay, as near to the primitive man of
America, that night, as any of its discoverers ever did.*
  —Henry David Thoreau, The Maine Woods

*As soon as possible after my arrival, I design to build myself a wigwham,
after the same manner and size with the rest . . . and will endeavour that
my wife, my children, and myself may be adopted soon after our arrival.
Thus becoming truly inhabitants of their village, we shall immediately
occupy that rank within the pale of their society, which will afford us all
the amends we can possibly expect for the loss we have met with by the
convulsions of our own. According to their customs we shall likewise
receive names from them, by which we shall always be known. My young-
est children shall learn to swim, and to shoot with the bow, that they
may acquire such talents as will necessarily raise them into some degree
of esteem among the Indian lads of their own age; the rest of us must
hunt with the hunters.*
  —J. Hector St. John Crèvecoeur, Letters from an American Farmer

With thanks to the Blackfoot tribe who adopted me.
  —Leslie A. Fiedler, The Return of the Vanishing American

Taken together, the three quotes above are good examples of a very old—
yet ongoing—process of the American imagination: the white discovery
of and the renaming and adoption into the tribal society of the American
Indian. In this essay[1] I describe a mythopoeic process that recurs often

enough in American history to merit more attention, especially after the apparent resurrection and further development of this gesture in Kevin Costner's tremendously popular *Dances With Wolves*, released too long since any other great, epic Western to be anything but a boondoggle—or so we thought until "Costner's folly" was seen by millions and had won seven Academy Awards.[2]

A traditional goal in American studies has been the search for *Americanness*. Crèvecoeur's third letter asked, "What is an American?" and his famous melting-pot response testified to the seriousness Crèvecoeur brought to the question. Tautologically, the defining American characteristic has been the continual redefinition of the American character. It is the question itself and its rhetorical immortality (a significant addition to Martin Lipset's "American exceptionalism") that mark this nation as unique. One answer to the question of national identity proposes that the original inhabitants of North America represent "True Americans," whose character deserves emulation. *Dances With Wolves* accepted this not-new proposal and sought to convince modern motion-picture audiences that only by going backward into history, back into tribalism, could the American hero hope to go forward.

D.H. Lawrence argued that Europeans "came to America for two reasons. . . . To slough the old European consciousness completely . . . [and] to grow a new skin underneath, a new form. This second is a hidden process" (53). Leslie Fiedler praised Lawrence's insight, suggesting that "he knew something . . . which we are born not knowing we know, being born on this soil . . . that the essential myth of the West and, therefore, of ourselves . . . [is] the myth of Natty Bumppo and Chingachgook. Here is, for us—for better or for worse, and apparently forever—the heart of the matter: the confrontation in the wilderness of the White European refugee from civilization and the 'stern, imperturbable warrior'" (167).

This meeting, Fiedler noted, occasioned two possible outcomes: "a metamorphosis of the WASP into something neither White nor Red" or "the annihilation of the Indian" (24). The later option was the most frequently chosen path of storymakers for the "penny dreadfuls" and nickelodeons, but the metamorphosis of White into Red developed rapidly in the 1950s with the "sympathetic Western," reaching its mythical cinematic culmination in *Dances With Wolves*.

Three famous ideas help explain how a motion picture of the 1990s would attempt a big-budget dramatization of the going-Indian myth, and, secondly, reach an appreciative audience in the process. First is Claude Lévi-Strauss's notion that myths and narratives reconcile cultural contradictions and bring opposing forces and values together. With the going-

Indian myth, the contradiction is between Nature and Industry, hunting and agrarianism, innocence and decadence, Manifest Destiny and the Sacred Homeland. Thus, *Dances With Wolves* is a cinematic myth that addresses still unresolved traumas and contradictions of American history, as well as current contradictions between industrialism and environmentalism, tribal society and industrial society, the melting-pot (assimilation) and multiculturalism (racial/ethnic pride).

The second theory was propounded by R.W.B. Lewis in *The American Adam*, where the author described the historical development of the idea of a new American "hero" who would be "emancipated from history, happily bereft of ancestry, untouched and undefiled by the usual inheritances of family and race" (5). That the American continent triggered images of the Garden among European immigrants has been ably documented by many scholars. But the Garden was not empty, and for those uncomfortable with the demonization of native inhabitants of this continent, the American Indian provided a ready-made adamic figure. The American Adam and Garden myths were easily transposed into American westerns and musicals, including the mythic/cinematic forerunner of *Dances With Wolves*, Delmer Daves's *Broken Arrow* (1950), considered the first of the sympathetic westerns of the 1950s. This film traces the transformation of an Indian fighter (played by Jimmy Stewart) into a man who befriends Cochise, marries an Apache maiden, and fights to establish some truce between the land-hungry settlers and the Apache. The American Adam undercurrent is manifested in *Broken Arrow* during a pastoral "honeymoon" scene that takes place on the banks of a wild pond. Stewart and the Apache maiden Morning Star have just been married; Stewart rests beside the still waters as the camera follows Morning Star; she walks majestically toward her lover, and lies in his arms. She asks:

> MORNING STAR: "You are asleep?"
> STEWART: "No. . . . I'm quiet because I'm so happy. I'm afraid if I open my mouth my happiness will rush out in a funny noise like, Ya Hoo!"
> MORNING STAR: "What does that mean? It is an American word?"
> STEWART: "Uh huh. I think it was a word made by Adam when he opened his eyes and saw Eve."

The dream of Pocahontas cannot last too long, however, and, even in this first "sympathetic" Western, Morning Star dies before the last reel. In contrast to the deluge of conventional Westerns, *Broken Arrow* was, for its time, the most pointed liberal critique of Manifest Destiny and the sad history of relations between Indians and whites.

The third theory comes from Freud's limited work with the family romance, where he attempted to account for certain fantasies of young children who denied their literal parentage in favor of more noble, imaginary mothers and fathers (236–41). Freud claimed that all young people must break with their parents at some point, that each generation must break with the previous. A "family romance" might be created in response to various motivations: loss of parental love, fear of breaking the incest taboo, realization of parental fallibility. This theory suggests a psychological mechanism that can account for the success of those narratives wherein the white protagonist goes Indian. Working on the personal and collective psychological levels, the romance of Native American parentage would satisfy the wish for a return to the Garden, where strong and noble parents live in abundance and harmony, free of the decay, pollution, and anxiety of industrial society. Crèvecoeur's letters were written during the troubled context of the American Revolution, when the author found himself pulled between British allegiance and colonial rebellion. His "Romance" of living with the Indians was never enacted in reality, but was exactly the tale of the noble savage Europeans would find appealing.[3]

Elizabeth Stone provides evidence that many modern, adult Americans engage in family romances of Indian ancestry. In a study of the psychological dynamics of family stories, Stone interviewed black and white Americans who claimed Indian ancestry even against rather conclusive evidence to the contrary. In spite of the truth of a family's history and the Indian's oppression and negative stereotyping in our culture, Stone found a number of Americans who claimed Indian blood in the manner that others would pridefully recall European royalty or illustrious Puritan ancestry. It is "the idea of the Indian," "a powerful symbol, especially since World War II," that Stone finds in American literature from Hemingway to Kesey, an idea "suggestive of our mourning for our lost pre-industrial Eden" (131).

These three theories offer a rudimentary dynamic in which *Dances With Wolves* can be seen to function as mythical narrative (Lévi-Strauss) through collective wish-fulfillment patterns (Freud) and in the context of America's historical legacy (Lewis). As such, this dynamic helps contextualize historical and fictional prototypes of the going-Indian myth in *Dances With Wolves*.

Thoreau was, Leslie Fiedler believed, "at his mythological core an Indian himself, at home in the unexplored regions where women flinch," and Fiedler adds that Thoreau himself claimed that "all poets are Indians" (106). Thoreau's Walden adventure strikes me as a case study of the limits of how far a Harvard man can "go Indian," and, although he does not ever entertain the notion of becoming a "squaw-man"—the "idea of the Indian" infuses every page of *Walden*. At one point in his masterpiece, Thoreau muses; "My days were not days of the week, bearing the stamp of any heathen deity, nor were they minced into hours and fretted by the ticking of the clock; for I lived like the Puri Indians, of whom it is said that 'for yesterday, to-day, and to-morrow they have only one word, and they express the variety of meaning by pointing backward for yesterday, forward for to-morrow, and overhead for the passing day" (112). Besides the explicit reference to living "like the Puri Indians," I also like here the notion of near timelessness, so central to any mythological state, as well as the privileging of the Indian lifestyle in contrast with the rush to keep European time. Although Thoreau draws no special attention to it when he mentions it, the story of the naming of Walden offers evidence, both literary and historic, of the claim the Indian holds not only on the American landscape, but on Thoreau's and our imaginations: "My townspeople have all heard it in their youth, that anciently the Indians were holding a pow-wow upon a hill here . . . and while they were thus engaged the hill shook and suddenly sank, and only one old squaw, named Walden, escaped, and from her the pond was named" (182).

Thoreau best shows where he has been and where he would like to go in *The Maine Woods*, where he admits, "One revelation has been made to the Indian, another to the white man. I have much to learn of the Indian, nothing of the missionary. I am not sure but all that would tempt me to teach the Indian my religion would be his promise to teach me his" (248).

Thoreau never wrote his planned work on the American Indian. His notebooks, though, were full of carefully collected details of Native dress and behavior. Most important, his greatest book may have captured more of the "idea of the Indian" than any scientific work he could have written.

Although he called himself an "illustrator" (*Trails Plowed Under*), Charles M. Russell is, along with Remington, the most famous of the Western artists. Russell, who began life as the son of a wealthy St. Louis family, eventually lit out for the territory of Montana (McCracken 13–36). As a painter, sculptor, and writer, Russell focused his attention on the lifestyles of cowboys, trappers, desperadoes, and Indians, all of which he captured in his seemingly simple, rough-hewn style. In a 1922 painting of a "squawman" titled, "When White Men Turn Red," Russell depicted a leather-clad, mounted white man descending into a river valley with his two Indian wives, three horses, and four dogs. Russell has poured a luminous golden sunlight over the distant mountain range and lower sky of this painting, and this golden sidelight outlines his figures, the effect being boldly romantic and serene. In commentary accompanying this painting in his *Remington and Russell*, Brian W. Dippie notes that "Russell himself had felt the lure of Indian life and knew that he, like several of his cowboy friends, would have been quick to take an Indian wife had the right woman come along" (156). Dippie mentions a short story from Russell's *Trails Plowed Under*, "How Lindsay Turned Indian." In this tale, Russell relates how, as a young boy, Lindsay ran off from a mean stepfather (a fictional "literalization" of Freud's family romance?) to find himself eventually following a tribe of Piegan Indians with no where else to turn. After meeting the rear-guard of the traveling Piegans, the young Lindsay uses his magnifying glass to light the pipe of the Piegan chief. Of course, for a people who worship the sun, this is no small feat, and the chief intones, "The grass has grown twice since my two sons were killed by the Sioux. . . . My heart is on the ground; I am lonesome, but since the sun has sent you, it is good. I will adopt you as my boy. . . . Child of the Sun, it is good" (139). Much like Lt. John Dunbar, Lindsay's important transition comes with his first buffalo hunt. In both cases the adopted whites get their first kill, eat the fresh liver of their killed animal, and consider that moment as the important point of no return in their going Indian: "My boy . . . that's been sixty-five years ago as near as I can figure. I run buffalo till the whites cleaned 'em out, but that's the day I turned Injun, an' I ain't cut my hair since" (144).

The hunt has long been an initiation ritual for many different groups, and the buffalo-hunt scene and subsequent feast in *Dances With Wolves* mark Dunbar's almost complete assimilation into the tribe, shown by his trading of pieces of his cavalry blues for Indian gear; his winning over of Wind In His Hair (earlier, a strong doubter of Dunbar's intentions toward the tribe); and his participation in the culturally important role of storyteller, where Dunbar recounts his own hunting feat over and over to the tribe's great enjoyment. In short, the buffalo hunt's central position in plains tribe culture would have made it the perfect path, both fictionally and historically, for any non-Indian to follow if he sought access to the flesh-and-bone existence of a tribe.

Since the *Narrative of the Captivity and Restoration of Mrs. Mary Rowlandson* (1682), any white seeking to go Indian has had to confront The Massacre. The historical and mythic power of The Massacre is so pervasive that it seems all Westerns that deal with the confrontation of white and red people must address this issue in some manner.

An interesting negotiation of The Massacre occurs in *Broken Arrow*, where Jimmy Stewart's character saves his life by aiding a wounded Cheyenne boy. When Stewart and the young boy are eventually surrounded by a group of warriors, the grateful Indian successfully pleads for Stewart's life with the menacing warriors. But when a group of unsuspecting whites interrupt the Cheyenne just as they are about to release Stewart, he is bound and gagged and forced to watch the resulting massacre. He must "witness" as well the torture of three white survivors of the battle—two are "crucified" and one is buried up to his neck, smeared with cactus pulp, and eaten by ants. Later in the film Stewart must pass through the "civilized," industrial equivalent of the Indian massacre nightmare—the lynching—when his own society tries to string him up for his defense of the Indian, only to be saved at the last minute with the rope already around his neck. Stewart's near-lynching by the townspeople, like Dunbar's beating at the hands of his fellow cavalrymen in *Dances*, signifies the one side of the cultural dialectic the hero must pass through in order to "prove" his commitment to the synthesis of cultural contradiction. The binding and gagging of Stewart is evocative of the deep psychological chasm the modern viewer must negotiate between the archetypal Massacre and the Noble Indian; that is, atrocities of history cannot be erased, but must be witnessed, and then passed through. Although sometimes suppressed, historical atrocities will, when they eventually force their way into cultural narratives, be dichotomized into the poles of evil aggressors and innocent victims; sometimes this dichotomy is inverted, as when the "good" (morally/historically justified) Indians attack the U.S. cavalry in *Dances With Wolves* and in the made-for-television *Son of The Morning Star* (1991).

Arthur Penn's "progressive" Western, *Little Big Man*, begins with (what else?) a massacre of the family of the young Jack Crabb. The film, and Berger's book, however, cannot exhaust the psychic energy and mythic trauma of The Massacre with this single blood-letting; and so, following the general reversal of the Western tale we find throughout *Little Big Man*, Penn gives us another "slaughter" by inverting the conventions of The Massacre by presenting Custer's infamous "battle" with the Cheyenne beside the Washita River. This time the cavalry does the massacring.

Almost twenty years after the sympathetic Western *Little Big Man*, the even more "sympathetic" *Dances With Wolves* cannot circumvent The Massacre, and, in fact, includes three massacres, one of which is told as a flashback of Stands With A Fist (Dunbar's future wife and herself a white adopted by the Lakota). The flashback is as distilled and powerful an embodiment of the Massacre trauma as has ever been presented by Hollywood. Shot in soft focus and at sunset, the scene begins, slow-motion, as an idyllic view of a rustic farm and cabin; two frontier families are eating outdoors on a large table when ominous-looking Pawnee warriors ride slowly in on horseback, their faces painted in bilious blues and bloody reds. At first it seems a peaceful meeting of the two cultures, but then a tomahawk flies through the air, and the scene takes on added poignancy as the next image is that of the horrified gaze of the young witness, which then dissolves into the still haunted Stands With A Fist.[4]

The third massacre in *Dances* transforms the horror associated with that depiction into the Hollywood sanctioned celebration of dispatching the badmen—the U.S. cavalry. Dunbar has been captured by the cavalry as a renegade and is being taken by wagon in shackles to a frontier prison. When the Lakota attack and kill Dunbar's tormentors, one realizes that even with ninety years of Hollywood history turned on its head—we have here the same cheer for the good guys; the skillful and precise application of violence in order to right the world; the promise of "regeneration through violence," which Richard Slotkin has so eloquently elaborated.

Another strategy for resolving the historical trauma and contradiction of The Massacre is, through sleight of hand, to present viewers a tribe of "Noble Savages" (The Sioux in *Dances* and the Cheyenne in *Little Big Man*), and then a tribe of just plain old fashioned savages (the Pawnee in both films). This strategy has the function of addressing white historical fear and guilt within the same narrative, providing a way in which a fiction can remain simultaneously true to contradictory emotional responses to history.

In *A Man Called Horse* Lord Morgan (Richard Harris) is captured by a band of Sioux in 1825. Yellow Hand decides to save this strange white man to be a slave of some sort and, after tying a rope around his neck, proceeds to ride Morgan like a horse before the other laughing warriors of the raiding party. Taken back to the Sioux camp, Morgan is mistreated until he eventually earns the Sioux's respect through his endurance, slaying of attacking Shoshone braves, and his successful completion of the Sun Dance ritual. Although never expressed in the film, Morgan's Indian name itself is transformed from the beast-of-burden connotations of that word, to the more noble connotations for "horse" one would expect from a horse culture. *Little Big Man's* young Jack Crabb (Dustin Hoffman) gets his name from old Chief Lodge Skins (Chief Dan George) who gives Jack his name—Little Big Man—by way of a story the old chief tells the short young man to inspire his confidence. Later, Jack kills a Pawnee during a war party and strengthens his bond to the tribe, eventually becoming a "squawman" in more ways than one.

In *Dances With Wolves*, Lt. John Dunbar is named, at first without his knowledge, by his Sioux brothers who have seen him "dancing" with his "pet" wolf, Two Socks. Dunbar had been trying to get Two Socks to return to his fort as he rode out to the Indian's camp, but the wolf would playfully snap at his heals as Dunbar tried to chase him back. The Indians watched in the foreground of the shot, incredulous that a white man could have such a relationship with a wild animal. This scene in the film is presented with no fanfare, narration, or dialog with which to signify its tremendous importance to the film's mythopoeic task; thus, viewers take Dunbar's frolic with Two Socks as just another day in the life of John Dunbar—that is, as natural and spontaneous. Because viewers do not hear the Lakota warriors name Dunbar, and because they already know the title of the film, the scene achieves two brilliant effects. First, the renaming scene is one of the most calculated moments of the film, yet it comes off as an utterly natural occurrence (accentuated by being filmed in long shot, soft-focus, and a PBS nature-documentary style). Second, Costner, in effect, lets every viewer rename Dunbar with his Lakota name, since the scene plays without dialog or even gesture from the Lakota. This has the effect of making filmgoers active participants in the sacred ritual of renaming a man into Nature and the tribe.

Although this renaming fits nicely with the standard Hollywood story convention of depicting an *evolving* character, this infrequent, but telling tendency says more about American romantic concepts of the Indian and the natural than it does about Hollywood storytelling. This renaming of a white man with a "natural name" and the shedding of his European name is the quintessential American myth—the self-made man rediscovering both America, and, most importantly, his own true self in the process. Freed from the oppressive yoke of European tradition, self-made even to his name (founder of his self—the task of Whitman's *Leaves of Grass*), this character of literature and film has, after two hundred years, become only more solidified in our consciousness: from a string of names with no "direct relation to the universe"—Natty Bumppo, Lewis Henry Morgan, Lord Morgan, Jack Crabb, and John Dunbar—emerge Indian names, true names—Leather Stocking/Deerslayer/Hawkeye, Tayadaowuhkuh, Horse, Little Big Man, Dances With Wolves. European interest in Indian names did not develop solely from fictional romances of the noble savage; the real contrast between Indian naming and European naming sparked the imaginations of many explorers, trappers, and immigrants who sought to communicate and understand that first task of language, naming.

As I heard my Sioux name being called over and over, I knew for the first time who I really was.
—from the Diary of John J. Dunbar

Figure 10.1. After shedding much of his uniform, Dunbar affects a renegade look familiar from Wild West shows, Hollywood Westerns, and the 1960s counterculture. The look is still evoked, an emblem of American outlaw heroism.

Dances With Wolves seems to me to be the latest, most important development in this mythopoeic founding of the "only real American."[5] It is a different myth from what Fiedler called the "anti-feminist" myth of the runaway male who flees from the white woman to his native, dark-skinned companion, for Lt. John Dunbar marries Stands With A Fist, a white survivor of The Massacre, who has nearly forgotten her first family and language. *Dances With Wolves* accomplishes, I think for the first time in our American imagination, the transmigration of the white family unit into the mythical hunting ground of The Indian. By the end of the film Dances With Wolves and Stands With A Fist have already transfigured into buckskins, the Sioux language, the Sioux way. Edward D. Castillo, a Native American academic, has written an excellent review of *Dances With Wolves* that explores many of the same issues analyzed here. Castillo asserts that *Dances* is "really about the transformation of the white soldier Lt. John Dunbar into the Lakota warrior Dances With Wolves" (16). Recalling Dunbar's hope to "see the frontier . . . before it's gone," Castillo notes, "That simple childlike desire touches an unspoken yearning in many Americans, young and old" (19). His words "childlike desire" recall Freud's family romance as well as the wish-fulfillment aspect of *Dances*. Even more interesting is this passage in Castillo's essay: "While exchanging parting gifts, Dances With Wolves tells Kicking Bird, 'You were the first man I ever wanted to be like. I will not forget you.' Indians know that no white man or woman can become Indian, but many of us hope those who have learned of our cultures and appreciate their unique humanity will be our friends and allies in protecting the earth and all of her children" (20).

Because *Dances With Wolves* starts with Lt. John J. Dunbar near death on a Civil War operating table, and never once flashes back to any fictional family or past, Dunbar's line to Kicking Bird—"You were the first man I ever wanted to be like"—becomes illustrative of a close adherence to the imaginative logic of the family romance, embossed with the American Adam myth and the historical legacy of Native American cultures. In retrospect, one should not be surprised at *Dances With Wolves'* enthusiastic reception, nor at the many modern Americans who found going Indian a still viable trail to follow through the American imagination.

During the November 1993 ratings sweeps, ABC broadcast a new, expanded version of *Dances With Wolves*. At fifty minutes longer than the original, the new *Dances* exploited the TV Western miniseries formula that worked so well with *Lonesome Dove*. The new *Dances* was originally composed by Costner and producer Jim Wilson for foreign distribution and simply reintegrated footage originally trimmed for the American theatrical release. As can be expected, much of the footage simply expanded on plot, characters, and themes in the original American version. A few additions bridge minor gaps in the narrative and flesh out issues that might have puzzled some original viewers. The crazy Major Fambrough, who sends Dunbar on his "knight's errand" is shown, through added footage, to be certifiably insane. The environmental destruction theme is pushed even further in a number of additions and in one wholly new scene. One addition has the slothful mule driver Timmons littering as he crosses the prairie, tossing a tin can to the ground as Dunbar registers the appropriately modern reaction of indignation. The horror of Fort Sedgewick's polluted pond grows through the addition of animal carcasses and by witnessing Dunbar having to swim into the pond, bandanna over nose, to struggle with the wet dead weight of the animals before he burns them. The wholly new scene of environmental devastation occurs when Kicking Bird and Dunbar journey alone to the sacred Sioux mountains (Kicking Bird: "The animals were born here") but find instead an ominous silence and the remnants of a hunting camp strewn with animal corpses and empty whisky bottles. The mystery surrounding the prior inhabitants of Fort Sedgewick is also settled. Before Dunbar reaches the deserted fort, the last of the fort's troops are shown cowering in their caves until their officer assembles them, commends them for staying after the others deserted, and suggests they mount an orderly mass desertion, saying, "The Army can go to Hell!" The new version also fleshes out a few of the minor characters. Two Socks, Dunbar's friendly wolf, gets much more onscreen time and the trio of young Sioux boys that includes Smiles A Lot turn up in a number of scenes of teenage drama and hijinks: last-minute jitters before the unsanctioned raid on Dunbar's horse, a vigorous but denied attempt to join the men during the buffalo hunt, and a foiled prank to close the smoke flap on the teepee of the honeymooning Dances With Wolves and Stands With A Fist. The inversions of cultural prejudice occasionally seen in the original film are seconded with one more quite pointed jibe that takes place during the massacre of Timmons. A Pawnee brave starts to take Timmons's quilt for a trophy until he sniffs it suspiciously, throws it on the ground in disgust, and cleans his hands with dirt. On a more romantic note, the new film elaborates on the courtship between Dances With Wolves and Stands With A Fist, including Dunbar's need to rely on tribal gifts of horses and clothing in order to purchase his new bride, in the traditional Sioux way, from her father/guardian, Kicking Bird.

But the most substantial difference between the new and original versions of *Dances* involves the night scene just before the buffalo hunt. In the original film, this night scene is one long take of twenty-eight seconds. The Sioux camp appears in the background, ponies in the middle ground, and Dunbar, resting on his bedroll, stretched out in the foreground, his voice over narration intoning: "As they celebrated into the night, the coming hunt, it was hard to know where to be. I don't know if they understood, but I could not sleep among them. There had been no looks, and there was no blame. There was only the confusion of a people not able to predict the future." One assumes simply that Dunbar is finding some time alone before the next day's big hunt. In the expanded version, however, one witnesses two minutes of footage and twenty-five shots that change not only the meaning of this one scene, but imbue the entire film with a greater moral complexity. The scene begins with Dunbar riding into camp with a small band of warriors. A large fire is burning in the center of camp as the Sioux dance around it. Dunbar holds back and sizes up the situation. He notices a wagon, filled with buffalo hides. His voice-over narration explains things: "It was suddenly clear now what had happened, and my heart sank as I tried to convince myself that the white men who had been killed were bad people and deserved to die, but it was no use. I tried to believe that Wind in His Hair and Kicking Bird and all the other people who shared in the killing were not so happy for having done it, but they were. As I looked at the familiar faces I realized that the gap between us was greater than I could ever have imagined."

The narration accompanies a building intimacy of shot scales, growing closer to the dancing Sioux as well as Dunbar's reaction shots. Two crucial insert shots provide gory emphasis: a severed white man's hand tied in rope and hanging over the flames of the campfire; a long blonde scalp at the end of a pole, reflecting the reddish glow. This unexpurgated scene then ends with the same thirty-second shot and voice-over found in the original; but now Dunbar's comment about not being able "to sleep among them" takes on a pointed meaning. The scene in the original *Dances*, then, is literally a repression of the novel and the shooting script, a repression of The Massacre.[6]

The other material in the film merely expands and explains themes already extant in the first release, but this new (old) material marks a radical addition, I should say a return, to the film. While trimming *Dances* to a tight (!) 181 minutes kept the film distributable and positioned for Oscar contention, Costner might have deflected a great deal of subsequent criticism that his Sioux were too wholesome by keeping just this one moment of unbridgeable cultural difference in the original film (or including, as the new film does, another moral complication of the Sioux: a brief scene early in the narrative makes it clear that Stands With A Fist's husband died not while defending the tribe from the marauding Pawnee,

Figure 10.2. In *Dances With Wolves,* a number of nighttime campfire scenes serve to summon the primitive, the animistic, the predatory. Both releases contain a scene in which Dunbar, alone, dances around a campfire in a type of wild-man epiphany. But only the television release includes the Sioux's post-massacre campfire celebration, a ceremony from which Dunbar excuses himself.

but during a raid on the Utes, explicitly undercutting the assumption the first film may have given that these Sioux practice only defensive tribal warfare).

This is not to deny *Dances'* radical inversion of the Western. Where *The Searchers* turns on a white man's obsessive attempts to find and retrieve a white woman from her tribal life, *Dances* at midpoint gives us a white cavalry officer who returns a white woman to her tribal life as a simple matter of course. But what I find so interesting is how the latest word in the progressive Western cannot live by genre inversion alone, but ends up negotiating, deflecting, and ultimately retrieving The Massacre. Neither film, I think, is the definitive, authoritative edition, the "director's cut." Multiple versions of narratives, sometimes, betray tensions not so easily written off as just more of the same. Thus, I think we have two films now, *Dances With Wolves* and *(The Return of) Dances With Wolves.*

Notes

1. This essay was previously published in the *Michigan Academician* 25:2, (Winter 1993): 133–146; in *Film & History* 23 (1993): 91–102; and in *Dressing in Feathers: The Construction of the Indian in American Popular Culture*, ed. Elizabeth Bird (Boulder: Westview Press, 1996): 195–209.

2. Wry, populist cartoonist Gary Larson hints at the success of *Dances With Wolves* in one of his famous *Far Side* pieces. Three odd-looking characters stand around a punch bowl in a massive, vacant ballroom. Above them hangs a cryptic banner: "DLDWWS." One man complains about the "insensitive" portrayal of the cavalry. A woman intones, "Those buffaloes weren't really killed. . . . That was all faked!" Thus goes another meeting of the "international" "Didn't Like Dances With Wolves Society." The film's widespread success had, I argue, much to do with its updating of the going-Indian myth; in this light, it is not at all innocent that Kevin Costner just happened to be the star who went Indian. Costner was, at the time and perhaps even after *Waterworld*, Hollywood's leading icon of masculine Americana, a descendant of the mantle passed down from Gary Cooper and Jimmy Stewart. But not everyone believed in Costner's Dunbar or fell in love with *Dances*. Pauline Kael called the film "childishly naive." Others complained the film was anachronistic, an allegory of Hollywood liberalism (historical guilt, environmentalism, middle-class feminism, and the New Age Indian wannabe syndrome) rather than an accurate history of the meeting of white and Sioux cultures during the 1860s. Not incidentally, *Dances'* most direct ancestor was *Little Big Man*, itself a product of the counterculture, which borrowed, Thodore Roszak has held, a "garish motley" of ideas from "depth psychiatry . . . mellowed remnants of left-wing ideology . . . the oriental religions . . . Romantic Weltschmerz . . . anarchist social theory . . . Dada and American Indian lore" (xiii). Nonetheless, millions of viewers embraced *Dances* in spite of its historical liberties and long running time (over three hours). Nominated for twelve Academy Awards, *Dances* won seven: Best Picture, Best Director (Kevin Costner), Best Adapted Screenplay (Michael Blake), Best Cinematography (Dean Semler), Best Film Editing (Neil Travis), Best Original Score (John Barry), and Best Sound (Russell Williams II, Jeffrey Perkins, Bill W. Benton, and Greg Watkins).

3. For an exhaustive, scholarly, but unrelentingly cynical examination of American mythology, including what he calls "Indianization," see Richard Slotkin's *Regeneration Through Violence* (1973) as well as his *Gunfighter Nation* (1992).

4. Men are not the only ones to gain an Indian name. The historical figure Virginia Dare, who was the first European child born in the New World and disappeared in 1587 with the rest of Sir Walter Ralegh's colony, has presented a puzzling mystery to historians ever since her disappearance. In the children's book *Virginia Dare: Mystery Girl*, part of a series called Childhood of Famous Americans, Augusta Stevenson creates a fictionalized conclusion to Virginia's story. Given the problems of presenting a children's story that must deal with The Massacre, Stevenson seems to have followed the mythical tradition, and given Virginia an adoptive tribe and an Indian name: White Flower.

5. Charles M. Russell left a number of comments concerning his vote for the "true American." In a 1914 letter to Judge Pray, Russell used pen, ink, and watercolor to depict a rather forlorn, mounted Indian. Beside the brave Russell inked, "This is the onley [sic] real American. He fought and died for his country. Today he has no vote, no country, and is not a citizen, but history will not forget him" (Broderick 84). Russell expressed much the same sentiment in another letter to Joe Scheurle, possibly around 1916: "The Red man was the true American. They have almost gon [sic]. But will never be forgotten. The history of how they fought for their country is written in blood, a stain that time cannot grind out" (Russell, *Good Medicine*, 127).

6. Michael Blake's novel makes Dunbar's cultural anxiety even more apparent than the expanded film. Some relevant passages:

> Suddenly it was clear as a cloudless day. The skins belonged to the murdered buffalo and the scalps belonged to the men who had killed them, men who had been alive that very afternoon. White men. The lieutenant was numb with confusion. He couldn't participate in this, not even as a watcher. He had to leave (167).

The scene concludes with Dunbar wracked with existential anxiety over his indeterminate place in the world:

> More than anything he wanted to believe that he was not in this position. He wanted to believe he was floating toward the stars. But he wasn't. He heard Cisco lie down in the grass with a heavy sigh. It was quiet then and Dunbar's thought turned inward, toward himself. Or rather his lack of self. He did not belong to the Indians. He did not belong to the whites. And it was not time for him to belong to the stars. He belonged right where he was now. He belonged nowhere. A sob rose in his throat. He had to gag to stiffle it. But the sobs kept coming up and it was not long before he ceased to see the sense in trying to keep them down (167–68).

Works Cited

Blake, Michael. *Dances With Wolves*. New York: Fawcett, 1988.

Broderick, Janice K. *Charles M. Russell: American Artist*. St. Louis: Jefferson National Expansion Historical Association, 1982.

Castillo, Edward D. *"Dances With Wolves." Film Quarterly* 44 (Summer 1991): 14–23.

Crèvecoeur, J. Hector St. John. *Letters from an American Farmer*. Gloucester, Mass.: Peter Smith, 1968.

Dippie, Brian W. *Remington and Russell*. Austin: University of Texas Press, 1982.

Fiedler, Leslie A. *The Return of the Vanishing American*. New York: Stein and Day, 1968.

Freud, Sigmund. *The Standard Edition of the Complete Psychological Works of Sigmund Freud* vol. 9. London: Hogarth Press, 1959.

Lawrence, D.H. *Studies in Classic American Literature*. New York: Viking Press, 1923.

Lewis, R.W.B. *The American Adam: Innocence, Tragedy, and Tradition in the Nineteenth Century*. Chicago: University of Chicago Press, 1955.

McCracken, Harold. *The Charles M. Russell Book: The Life and Work of the Cowboy Artist*. Garden City, N.Y.: Doubleday, 1957.

Roszak, Thodore. *The Making of A Counter-Culture: Reflections on the Technocratic Society and Its Youthful Opposition*. New York: Doubleday, 1969.

Russell, Charles M. *Good Medicine: The Illustrated Letters of Charles M. Russell*. New York: Doubleday, 1929.

———. *Trails Plowed Under*. New York: Doubleday, 1935.

Slotkin, Richard. *Gunfighter Nation: The Myth of the Frontier in Twentieth-Century America*. New York: Atheneum, 1992.

———. *Regeneration Through Violence: The Mythology of the American Frontier, 1600–1860. Frontier, 1600–1860*. Middletown, Conn.: Wesleyan University Press, 1973.

Stevenson, Augusta. *Virginia Dare: Mystery Girl*. New York: Bobbs-Merrill, 1958.

Stone, Elizabeth. *Black Sheep and Kissing Cousins: How Our Family Stories Shape Us*. New York: Penguin Books, 1988.

Thoreau, Henry David. *The Illustrated Walden*. Princeton: Princeton University Press, 1973.

———. *The Maine Woods*. 1864. New York: Harry N. Abrams, 1989.

Deconstructing an American Myth
The Last of the Mohicans (1992)

Since its initial two-volume publication on February 6, 1826, by the Philadelphia publishing house of Carey and Lea, James Fenimore Cooper's
The Last of the Mohicans; A Narrative of 1757 has probably generated
more attention from Hollywood filmmakers than any other American
novel. From its first adaptations in 1909 as a D. W. Griffith one-reeler
and in 1911 as two different one-reelers by the Powers and Thanhouser
Film Companies to its latest incarnation in 1992 as a Michael Mann pot-
boiler, more than a dozen interpretations of the novel have appeared in
various forms: silent picture, Mascot serial, animated version, BBC television series, and Hollywood epic.[1] Considering the popular reception of
the novel in Cooper's day, and the mythic story it spins about American
frontier heroes, this attention seems deserved. Most Americans, if they
have not read the novel (and most have not), have nonetheless read about
it or read abridged versions of it, and our own popular culture has embraced it in a number of curious ways. Mark Twain made Cooper and his
"offenses" against literary art in the Leather-Stocking Tales part of his
traveling lecture shows. More recently, the antihero of television's
M*A*S*H, Captain Benjamin Franklin Pierce, we are told, received his
sobriquet "Hawkeye" because the Cooper tale was supposedly the only
novel his father had ever read.

That most Americans have never read *The Last of the Mohicans* is
not surprising. Until the Fenimore Cooper family agreed to cooperate in
the production of a responsibly edited series of Cooper's fiction and non-
fiction in the mid-1960s, *The Last of the Mohicans* (appearing in 1983 as
part of that NEH-sponsored, CSE-sealed, SUNY Press-published series)
was available for readers only in a plethora of corrupt texts. And while the
absence of reliable Cooper texts has been partially responsible for Cooper's

less than highly touted reputation as a man of letters, Twain certainly had something to do with this offense against the American literary canon. The fact remains that the novel has been praised more often for what it did not do than for what it did. Film versions of the novel illustrate this strange reaction to Cooper's masterpiece and explain the distortion of the text; yet, ironically, Hollywood filmmakers are probably as responsible for generating interest in Cooper's novel over the years as literary critics or college and university professors. In translating Cooper's work for the screen, they highlight and make popular those elements of *The Last of the Mohicans* that have little to do with Cooper's original story but have everything to do with twentieth-century American popular culture and taste. Although most of the directors do a sterling job of presenting Cooper's mise-en-scène, none of the film versions of the novel accurately reproduce Cooper's plot, and few come close to understanding Cooper's theme. Despite these problems, film versions continue to be made because Hollywood sees the novel as containing the ingredients of an American film classic—albeit for all the wrong reasons.

When *The Last of the Mohicans* appeared in 1826, it was hailed by some as an American masterpiece. In the February 18, 1826, issue of the Philadelphia *National Gazette*, Robert Walsh remarked, "Never since the days of our childhood has Fairy hand sported so with our feelings. . . . Never has necromancer, or poet, held us so long enchanted. The work, from the beginning to the close, is one tissue of harrowing incidents, beautiful and chaste imagery, and deep pathos, and what adds to the charm, is, though we yield a willing credence to every turn of the narrative, we know that every thing is true" (163). William Leete Stone's review in the New York *Commercial Advertiser* of February 6, 1826, concurred with Walsh's praise of Cooper's novel: "'It is American books,' says a late English Review, 'that are wanted of America; not English books, nor books made in America by Englishmen. We want, in a word, from the people of North America, books, which, whatever may be their faults, are decidedly, if not altogether, American.' Well, here they have one—a description of the aboriginal character—in all its native, wild, and lofty grandeur—powerful warm, rich, glowing, and animated, from the hand of a master, though they may be unwilling to acknowledge him as such" (238).

Such contemporary reviews of the novel addressed issues that have affected the literary interpretation of *The Last of the Mohicans* in the almost two centuries since its publication, but have had seemingly little impact on the twentieth-century filmmaker's response to the text. Historically praised either for the inclusion of harrowing incidents in his fictions or for the creation of truly American books, Cooper has been generally misinterpreted and misrepresented by filmmakers. Almost all of the film adaptations have concentrated on his plots, always to the novel's detriment, and the result has been chaos with Cooper's text.

With the exception of the 1920 silent version of *The Last of the Mohicans* (directed by Maurice Tourneur and Clarence Brown, and starring Wallace Beery as Magua, Barbara Bedford as Cora, Albert Rosco as Uncas, Harry Lorraine as Hawk-eye, and Theodore Lerch as Chingachgook), none of the other versions comes close to reliably retelling the story. In this 1920 interpretation, the directors concentrated on the relationship between Cora and Uncas, with Hawk-eye reduced to a secondary position. It is generally faithful to the novel, although it includes an extremely long section on the Fort William Henry massacre and introduces a villainous British officer who lusts for Cora and betrays the fort to the French. (These are minor distortions in the text in comparison to those in later versions.)

In 1924, for example, Pathé produced a composite film of *The Leatherstocking Tales* directed by George B. Seitz. With Harry Miller as Leatherstocking and David Dunbar as Chingachgook, the film also features Edna Murphy as Judith Hutter and Lillian Hall as Hetty Hutter (both characters from *The Deerslayer*, not *Mohicans*), and depicts such historical figures as Montcalm, Braddock, and Washington. Columbia Pictures produced a similar distortion in 1947 called *The Last of the Redmen*. In addition to making Hawk-eye an Irish scout and Cora Munro a redhead, the film also introduces a new character into the text, Davy Munro, the Munro girls' kid brother, as well as a standard bromide of the classic Western, the circling of the wagon train. Equally Western in its mise-en-scène is Harold Reinl's direction of a 1965 German adaptation called *The Last Tomahawk*. Set in the American West of the 1880s, the action takes place at Ranch Munro and contains such imaginative variations as a chest of government gold, an exploding mountain, and a cavalry charge.

In the 1930s, two film versions of the novel were produced. The first, a Mascot serial directed by Reaves Eason in 1932, is a classic twelve-chapter nail-biter that includes almost as many textual distortions of the novel as it has cliffhanger endings. Known chiefly for its casting of Harry Carey as Hawk-eye, the twelfth installment ends with an equally bizarre violation of textual integrity: Chingachgook is killed, Uncas lives, and Hawk-eye tells the young Mohican that he is the last of his race. The second cinematic version filmed in the 1930s is probably the most famous of all the film adaptations, primarily because its script was used as the source for the 1992 Michael Mann blockbuster. Based on a screenplay by Philip Dunne and directed by George B. Seitz, who remade his 1924 silent film in 1936 for United Artists, *The Last of the Mohicans* stars Randolph Scott as Hawk-eye and Binnie Barnes as Alice Munro. Seitz introduces most of the plot changes used in the 1992 film, but the chief plot difference portrays Seitz's Hawk-eye and Alice Munro as the two white star-crossed lovers rather than Mann's Hawk-eye and Cora. In spite of his misrepresentation of Cooper's novel, which has Uncas, the Native American, and Cora, the part-white woman herself the product of miscegenation, as the principals in an interracial romance, Seitz's plot twist was not surprising in 1936, given Hollywood and the Hays Office's horror of miscegenation.[2] It would have been distasteful to Cooper, too, not only because of the violation of plot, but also because he attempted in his Leather-Stocking Tales to deemphasize the love interest so important to the European Gothic novel.

When Michael Mann produced his 1992 film, the Hawk-eye and Cora love affair took center stage. In choosing to pair Hawk-eye with the dark-haired Cora and Uncas with the fair-haired Alice, Mann revised Cooper's original story which showed Hawk-eye as a "man without a cross" (and without a girlfriend) and Uncas drawn to Cora, a dark-haired mulatto, rather than to the blonde Alice, a coupling representing Cooper's own attitudes toward miscegenation. Of all the many revisions of Cooper's novel that appear in the 1992 version, Mann's decision to turn *The Last of the Mohicans* primarily into a love story and to ignore the essence of the Native American theme is the strangest and most damaging plot twist of all. It is one thing to borrow scenes from other Leather-Stocking novels (the canoe chase from *The Pathfinder*, for example), to invent scenes (Hawk-eye's shooting of Duncan Hayward to prevent his suffering at the burning stake, Magua's killing of Colonel Munro), or to mismatch lovers (Duncan and Cora rather than Duncan and Alice, Uncas and Alice rather than Uncas and Cora) to sell theater tickets. But to manipulate the story's plot in an attempt to make history more vivid and realistic for the contemporary filmgoer is questionable directing and screenwriting—although the ploy has many precedents in films about Native Americans. To focus on the love affair between American literature's most strongly individualistic, anti-authoritarian, and anti-British mythic hero and Cora Munro is to miss the essential theme and flavor of Cooper's classic tale. As James Franklin Beard informs us in his historical introduction to the SUNY Press edition of the novel, *The Last of the Mohicans* is not finally about such peripheral action as two lovers (particularly white ones), but about the "unremitting, frequently violent, always exasperating contest between the Native Americans and the intruders, white immigrants and settlers of

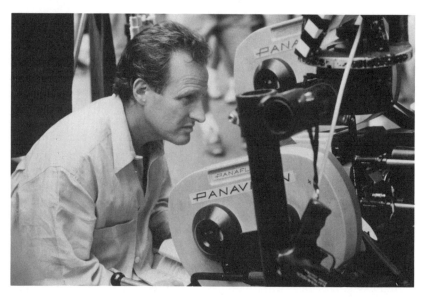

Figure 11.1. Writer-producer-director Michael Mann on the set of *The Last of the Mohicans*. Courtesy of the Museum of Modern Art/Film Stills Archive.

every description" (xxx) and its consequences: the destruction of the last vestiges of a race of Native Americans.

In the current climate of political correctness, where the rights and heritage of all Americans demand celebration and recognition, it is unusual that none of the filmmakers who have translated *The Last of the Mohicans* for the screen have taken this theme into consideration. Cooper's early nineteenth-century reviewers certainly recognized his strengths and his weaknesses as a writer and a social critic. An anonymous pundit wrote in the pages of the July 1826 issue of the *North American Review* that "we do not find that he [Cooper] describes with great effect the secret workings of the passions of the human heart; or that he moves our affections, by any other than mere external agents, and such commonly as are calculated to excite no softer or more sympathetic emotion than terror or surprise" (153). Charles Sealsfield agreed in his February 12, 1831, *New York Mirror* essay on the newly published Bentley Standard Novels series of Cooper's novels, writing, "Our author does not excel in painting civilized men and manners; and, least of all, civilized woman" (252). Cooper, of course, was not, nor did he intend to be, a novelist of manners. As another anonymous critic pointed out in his biographical sketch of Cooper in the June 1838 issue of the *Southern Literary Messenger*, "In painting Indian scenes of still life, or in delineating the warrior and hunger, the battle

Figure 11.2. American epic or Hollywood love story? Courtesy of the Museum of Modern Art/Film Stills Archive.

or the chase, our novelist, as he is the first who seized upon subjects so full of interest for the romance, so is he alone and unrivalled in this branch of his art" (375). An earlier anonymous writer's diagnosis in *The New-York Mirror* concurs: "In this novel the American aborigines are introduced with better effect than in any work of fiction that has ever been written. The gentle Uncas and his valiant sire, the fiend-like Magua, and the venerable patriarch of the Delawares, are perfect masterpieces of their kind. . . . They are immensely superior to all that Chateaubriand, or any others, have made to delineate the character of the American savage" (39).

Cooper's strengths certainly did not lie in his portrait of domestic interacation, and the contemporary reviews showed it; instead reviewers like the critic in the April 1826 issue of the *Literary Gazette* admired his Native Americans and praised them as "original and interesting" portraits never "so well, so truly, and so vividly drawn as in his pages" (198).

How then have twentieth-century America and Hollywood strayed so far from Cooper's original theme in *The Last of the Mohicans*? What is it about Cooper's story that readers and filmmakers have refused to understand or acknowledge? Does the problem lie in ignoring the source and history of Cooper's tale, or perhaps in falling prey to the bad reputation Cooper as novelist has received in American literature ever since Mark Twain penned his hilarious satire "Fenimore Cooper's Literary Offenses" and condemned Cooper forever as a second-rate hack? The problem lies somewhere in between. On the one hand, American readers have not stopped laughing long enough over Twain's essay to recognize that it was not serious literary criticism, but primarily a tour de force in the history of American humor. To some degree this lack of reconsideration has prevented American readers and filmmakers from listening closely enough to what scholars have been claiming to be Cooper's contributions to American literature, or to what we have learned about the historical background and composition of the novel.

When Twain wrote his grossly exaggerated lampoon in the July 1895 issue of the *North American Review*, he accused Cooper of literary incompetence by attacking his use of imprecise language, his development of improbable characters, and his creation of impossible plots in the Leather-Stocking novels (in particular, *The Deerslayer*, *The Pathfinder*, and *The Last of the Mohicans*).[3] In recent years, as the *Writings of James Fenimore Cooper* series has worked to produce seventeen textually reliable editions of his novels, we have learned that Cooper was not the slipshod writer Twain portrayed him to be in his essay. Although it is true that the editions of his novels were remarkably corrupt because compositors had difficulty reading his script, because he did not read proof against printer's copy, and because numerous resettings had left a heavy toll of corruptions, Cooper did revise, as the textual evidence discovered by the editors of the Cooper series has demonstrated conclusively. In *The Last of the Mohicans*, for example, Cooper, in a letter from Paris dated August

29, 1831, to his publishers Colburn and Bentley, noted that "there are errors in the Preface of the Mohicans, and in one instance bad grammar—'As the verdure of their native forests fall.' Verdure is the nominative case of fall, and it should have been falls" (*Letters and Journals* 2: 137). Such authorial revisions were commonplace with Cooper. Furthermore, Twain's charges have also been challenged and disproven by Lance Schachterle and Kent Ljungquist in their rejoinder to Twain appropriately called "Fenimore Cooper's Literary Defenses: Twain and the Text of *The Deerslayer*." In their essay, they attempt to prove that Twain's charges against Cooper's art are both fallacious and inaccurate. Based upon their own work editing Cooper's writings, they determine that "by carefully manipulating Cooper's texts, willfully misreading, and sometimes fabricating evidence, Twain leaves the reader with the impression that he has polished Cooper off." However they continue, "By looking at Twain's treatment of plot, characterization, and especially diction in *The Deerslayer*, we lay bare Twain's rhetorical strategy and satirical distortions" (402). Despite the overwhelming evidence they present in their essay that Cooper was a careful craftsman, most American readers continue to laugh at Cooper. Hollywood has unfortunately contributed to this offense against literary history by repeatedly telling the wrong tale of *The Last of the Mohicans*.

Cooper first conceived the idea for his novel in early August 1824. As James Franklin Beard tells the story, *The Last of the Mohicans* was born out of an excursion Cooper took with four young English noblemen (Edward Stanley, Henry Labouchere, Evelyn Denison, and John Wortley) to Glens Falls and Lake George. Cooper was struck by the scenery at the falls and declared (recorded in a footnote in Stanley's journal appended to his description of the Falls) that he had to "'place one of his old Indians here'—'The last of the Mohicans' was the result." Beard notes that "the word Indian or Indians in both accounts is probably significant; for the Leatherstocking Tales had not yet been conceived as a series, and the introduction of Hawk-eye may have been an afterthought" (*Mohicans* xx). If Stanley's note and Beard's interpretation of Cooper's words are correct, then *The Last of the Mohicans* as a novel focusing exclusively on the character of Hawk-eye as its central hero is as much an American literary myth as are the Hollywood films that not only place him at the center of their adventure tale, but also represent him as the principal male lead in a love story.

Of course, Hawk-eye's role in the novel is certainly important and central to the significance of the action, but it is not necessarily as the quintessential American white hero that this centrality functions. Following the massacre at Fort William Henry, Hawk-eye recognizes that the decisions made by his fellow white men (Munro, Heyward, Montcalm) have led to an unmitigated disaster. As he discussed with Chingachgook and Uncas the path they should take to recover the Munro sisters, "he arose to his feet, and shaking off his apathy, he suddenly assumed the manner of an Indian, and adopted all the arts of native eloquence. Elevating an arm, he pointed out the track of the sun, repeating the gesture for every day that was necessary to accomplish their object" (199). This scene is crucial, not only because Hawk-eye shakes off his apathetic mood, but also because he undergoes a metamorphosis and realizes that the "manner of an Indian" is one he must assume to successfully rescue the women. It is in the second half of the novel that Cooper reinforces his decision to select the Native American (and his ways) as the hero and the subject of his story.

Cooper's interest in Native Americans and their story appears throughout *The Last of the Mohicans*. He was certainly aware of the significance of statements by Chief Justice John Marshall in 1823 and President James Monroe in 1824 that would be the basis of the official Federal Indian Removal Policy instituted years after the publication of his novel,[4] as well as the popularity of Indian captivity narratives throughout the colonial period of American history and historical treatments of the massacre of Fort William Henry, all of which he used as inspiration for his narrative of 1757.[5] Cooper's task, as Beard suggests, "whether or not he formulated it consciously, was to invent an infrastructure to make the outrage dramatically intelligible and humanly meaningful" (*Mohicans* xxxi). *The Last of the Mohicans* was that infrastructure.

Seventeen years after the publication of *The Last of the Mohicans*, Cooper wrote to Rufus Wilmot Griswold telling him that his book was "an experiment, being quite original as to manner and subject" (*Letters and Journals* 4: 343). A year later, in another letter to Griswold, he remarked that his narrative was "an original book. . . . I do not know where to find its model. It succeeded perfectly, forming a totally new class of romance" (*Letters and Journals* 4: 461). Noting the book's originality, Cooper implies that *The Last of the Mohicans* was not a novel intended to continue the Leather-Stocking saga first addressed in *The Pioneers*, or simply a tale that would address his fascination from youth with Indian culture; instead, as he said in the introduction to the 1831 Bentley Standard Novels edition, "the business of a writer of fiction is to approach, as near as his powers will allow, to poetry" (*Mohicans* 7). Cooper meant that he would deemphasize realism and, as Beard notes, present "himself as a writer of romance, stressing the tragic element Aristotle identified as

Figure 11.3. Hawk-eye goes Native. Courtesy of the Museum of Modern Art/Film Stills Archive.

endemic in epic structure" (*Mohicans* xxxii). *The Last of the Mohicans* fits this definition, but it becomes not so much a romance demonstrating Hawk-eye and his woodmanship as a tragic tale of the extinction of a Native American race and the recognition of man's mortality.

Cooper did not write *The Last of the Mohicans* because he wanted to vilify Native Americans or to celebrate Manifest Destiny. He examined human nature and did not care much whether he exposed the evils of one race or another. Magua is probably the blackest villain in Cooper's fiction, but Montcalm's inability (or unwillingness) to anticipate and prevent the Fort William Henry massacre does not speak well for Europeans. Similarly, those characters who promote their own education and sophistication as the chief virtues of the civilized world (Montcalm again, Colonel Munro, Duncan Heyward, the Munro sisters) have little or no compassion or understanding of human nature. Even Hawk-eye and the two Mohicans commit their own acts of transgression in the course of the narrative and do not escape blame for the tragedies that befall either race. Cooper was far more interested in exploring larger moral issues in *The Last of the Mohicans*, something that Hollywood has not recognized in its adaptations of the novel.

To explore these ideas, Cooper did not write a Gothic romance; instead he constructed a plot that borrowed from several popular genres of the period, ones that were certain to address moral issues in 1826 America and to evoke emotional responses from his readers. Certainly the most prominent genre appearing in *The Last of the Mohicans* is the Puritan captivity narrative.[6] Cooper adopts many of its conventions and invents some new variations, so as to transform the captivity genre into his own secular adventure story. By doubling the number of captivities, Cooper also doubles the number of the traditional attack–capture–escape scenes in the novel and makes the centerpiece of the tale—the massacre at Fort William Henry—more atrocious and dehumanizing. Cooper also invents two heroines instead of one, doubling the love interest borrowed from the British Gothic romance. He introduces the psalmist David Gamut into the novel for comic relief and to satirize the Calvinist theme of the triumph of the godly over the savage wilderness and the pagans who inhabit it. And by describing Magua and his actions in both Miltonic and Shakespearean terms to broaden his historiographic strategy (his use of literary allusion in the novel is extensive), Cooper borrows and modifies for his own use traditional literary tropes.[7] But *The Last of the Mohicans* is anything but a traditional novel.

Almost every convention and motif Cooper adopts in his narrative of 1757 helps him address in one way or another the conflict between Native Americans and European settlers. His use of two captivity narratives not only provides structure for the novel (the first occurs in chapters 1–17 and describes the journey to Fort William Henry and the events leading up to the massacre; the second, in chapters 18–33, charts the course of Hawk-eye and the Mohicans as they track Magua and the captive Munro sisters), but also provides an important context for the tragic conclusion.[8] Following the massacre scene in chapter 17, Cooper describes, almost immediately, in the very next chapter the change in the season: "The whole landscape, which, seen by a favouring light, and in a genial temperature, had been found so lovely, appeared now like some pictured allegory of life, in which objects were arrayed in their harshest but truest colours, and without the relief of any shadowing" (181). The grass is arid, the mountains are barren, the wind blows unequally; as Cooper paints it in allegorical terms, "it was a scene of wildness and desolation; and it appeared as if all who had profanely entered it, had been stricken, at a blow, by the relentless arm of death" (181–82). The world of the novel has abruptly changed, but so too has the character of the participants also changed. Munro and Heyward, the heroes of the European world of the first half of the novel, seem unimportant, while Uncas, "who moved in front" (183), takes the lead in the chapter following the massacre and discovers the telltale signs of Magua and the fleeing party. Magua is transformed from the victim of the European settlement of the colonies to its destroyer, the "Prince of Darkness, brooding on his own fancied wrongs, and plotting evil" (284). It is Uncas and Magua who become the central figures in the second half of the novel; as the last of the Mohicans, Uncas asserts his mythic stature in a battle on a mountain top with Magua, not only to determine the winner in a struggle between good and evil but also to decide the destiny of a race.[9] Uncas's ultimate death signifies not only the end of the Mohicans, but also, in a larger context, the end of a time in history. In the final paragraph of the novel, Tamenund, the Delaware sage, elegizes, "The pale faces are masters of the earth, and the time of the red-men has not yet come again" (350).

Cooper's decision to concentrate on the end of a race and on the dramatic battle between white and red, rather than on the romantic adventures of a frontiersman in *The Last of the Mohicans*, surfaces everywhere in the novel. Hawk-eye, for all his centrality in the tale, never serves as the romantic lead or as the hero, of the story, the role that Hollywood has assigned him in all screen adaptations of Cooper's work. In the first half of the novel, Cooper casts Hawk-eye as a guide to lead Heyward and the Munro sisters to Fort William Henry. In the second half, Cooper uses him again as guide, this time to prepare Uncas to seek his destiny in the land of the Delawares. Although he voices many of Cooper's concerns regarding the settlement of America by Europeans throughout the novel, fulfills his role as sharpshooter when the events demand, and serves as the stage manager of much of the plot in the tale, he guides—but never directs—

the action. Similarly, none of the other white male characters in the novel take the lead in anything other than their own culpability. Duncan Heyward never understands that the methods of white warfare will not work in the wilderness; Colonel Munro's and Montcalm's blindness to the realities of "honor" (whether white or red) brings destruction; David Gamut's belief in the goodness of men is both facetious and ironic. Hollywood has consistently portrayed these important Europeans in their true light in all of the film versions of *The Last of the Mohicans*, but scriptwriters and directors continue to misrepresent Hawk-eye and the Native Americans in the tale.

Even the two heroines in the tale surface on film as the opposite of what Cooper intended them to represent. It is Cora Munro, the dark-haired sister to the fair-haired Alice, that Cooper intends to fall in love with Uncas. By using Cora, the product of two races, not Alice, as the love interest of Uncas (and in an even more aberrant moment, of Magua), Cooper intensifies the tragic consequences of their fatal attraction and heightens the importance of Uncas's responsibilities to his hereditary responsibilities and customs. The Hollywood of the 1930s could not have portrayed on celluloid such an interracial relationship, but the Hollywood of the 1990s certainly could have portrayed such a match. To pair Hawk-eye with either woman or to match Uncas with the fair-haired Alice, as Hollywood filmmakers continue to do, is to misunderstand the very essence of Cooper's theme in *The Last of the Mohicans*. Cooper did not condone interracial relationships; his attitude toward interracial marriage was pragmatic. In his *Notions of the Americans* (1828), he explained, "As there is little reluctance to mingle the white and red blood . . . I think an amalgamation of the two races would in time occur. Those families of America who are thought to have any of the Indian blood, are rather proud of their descent; and it is a matter of boast among many of the most considerable persons of Virginia, that they are descended from the renowned Pocahontas" (490). For Cooper, neither interracial marriage (the proposed match of Uncas and Cora) nor miscegenation (Colonel Munro and his mixed-blood mistress) was a racial judgment, but instead a plot device.[10]

As a plot device, the suggestion of interracial marriage or miscegenation raises important issues in the novel on a number of levels. As a product of an "unnatural union" (her mother was "the daughter of a gentleman of those isles, by a lady, whose misfortune it was, if you will . . . to be descended, remotely, from that unfortunate class, who are so basely enslaved to administer to the wants of a luxurious people!" [159]). Cora herself is tainted. Yet it is Cora who anticipates a marriage with a red man, and it is Cora who is the object of both the lust and protection of Magua. As a tainted woman, however, Cora also is the only character in

Figure 11.4. Michael Mann interprets Cooper on the set. Courtesy of the Museum of Modern Art/Film Stills Archive.

the novel who represents Christian forgiveness. As Robert Milder reminds us, she "pardons Magua for his obscene proposal to her and his malignant ferocity with a Christ-like 'he knows not what he does,' . . . and in the trial scene . . . she is cast in the role of the eloquent advocate for mercy, Shakespeare's Portia" (426–27). Milder concludes that "Cora's history establishes her as a symbol for the injustice done the Negro," and "she is made to embody both the problem itself and the potential solution to the problem. . . . As the product and victim of racial injustice Cora represents the sufferings of the Negro in the New World; as the most eloquent and admirable Christian in the book she offers a principle of reconciliation founded upon the equality of souls before God" (427–28). Everyone loves her: Magua, Uncas, Alice, Colonel Munro, and Duncan Hayward (ironically, a Southerner himself). It is unusual in another sense that Hollywood has not grasped the significance of Cooper's treatment of Cora and developed her role in their versions of *The Last of the Mohicans* as something more than the love interest of Hawk-eye, who in the novel admires her also, but certainly is not in love with her.

Hollywood has seldom missed an opportunity to tell a story on film about interracial relationships, independent men and women, Native Americans, and the historical truth behind the real violence that generated American culture. They missed their chance this time, however.

Filmmakers should follow D.H. Lawrence's advice for readers in regard to Cooper, and trust the (text of the) tale, not the (misunderstood reputation of its) teller (2). Although *The Last of the Mohicans* seems a natural choice for the wide screen—at least to those who believe that Fenimore Cooper was a writer of children's frontier-adventure stories—it is a tale with a far more profound significance than Hollywood has given it in any of its superficial film interpretations. None of them are accurate representations of Cooper's novel. Hollywood has regrettably conducted its own campaign against historical and textual veracity and committed its own set of literary offenses. In their versions of *The Last of the Mohicans*, filmmakers have rewritten Cooper's plot,[11] miscast and mislabeled his characters, modernized his dialogue, misunderstood his themes, and misrepresented history. As Mark Twain himself would have to confess, "Counting these out, what is left is Art. I think we must all admit that" (12).

Notes

1. I would like to thank Hugh C. MacDougall of the James Fenimore Cooper Society, Cooperstown, for providing me with a description of the film versions of *The Last of the Mohicans*.

2. The Motion Picture Production Code was adopted by the Association of Motion Pictures producers in February 1930, and by the Motion Picture Producers and Distributors of America the following March. The Code was amended several times over the years and included new sections on crime, costumes, profanity, and cruelty to animals. A complete copy of the code is included in the appendix to Leff's and Simmon's *The Dame in the Kimono* (283–92). In section "II—Sex," under "Particular Applications," number 6 deals with miscegenation: "Miscegenation (sex relationships between white and black races) is forbidden" (285).

3. Twain also wrote a second essay on Cooper, edited by Bernard DeVoto under the title "Fenimore Cooper's Further Literary Offences."

4. Marshall's 1823 decision removed the "right of discovery" as the legal basis for titles to Indian land conveyed in treaties and agreements; Monroe argued that "unless the tribes be civilized they can never be incorporated into our system in any form whatsoever." See Beard's "Historical Introduction," especially xxviii–xxix.

5. For a discussion of Cooper's sources for the Fort Willam Henry massacre, see French and Philbrick; see also Butler and Philbrick, "Sounds of Discords," for a discussion of Cooper's historical process.

6. Numerous critics have drawn connections between the captivity narrative and *The Last of the Mohicans*, but David Haberly's essay is the best.

7. William Kelly calls *The Last of the Mohicans* Cooper's most allusive of novels, not only in his use of material for the epigraphs, but also in his extensive use of literary allusions to reveal the character of his players.

8. See Peck's chapter on *The Last of the Mohicans* and the parallels he draws between the first and second halves of the novel.

9. See Darnell's treatment of Uncas as the hero of the novel in the tradition of the ubi sunt formula, as well as John McWilliams's essay and chapter on the novel as an American Indian epic.

10. Leslie Fiedler's treatment of the miscegenation theme in *The Last of the Mohicans* remains the most celebrated.

11. Michael Mann's 1992 version of *The Last of the Mohicans* contains a number of significant plot variations. Cooper's original plot (in italics) is followed by Mann's version: *the scout is called Nathaniel Bumppo*, the scout is called Nathaniel Po; *Natty does not fall in love with any of the women in the novel*, Natty falls in love with Cora; *Cora is attracted to Uncas*, Cora falls in love with Natty; *Uncas falls in love with Cora*, Uncas falls in love with Alice; *Heyward falls in love with Alice*, Heyward falls in love with Cora; *Heyward lives (and eventually marries Alice)*, Heyward dies at the burning stake in the Delaware camp (shot by Natty); *Colonel Munro lives a disillusioned and broken man*, Colonel Munro dies (killed by Magua); *two captivities*, one captivity; *Cora dies (killed by a Huron)*, Cora lives and travels with Natty and Chingachgook at the end; *Alice lives*, Alice dies (by jumping over a cliff); *Natty shoots and kills Magua*, Chingachgook kills Magua; *Natty as guide*, Natty as hero.

Works Cited

Beard, James Franklin. Historical Introduction. xv–xviii In *The Last of the Mohicans; A Narrative of 1757* by James Fenimore Cooper, James A. Sappenfield and E.N. Feltskog, eds. Albany: SUNY Press, 1983.

"Biographical Sketches of Living American Poets and Novelists. No. II. James Fenimore Cooper, Esq." *Southern Literary Messenger* 4 (1838): 373–78.

Butler, Michael D. "Narrative Structure and Historical Process in The Last of the Mohicans." *American Literature* 48 (1976): 117–39.

Cooper, James Fenimore. *The Last of the Mohicans; A Narrative of 1757*. James A. Sappenfield and E.N. Feltskog, eds. Albany: SUNY Press, 1983.

———. *The Letters and Journals of James Fenimore Cooper*. 6 vols. James Franklin Beard, ed. Cambridge: Harvard University Press, 1960–68.

———. *Notions of the Americans: Picked up by a Travelling Bachelor*. Gary Williams, ed. Albany: SUNY Press, 1991.

"Cooper's Novels, No. 2." *New-York Mirror*, Aug. 11, 1827: 39.

Darnell, Donald. "Uncas as Hero: The *Ubi Sunt* Formula in *The Last of the Mohicans*." *American Literature* 37 (1965): 259–66.

DeVoto, Bernard, ed. "Fenimore Cooper's Further Literary Offences." *New England Quarterly* 19 (1946): 291–301.

Fiedler, Leslie. *Love and Death in the American Novel*. New York: Dell, 1966.

French, David P. "James Fenimore Cooper and Fort William Henry." *American Literature* 32 (1960): 28–38.

Haberly, David T. "Women and Indians: *The Last of the Mohicans* and the Captivity Tradition." *American Quarterly* 28 (1976): 431–43.

Kelly, William P. *Plotting America's Past: Fenimore Cooper and the Leatherstocking Tales*. Carbondale: Southern Illinois University Press, 1983.

Lawrence, D.H. *Studies in Classic American Literature*. New York: Viking, 1961.

Leff, Leonard J., and Jerold L. Simmons. *The Dame and the Kimono: Hollywood Censorship and the Production Code from the 1920s to the 1960s*. New York: Grove Weidenfeld, 1990.

McWilliams, John P. *The American Epic: Transforming a Genre, 1770–1860*. Cambridge: Cambridge University Press, 1989.

———. "Red Satan: Cooper and the American Indian Epic." In *James Fenimore Cooper: New Critical Essays*, 143–61. Robert Clark, ed. New York: Vision Press, 1985.

Milder, Robert. "*The Last of the Mohicans* and the New World Fall." *American Literature* 52 (1980): 407–29.

Peck, H. Daniel. *A World By Itself: The Pastoral Moment in Cooper's Fiction*. New Haven: Yale University Press, 1977.

Philbrick, Thomas. "*The Last of the Mohicans* and the Sounds of Discord." *American Literature* 43 (1971): 25–41.

———. "The Sources of Cooper's Knowledge of Fort William Henry." *American Literature* 36 (1964): 209–14.

Schachterle, Lance, and Kent Ljungquist. "Fenimore Cooper's Literary Defenses: Twain and the Text of *The Deerslayer*." In *Studies in the American Renaissance*, 401–17. Joel Myerson ed. Charlottesville: University Press of Virginia, 1988.

Sealsfield, Charles. "The Works of the Author of the Spy." *New-York Mirror* Feb. 12, 1831: 252–54.

Stone, William Leete. Review of *The Last of the Mohicans*, by James Fenimore Cooper. *Commercial Advertiser*, Feb. 6, 1826: 162.

Twain, Mark. "Fenimore Cooper's Literary Offences." *North American Review* 161 (1895): 1–12.

Walsh, Robert. Review of *The Last of the Mohicans*, by James Fenimore Cooper. *National Gazette* Feb. 18, 1826: 138.

Playing Indian in the Nineties
Pocahontas and *The Indian in the Cupboard*

Hollywood has long taken a leading role in shaping the American tradition of "playing Indian." This chapter considers how this tradition is mobilized in two family films released in 1995: Disney's heavily marketed *Pocahontas* and the Columbia/Paramount adaptation of Lynne Reid Banks's popular children's novel *The Indian in the Cupboard.* Borrowing a concept from Donna Haraway, I would place my "situated knowledge" of these films and their associated playthings at the intersection of, first, my scholarly interest in the production and significance of imagined Indians in Anglo-American culture; second, my memories of "playing Indian" at school, at summer camp, and in Camp Fire Girls during my childhood; and, finally, my experiences rearing two daughters (ages seven and ten when the films were released). In other words, this is what Kathleen Stewart would call a "contaminated" critique, one that is complexly influenced by my participation in the cultural phenomena that it analyzes. I write as a pianist who has played "Colors Of The Wind" (the theme song from *Pocahontas*) so often for my daughters' school choir that it runs unbidden through my mind; as a parent who has spent much of a weekend "playing Indian" on CD-ROM, helping seven-year-old Tina "earn symbols" for a computer-generated wampum belt so that we could be inducted as "Friends of the Iroquois"; and, above all, as a cultural critic whose views are influenced both by the insights of my daughters and by my hopes for their generation.

As I sit at my computer composing this essay, a three-inch plastic Indian stands beside the monitor. He wears a scalp lock, yellow leggings and breechcloth, a yellow knife sheath, and a yellow pouch. Next to him is the case for our videocassette of *The Indian in the Cupboard,* with the cover reversed, as directed, so that the case simulates a weathered wooden

Figure 12.1. Video, CD-ROM, and plastic versions of *The Indian in the Cupboard*. The cupboard is made by reversing the cover of the video case. The other side pictures Omri holding the miniature Indian and announces "FREE! Indian, Cupboard and Key Included!" Photo © 1997 by Suzanne McEndree.

cabinet. Beside the cabinet is a plastic skeleton key, almost as large as the miniature Indian, that can be used to open the cabinet. Although it is possible to purchase the Indian figurine and the key independently, as well as figurines of other characters in the film, ours were packaged with the video, just as a locket was packaged with *The Little Princess.*

Equipped with the miniature Indian, the cabinet, and the key, I can, if I wish, imitate Omri, the nine-year-old American boy whose coming-of-age story is told in the film. Omri, like his English namesake in the novel, is given an Indian figurine that comes to life when locked inside a magical cabinet. My figurine does not come to life, but it nevertheless mocks me as it stands by my computer, underscoring my embeddedness in several traditions—European and Anglo-American, popular and schol-arly—that have locked miniature Indians in cabinets, be they late-Re-naissance wonder cabinets, children's toy collections, tourists' and collectors' displays, or museum dioramas.

If I wish to simulate Omri's mastery over life I must turn to the CD-ROM version of *The Indian in the Cupboard,* where with my cursor I can animate an Indian figurine—one that, like the miniatures that open the film, appears to be "antique," made of painted porcelain or wood rather than plastic. The figurine reminds me of a miniature cigar-store Indian or a ship's figurehead, as do the seven other Indian figurines on Omri's toy shelf. When I move the cursor in order to place the figurine in the cabi-net and turn the key, it "comes to life" and begins to talk to me. Like Omri's miniature friend in the film, this animated Indian is named Little Bear. He identifies himself as an Onondaga of the Wolf clan and intro-duces me to his Ungachis, his "friends" on the toy shelf. He gives me the name of Henuyeha, or "player."[1] I accompany Little Bear to a promon-tory overlooking his palisaded village, where his people live in three longhouses.

Descending to the village I meet the Ungachis, whom I will later bring to life as my guides. I recall the many American Indians who have made their living as guides for hunters or anthropologists, as well as the YMCA organization Indian Guides, to which my brother and father once belonged (an organization parodied to good effect in the Disney film *Man of the House*). Foremost among my Onondaga "friends" is a clan mother, Gentle Breeze, who will introduce me to Onondaga words, stories, and symbols referring to the ancestors of the clans—Turtle, Bear, Wolf, Snipe, Beaver, Hawk, Deer, and Eel—as well as to the underwater Panther, the Keeper of the Winds and his Spirit Animals, the Peacemaker, and the Tree of Peace. Another Ungachi, a "chief" named He Knows the Sky, will point out and tell me stories about Grandmother Moon, the Path of the

Figure 12.2. The miniature Indians pictured during the credits to *The Indian in the Cupboard* and in the cupboard in the CD-ROM video game are reminiscent of nineteenth-century "cigar store Indians." The life-size wooden figure depicted here, dating from about 1865, stood in the streets of Cleveland, Ohio. It was painted about 1937 by Eugene Croe as part of a WPA folk art project. *Cigar Store Indian,* Index of American Design, © Board of Trustees, National Gallery of Art, Washington.

Dead, the Bear, the Seven Children, and Star Girl. ("What I like about the Onondaga," says ten-year-old Katie upon hearing the story of how Star Girl guided the starving people home, "is that it's not only boys and men who do important things.")

An Ungachi named Shares the Songs will teach me to play water drums, a flute, and a variety of rattles, challenging me to remember ever more complex rhythms. Swift Hunter will teach me to recognize and follow animal tracks, while Keeper of the Words will show me how to make a headdress in the style of each of the Six Nations of the League of the Onondaga. Two children will teach me their games: from Blooming Flower I will learn how to decorate carved templates with beads; from Runs with the Wind, how to play a challenging memory game with seeds of corn, squash, and several varieties of beans.

Succeeding in these various activities requires patience, attentiveness, and a well-developed memory. Each time I succeed I am rewarded with a symbol for my "wampum belt" and the kind of effusive praise Anglo-

American children expect. Upon its completion a ceremony is held to present me with the wampum belt and to name me an Ungachi, a "Friend of the Iroquois." I am feasted with a meal of corn, pumpkin, potatoes, squash, deer, roasted turkey, and cornbread. This concludes the ceremony, which I have experienced as a disconcerting example of what Michael Taussig calls "mimetic excess." The resonances are many and diverse: Camp Fire Girl "council fires" at which, proudly wearing my deerskin "ceremonial gown" and the beads I had "earned," I paid homage to Wohelo ("Work, Health, Love"); campfires under the stars at Camp Wilaha and Camp Kotami; classroom lessons and plays about the first Thanksgiving; the councils of "The Grand Order of the Iroquois," a fraternal organization founded by anthropologist Louis Henry Morgan (Bieder); the assimilationist group of reformers known as the "Friends of the Indian" (Prucha); and Vine Deloria's caustic dismissal of "anthropologists and other friends" in *Custer Died for Your Sins.*

Despite my initial discomfort with the power of bringing miniature Onondagas to life—and especially with the power to turn them back into mute "plastic"—I find myself intrigued and charmed by this simulated world. So is Tina, whose favorite game is one in which we bring an English trader to life and barter with him for trade goods. In the process we learn a fair amount about Iroquois hunting, farming, manufactures, and desires for trade goods. (The other Anglo-American figurine—and the only character drawn from the film besides Little Bear—is the cowardly cowboy Boone, with whom we experience the terrors of Omri's room from the perspective of a person three inches in height.) By the time Tina and I are presented with our wampum belts, we have been introduced to many aspects of Onondaga life in the early eighteenth century: the forest, the river, and the clearing; the architecture and layout of the village; corn, beans, and squash, the Three Sisters; the powers of various animals; the Onondaga names and legends of the moon, Milky Way, and several constellations; the manufacture of goods and the practice of reciprocity; the importance of clans and clan matrons. We have heard many Onondaga words and learned to recognize a few. With the exception of the trader and his goods, however, we have encountered no evidence of Iroquois relations with European colonists or with other indigenous peoples.

Little Bear's world is one of order, beauty, and tranquility, free of disruptions from warfare, disease, displacement, or Christian evangelism. It serves simultaneously to arouse powerful feelings of nostalgia and nostalgic feelings of power. This is a world under control; a world in which people treat each other with respect; a world pervaded by the soothing, rhythmic music of flutes, rattles, and vocables. It is a world in which human relationships tend to be free of conflict, a world in which—as both the textual and celluloid Omri teaches his friend Patrick—"you can't use people" (Banks, *Indian* 129). That we enter this world through the conceit of controlling the lives of miniature Indians and "mastering" the knowledge they have to teach us; that in this world the stereotypical Iroquois warrior is replaced by people living outside of history; that we feel we can be "Friends of the Iroquois" without confronting the political and economic claims that very friendship would make upon us, whether in 1720— the era in which the CD-ROM is set—or today: such ironies pervade *The Indian in the Cupboard* in all its incarnations.

Destabilizing stereotypes is tricky, as others easily rush in to fill a void. In L.R. Banks's original series of four novels, the figure of Little Bear explicitly replaces the stereotypical Plains Indian with a more localized and complexly rendered representation. When Little Bear comes to life, he does not live up to Omri's expectations of an Indian: he lives in a longhouse rather than a tipi, walks rather than rides a horse, and is unaware of the custom of becoming "blood brothers." In other ways, however, Little Bear more than meets stereotypical expectations: he is a fierce "Iroquois brave" who has taken some thirty scalps; he is volatile, demanding, and interested in "firewater"; he becomes "restive" while watching a Western on television; his English is broken and, early on, mixed with grunts and snarls; he initially thinks of Omri as the "Great White Spirit," only to be disillusioned when the boy fails to live up to his expectations of a deity (20–23, 148). Even so, the most racist typifications are voiced not by the narrator but by "Boohoo" Boone—who, when brought to life, denigrates "Injuns" and "redskins" as "ornery," "savage," and "dirty," only to be convinced otherwise by Omri and Little Bear (99–101). These passages and cover illustrations reminiscent of nineteenth-century dime novels have attracted some criticism (Slapin and Seale 121–22), but the moral of the tale is clear: although Omri at first cherishes his power over Little Bear, calling him "my Indian," he comes to respect Little Bear as an autonomous human being with his own life, times, country, language, and desires (Banks, *Indian* 70, 82).

Lynne Reid Banks is an Englishwoman who spent the war years in Saskatchewan, and the friendship between Omri and Little Bear plays on the alliance between the English and Iroquois during the French and Indian War (1754–63). The historical context of the books, however, is almost completely absent in both the film and the CD-ROM, which transpose Omri from England to New York City. In contrast to the CD-ROM, the film takes place completely in Omri's world, except for a brief visionlike sequence in Little Bear's world. For this reason the film has far less

Onondaga content than the CD-ROM, though what there is has been carefully rendered, following the advice of Onondaga consultants Jeanne Shenandoah[2] and Oren Lyons (Yankowitz 31). Nevertheless, the film is just as nostalgic as the CD-ROM. When Little Bear, preparing to return to his own time, asks whether the Onondaga are always a great people, Omri sadly answers in the affirmative, then reluctantly reveals that "it isn't always so good" for them. This is indisputable, but the scene misses a valuable opportunity to show something of the resiliency and the contemporary life of Iroquois people. Portrayed in the past or in miniature, and without visible descendants, Little Bear is out of place, out of time, and an object of intense longing (as Susan Stewart has suggested for miniatures more generally). The film does nothing to help viewers imagine Little Bear's descendants as persons who share a world with Omri even as they share a tradition with Little Bear.

Nevertheless, the film is more successful than the book or CD-ROM in presenting Little Bear as far more than a typification. As played by the Cherokee rap artist Litefoot (Yankowitz), Little Bear dominates the film, even at three inches tall. This Little Bear is not to be patronized. He earns Omri's respect and teaches him to appreciate the awesome responsibility that comes with power over other human beings. Given their relationship, it is particularly jarring to have power over Little Bear, voiced by Litefoot, when playing Omri's role on the CD-ROM. The CD-ROM encourages the Henuyeha, in the spirit of playful learning, to mimic just what Omri learned *not* to do—albeit in the spirit of understanding Little Bear's world. It is doubly disconcerting to possess a plastic figurine of Little Bear. Omri's rejection of objectifying human beings was, predictably, lost on the marketing department—and doubtless on many of its young targets, who may well have added Little Bear to their collection of *Pocahontas*-related figurines from Burger King.

Although the marketing of *The Indian in the Cupboard* and its translation onto CD-ROM undercuts the narrative's critique of objectifying and manipulating human beings, the tensions and contradictions among the message, the medium, and the marketing of Disney's *Pocahontas* are far more blatant. On one level *Pocahontas* can be dismissed as a commercial product through which Disney's powerful marketing machine has revived and exploited the public's perennial fascination with playing Indian—"bringing an American legend to life" in order to hawk beads, baubles, and trinkets to would-be Indian princesses and to those who would seek to please them.[3] On another level, however, Disney's interpretation of the Pocahontas legend—which, following Sommer, we might call the United States' "foundational romance"—makes a serious statement about ethnocentrism, androcentrism, commodification, and exploitation as barriers to the dream of interethnic harmony that Smith and Pocahontas represent. Disney's *Pocahontas* purports to offer a far broader and more devastating cultural critique than *The Indian in the Cupboard:* a critique of the commodity form itself, albeit a consummately commodified critique.

To consider *Pocahontas* in terms of how it meets the challenges posed by its own message takes us beyond the usual attempts to measure the film solely against an uncertain and elusive historical reality. Pocahontas may be the first "real-life figure" to be featured in a Disney film, but the pre-Disney Pocahontas was already a highly mythologized heroine known only through colonial and nationalist representations—from the beginning, a product of Anglo-American desire. Disney has drawn on various versions of what Rayna Green calls "the Pocahontas perplex," giving new life and ubiquitous circulation to those versions deemed resonant with contemporary preoccupations. That is to say, the animated Pocahontas is located within the colonial and neocolonial tradition of noble savagism that Berkhofer analyzes in *The White Man's Indian:* the natural virtues she embodies and self-sacrifice she offers are those found in Montaigne and Rousseau, Thoreau and Cooper, Helen Hunt Jackson and *Dances with Wolves.* This is not to imply, to be sure, that Pocahontas is entirely a product of Western colonialism, but that we "know" her only within that arena—which, after all, is tantamount to not knowing her very well at all.

Outside of promotional material, the film's message is articulated most fully in "Colors Of The Wind," the Academy Award–winning song advertised as summing up "the entire spirit and essence of the film." Responding to Smith's recitation of all that the English can teach the "savages," Pocahontas chides him for thinking "the only people who are people" are those who "look and think" like him. Adapting a famous saying of Will Rogers, she urges Smith to "walk the footsteps of a stranger," promising that he will learn things he "never knew" he "never knew."[4] This Pocahontas is, above all, a teacher. Not, as one might expect, a teacher of the Powhatan language, culture, and standards of diplomacy, for the time-consuming process of learning to translate across cultural and linguistic borders is finessed through her mystical ability, as another song puts it, to "Listen With Your Heart." Rather, Pocahontas, a veritable child of nature, is a teacher of tolerance and respect for all life.

This unfortunate impoverishment of Pocahontas's teachings produces a truly awkward moment in the film, when Pocahontas magically switches from English to her native language on first encountering Smith. ("She was just speaking English a moment ago!" observed my daughters when they first saw this scene.) Although a few Algonquian words are

Figure 12.3. This seventeenth-century engraving of Pocahontas's rescue of John Smith initiated the visual iconography that the Disney animated film continues almost four centuries later. Robert Vaughan, "King Powhatan commands Capt. Smith to be slain," in John Smith, *The Generall Historie of Virginia . . .* (1624). Photo courtesy of the Edward E. Ayer Collection, The Newberry Library.

sprinkled through the film, and Smith learns how to say "hello" and "goodbye," Disney's *Pocahontas* gives no sense of the intelligence, dedication, patience, and humility needed to "learn things you never knew you never knew." In being figured within the series of recent Disney heroines that includes Ariel, Beauty, and Jasmine (of *The Little Mermaid*, *Beauty and the Beast*, and *Aladdin*, respectively), this most famous of North American cultural mediators is removed from the series that also includes Malinche, Sacajawea, and Sarah Winnemucca. The ability to "listen with your heart" conquers all cultural distance for Pocahontas and John Smith.

This is not to say that it is entirely implausible that Pocahontas teaches Smith tolerance and respect for all life. One of the subtly effective moments in the film is the animated sequence corresponding to the passage in "Colors Of The Wind" about walking in the footsteps of a stranger. The footsteps shown are the tracks of a Bear Person, a concept as unfamiliar to most film viewers as it is to John Smith. "Colors Of The Wind" challenges not only ethnocentrism but also androcentrism, and the bear scene goes beyond Disney's ordinary anthropomorphizing to open a window onto an animistic view of the world. More often, however, Pocahontas's relationship to animals (for example, to Meeko the raccoon and Flit the hummingbird) is trivialized,[5] appearing not unlike Cinderella's relationship with her friends, the mice and birds, in the classic Disney film.

In another verse of "Colors Of The Wind" Pocahontas contrasts Smith's utilitarian and possessive thinking with her own intimate knowledge of nature. She scolds Smith for seeing the earth as "just a dead thing you can claim," for she knows that each rock, tree, and creature "has a life, has a spirit, has a name." Then, in the most sensual sequence of the film—or indeed of any previous Disney animation—Pocahontas entices Smith to run through the forest's hidden trails, to taste the earth's sun-ripened berries, to roll in the grasses of the meadow, enjoying all these riches "for once" without wondering "what they're worth." The seductive and precocious Pocahontas, who stalks Smith like a wildcat and then rolls with him in the grass, is a "free spirit" who embodies the joys of belonging to an enchanted and uncommodified world. This is not the first time the young Pocahontas has been sexualized—precedents include Smith's own writings as well as John Barth's *The Sot-Weed Factor*—but it is a startling departure for a Disney children's film. Pocahontas's overt sexuality no doubt has multiple motivations, but at one level it marks her as an intrinsic part of the natural world (as a "tribal Eve," according to Supervising Animator Glen Keane) (Hochswender 156).

It is the clear contrast between utilitarian possessiveness and sensual spirituality in scenes and lyrics like these that Russell Means pointed to in calling *Pocahontas* "the single finest work ever done on American Indians by Hollywood" by virtue of being "willing to tell the truth." But the film's critique of capitalist appropriation is enunciated by the same Pocahontas whose licensed image saturates the marketplace—along with that of her father, Powhatan, who, even more ironically, is modeled after and voiced by the same Russell Means who has demonstrated against the use of Indian images as mascots for sports teams. One can only wonder: what is the exotic, sensual, copyrighted Pocahontas if not the mascot for a feminine, earthy, New Age spirituality?

An eager and willing student of Pocahontas, John Smith learns to see maize as the true "riches" of Powhatan's land and presents the gold-hungry Governor Ratcliffe with a golden ear of corn. The play on "golden" makes for an effective scene, but totally excluded from the film is that other sacred American plant, tobacco, which became the salvation of the Virginia economy thanks to John Rolfe, the husband of a mature, Christian, and anglicized Pocahontas never seen in the film. Is this story—told in Barbour's biography and elsewhere—reserved for *Pocahontas II*? Probably not, for the historical Pocahontas's capture by the English as a hostage, transformation into Lady Rebecca Rolfe, and fatal illness during a trip to London does not resonate as well with an Anglo-American audience's expectations as the legend of Smith's capture and salvation by an innocent, loving, and self-sacrificing child of nature.[6]

Resonating with expectations, of course, is what creating a "timeless, universal, and uniquely satisfying motion picture experience" is all about. In imagining Pocahontas the filmmakers relied to some extent on consultation with Native people and scholars, but more on what resonated with their own experiences, desires, and sense of "authenticity" (so central to the Anglo-American tradition of "playing Indian," as Jay Mechling has pointed out). Lyricist Stephen Schwartz said of the composition of "Colors Of The Wind" that "we were able to find the parts of ourselves that beat in synchronicity with Pocahontas," while animator Keane declared, "I'm cast as Pocahontas in the film" (Hochswender 156). I suppose this is something like listening with one's heart, but there is a significant tension between such identification and "walk[ing] the footsteps of a stranger." This is not the Pocahontas we never knew we never knew, but the Pocahontas we knew all along, the Pocahontas whose story is "universal"—that is, familiar, rather than strange and shocking and particular. This is a Pocahontas whose tale, like that of Simba in *The Lion King* or Omri in *The Indian in the Cupboard*, fits into the mold of the Western coming-of-age story: Pocahontas, yearning to see (as the song goes) "Just Around

Figure 12.4. The film's Pocahontas is shown with her father Powhatan, modeled after the Indian who provided the voice of Powhatan, Russell Means. From Disney's *Pocahontas*. © 1995 Disney Enterprises, Inc.

The Riverbend," grows from youthful irresponsibility to mature self-knowledge through courage and love. It is a Pocahontas who speaks what is known in anthologies (for example, Suzuki and Knudtson) as "the wisdom of the elders," and communes with a Grandmother Willow who appears to be a kindly descendant of the animated trees in *Babes in Toyland*. It is a Pocahontas who, despite a tattoo and over-the-shoulder dress loosely consistent with John White's watercolors of sixteenth-century coastal Algonquians (Hulton, Josephy 183–93), has a Barbie-doll figure, an Asian model's glamour (Hochswender), and an instant attraction to a distinctly Nordic John Smith. In short, Disney has created a New Age Pocahontas embodying Americans' millennial dreams for wholeness and harmony while banishing our nightmares of savagery without and emptiness within.

Just as the dream of tolerance and respect for all life is voiced in song, so too is the nightmare of savagery and emptiness. While the dream is figured as feminine and Indian in the lyrical "Colors Of The Wind," the nightmare is presented as masculine and—at least initially—English in the driving and brutal "Savages." Mobilizing stereotypes akin to Boohoo Boone's, but considerably more vicious, this song describes Pocahontas's people as worse than vermin, as "filthy little heathens" whose "skin's a hellish red," as a cursed and disgusting race, as evil, "barely human," and "only good when dead."

Figure 12.5. John G. Chapman's *Baptism of Pocahontas at Jamestown, Virginia, 1613* (1837-47) hangs in the Rotunda of the U.S. Capitol. Contrasting markedly with Disney's representation of the young Pocahontas whose ultimate loyalty was to her people, Chapman's painting memorializes her conversion to Christianity. Her future husband, John Rolfe, stands behind her; her Powhatan family (in the right foreground) are relegated to the shadows, their dark clothing signifying savagery in contrast to the brilliant white of Pocahontas's English gown. Courtesy of the Architect of the Capitol.

"Savages" presents, at its dehumanizing extreme, the ideology of ignoble savagism—less typical, as Bernard Sheehan has shown, of the earliest years of the Jamestown colony than of the years after 1622, when Powhatan's kinsman Opechancanough launched a war of resistance against the English. In the context of the film, however, appearing as the English prepare to attack the Powhatan people, it is extremely effective, serving ironically to underscore the savagery of the English colonists rather than that of the "heathen." Earlier, in the opening to "Colors Of The Wind," Pocahontas had gently challenged the ideology of ignoble savagism by asking Smith why, if it was she who was the "ignorant savage," there was so very much he did not know. Characterized as wise and gentle, if mischievous and spirited, Pocahontas is clearly not an ignorant savage. With this already established, the colonists' rhetoric of savagery turns back upon them—at least until Powhatan, advised by a diviner, leads his people in a similar chorus, calling the "paleface" a soulless, bloodless demon distinguished only by his greed. It is the English who are "different from us," who are untrustworthy killers, who are "savages."

Figure 12.6. Pocahontas and John Smith converse with Grandmother Willow, a "four-hundred-year-old tree spirit." From Disney's *Pocahontas*. © 1995 Disney Enterprises, Inc.

Powhatan's portion of "Savages" purports to offer a portrait of the English colonists from the point of view of the colonized. Given what has gone on thus far in the film, and what we know of subsequent history, the accusation rings true. But this passage, too, ultimately rebounds against those who utter it. John Smith is captured and laid out, the executioner's tomahawk is raised, Smith is about to be mercilessly executed . . . and Pocahontas throws her body upon his, successfully pleading with her father for his life. The savagery of fear and intolerance is vanquished through the power of "listen[ing] with your heart."

So the story goes, in Smith's telling, at least. It may be, as Gleach suggests, that this was all an elaborate adoption ceremony in which Smith became a vassal of Powhatan, who ruled over an expanding group of villages. It may be, as I have proposed (in "Captivity in White and Red"), that Pocahontas was playing a traditional female role in choosing between life and death for a sacrificial victim. It may be that the incident is best understood as part of Smith's imaginative and self-serving fabrication of himself—what Greenblatt calls "Renaissance self-fashioning." I would not fault Disney for repeating the rescue as it is commonly known in a film advertised as "an American legend," but the litany "Savages! Savages!" is quite another matter. Its ideological work, in the end, is to level the English and the Powhatan people to the same state of ethnocentric brutishness, portraying ignoble savagism as natural and universal rather

Figure 12.7. John White's 1585 watercolor "A chief werowance's wife of Pomeiooc and her daughter of the age of 8 or 10 years" served as a model for Disney's precocious Pocahontas. The artist's fine eye for detail captured the woman's tatoos, deerskin apron, and freshwater pearls. The girl carries an English doll, probably obtained from a member of the English expedition to Roanoke. North Carolina Collection, University of North Carolina Library at Chapel Hill. © The Trustees of the British Museum, British Museum Press.

than as having particular cultural and historical roots. When these lyrics are disseminated outside the context of the film, in songbooks and on the soundtrack, they may have a particularly harmful impact upon a young and impressionable audience. We don't play the soundtrack in our house, but friends with younger children tell me that, to their horror, they have caught their children singing "Savages, Savages" among themselves, having internalized a racist epithet that remains potent and degrading.[7]

The filmmakers are quite aware that they are in risky territory here and characterize the episode as dealing with "one of the most adult themes ever in a Disney film." The theme is "the ugliness and stupidity that results when people give in to racism and intolerance," and it is refreshing to have it aired, particularly by a studio with a history, even recently, of racist animation. But a more responsible treatment of the theme would be considerably more nuanced, distinguishing between English colonialism and Powhatan resistance, and between the English ideology of savagism and coastal Algonquian attitudes toward their own enemies—whom, as Helen Rountree shows, they generally aimed to politically subordinate and socially incorporate, rather than exterminate and dispossess. This could be done by telling more of Pocahontas's and Powhatan's subsequent dealings with Smith, whom they treated, respectively, as "brother" and *weroance* (a ruler subordinate to Powhatan, the *manamatowick* or supreme ruler).

That *Pocahontas* raises a number of difficult and timely issues is a tribute to its ambition and seriousness of purpose. Indeed, the film begs to be taken as a plea for tolerant, respectful, and harmonious living in a world torn by prejudice, exploitation, ethnic strife, and environmental degradation. So, too, does *The Indian in the Cupboard,* albeit in a more limited fashion. That both films and their associated products and promotions are rife with tensions and ironies exemplifies the limitations of serious cultural critique in an artistic environment devoted to the marketing of dreams. That our children are bombarded with plastic consumables and impoverished caricatures while being admonished to treat other cultures, other creatures, and the land with respect should prompt us to find ways to teach them—and learn from them—the difference between producing and consuming objectified difference, on the one hand, and sustaining respectful relationships across difference, on the other.

In a society founded on objectification, differentiation, and commodification the lesson is a hard one, and one that has characteristically been expressed in an oppositional "Indian" voice. If *Pocahontas* and *The Indian in the Cupboard* can be viewed only with ambivalence because of their own participation in processes of objectification and commodification, the forms of "playing Indian" to which each gives rise may offer genuine possibilities for unlearning these processes and imagining new ones, that is, for learning things we never knew we never knew.[8]

"I love that part of the song," Katie has told me, and Tina and I agree. We often find ourselves singing Pocahontas's lines, and sometimes we stop to wonder at the paradoxical form of learning they suggest. As a first step on a transformative journey, we locked the plastic Indian in his video-case cupboard once and for all and stepped outside to find Star Girl in the night sky.

Notes

This essay, dedicated to Jane Cauvel upon her retirement from The Colorado College, is adapted from "Animated Indians: Critique and Contradiction in Commodified Children's Culture," *Cultural Anthropology* 11, 3 (August 1996): 405–24. It is published here with the permission of the American Anthropological Association. While certain new material is included, the original version contains more extensive references and acknowledgments, as well as lyrics and illustrations that were deleted from this version because of copyright restrictions.

1. Onondaga words are treated more or less as proper names on the CD-ROM, and I have anglicized them in this essay. Consulting the sparse published documentation on the Onondaga language, I am delighted to find that Little Bear's term for "player," Henuyeha, is a nominalization of the form used for playing the indigenous game of lacrosse (Hewitt 625). The term for "friend" that I anglicize as Ungachi is transcribed as *onguiatsi, mon ami* in Shea's French-Onondaga dictionary.

2. Jeanne Shenandoah was also a consultant for the CD-ROM, as were Rick Hill and Huron Miller.

3. This and subsequent unattributed quotations are taken from Disney press releases.

4. Paraphrasing the lyrics to "Colors Of The Wind" (because of copyright restrictions) does an injustice to Stephen Schwartz's fine poetry, which may be found in song books and on the notes to the soundtrack.

5. The trivialization of Pocahontas's relationship to animals was brought to my attention by a chastening response to the review of *Pocahontas* I posted on H-Net on June 30, 1995. On the electronic list devoted to "teaching social studies in secondary schools," Paul Dennis Gower Sr. replied, "PUHLEASE!!!!!! It is, after all, a cartoon. It has a talking raccoon, for crying out loud."

6. The rest of Pocahontas's story would make for an intriguing drama indeed if treated something like Disney's underpublicized *Squanto: A Warrior's Tale*, which does not hesitate to portray the brutality of Squanto's English kidnappers as well as a likely course of events leading to Squanto's allegiance to the English settlers at Plymouth. *Pocahontas: Her True Story*, a televised biography from the Arts & Entertainment network, provides a useful counterpoint to the Disney film but

does not do justice to Pocahontas's tale or to the historical context of visual imagery (which is treated transparently as illustrative material, unlike the more historicized treatments of Josephy and Strong's "Search for Otherness").

7. This was a key objection of an open letter regarding *Pocahontas* posted by more than a hundred members of the NatChat listserv on July 18, 1995.

8. This outcome—utopian, perhaps, but consistent with Omri's own course of development—requires that commodified images be taken as "teachable moments" pointing toward more complex, less objectified, understandings.

Works Cited

Banks, Lynne Reid. *The Indian and the Cupboard.* New York: Doubleday, 1981.
———. *The Mystery of the Cupboard.* New York: William Morrow, 1993.
———. *The Return of the Indian.* New York: Doubleday, 1986.
———. *The Secret of the Indian.* New York: Doubleday, 1989.
Barbour, Philip. *Pocahontas and Her World.* Boston: Houghton Mifflin, 1969.
Barth, John. *The Sot-Weed Factor.* Toronto: Bantam Books, 1980.
Berkhofer, Robert F. *The White Man's Indian: Images of the American Indian from Columbus to the Present.* New York: Random House, 1977.
Bieder, Robert E. "The Grand Order of the Iroquois: Influences on Lewis Henry Morgan's Ethnology." *Ethnohistory* 27 (1980):349–61.
Deloria, Vine. *Custer Died for Your Sins: An Indian Manifesto.* New York: Macmillan, 1969.
Gleach, Frederick W. "Interpreting the Saga of Pocahontas and Captain John Smith." In *Reading Beyond Words: Contexts for Native History,* 21–42. Ed. Jennifer S.H. Brown and Elizabeth Vibert, eds. Peterborough, Ontario: Broadview Press, 1996.
Green, Rayna. "The Pocahontas Perplex: The Image of Indian Women in American Culture." *Massachusetts Review* 16, 4 (1975): 698–714.
Greenblatt, Stephen. *Renaissance Self-Fashioning: From More to Shakespeare.* Chicago: University of Chicago Press, 1980.
Haraway, Donna J. *Simians, Cyborgs, and Women: The Reinvention of Nature.* New York: Routledge, 1991.
Hewitt, J.N.B. "Iroquoian Cosmology, Second Part." *43rd Annual Report of the Bureau of American Ethnology, 1925–26.* Washington, D.C.: U.S. Government Printing Office, 1928.
Hochswender, Woody. "Pocahontas: A Babe in the Woods." *Harper's Bazaar* (June 1995): 154–57.
Hulton, Paul. *America 1585: The Complete Drawings of John White.* Chapel Hill: University of North Carolina Press and British Musuem Press, 1984.
Jennings, Francis. *The Invasion of America: Colonialism and the Cant of Conquest.* New York: W.W. Norton, 1975.
Josephy, Alvin M., Jr. *Five Hundred Nations: An Illustrated History of North American Indians.* New York: Alfred A. Knopf, 1994.

Mechling, Jay. "'Playing Indian' and the Search for Authenticity in Modern White America." *Prospects* 5 (1980): 17–33.

Prucha, Francis Paul. *Americanizing the American Indians: Writings by the "Friends of the Indian," 1880–1900.* Cambridge: Harvard University Press, 1973.

Rountree, Helen. *The Powhatan Indians of Virginia: Their Traditional Culture.* Norman: University of Oklahoma Press, 1989.

Sharpes, Donald K. "Princess Pocahontas, Rebecca Rolfe (1595–1617)." *American Indian Culture and Research Journal* 19, 4 (1995): 231–39.

Shea, John Gilmary. *A French-Onondaga Dictionary, from a Manuscript of the Seventeenth Century.* 1860. New York: AMS Press, 1970.

Sheehan, Bernard W. *Savagism and Civility: Indians and Englishmen in Colonial Virginia.* Cambridge: Cambridge University Press, 1980.

Slapin, Beverly, and Doris Seale. *Through Indian Eyes: The Native Experience in Books for Children.* Philadelphia: New Society Publishers, 1992.

Smith, John. "A True Relation of Such Occurrences and Accidents of Noate as Hath Hapned in Virginia." In *The Complete Works of Captain John Smith (1580–1631)*, 1:3–117. Philip L. Barbour, ed. Chapel Hill: University of North Carolina Press, 1986.

———. "The Generall Historie of Virginia, New England, and the Summer Isles." In *The Complete Works of Captain John Smith (1580–1631)*, 2. Philip L. Barbour, ed. Chapel Hill: University of North Carolina Press, 1986.

Sommer, Doris. *Foundational Fictions: The National Romances of Latin America.* Berkeley and Los Angeles: University of California Press, 1991.

Stewart, Kathleen. "On the Politics of Cultural Theory: A Case for 'Contaminated' Cultural Critique." *Social Research* 58, 2 (1991): 395–412.

Stewart, Susan. *On Longing: Narratives of the Miniature, the Gigantic, the Souvenir, the Collection.* Durham, N.C.: Duke University Press, 1993.

Strong, Pauline Turner. "Captivity in White and Red." In *Crossing Cultures: Essays in the Displacement of Western Civilization*, 33–104. Daniel Segal, ed. Tucson: University of Arizona Press, 1992.

———. "The Search for Otherness." In *Invisible America: Unearthing Our Hidden History*, 24–25. Mark P. Leone and Neil Asher Silberman, eds. New York: Henry Holt, 1995.

Suzuki, David, and Peter Knudtsen. *Wisdom of the Elders: Sacred Native Stories of Nature.* New York: Bantam, 1992.

Taussig, Michael. *Mimesis and Alterity: A Particular History of the Senses.* New York: Routledge, 1993.

Yankowitz, Joan. *Behind the Scenes of "The Indian in the Cupboard."* New York: Scholastic, 1995.

⟨ Bibliography / Steven Mintz

Western Films
The Context for Hollywood's Indian

Preliminary Note: Most essays in this collection have a section for works cited, a segment designed to point students of the Hollywood Indian in directions for further study. However, it is most important to remember that Hollywood's Indian was affected by a popular genre, the Western film. Not every Western film comments on Native American culture, but the Western film genre helps define basic images of the frontier for viewers. Anyone interested in the Hollywood Indian must gain some understanding of the mise-en-scène and dynamics of the Western film.

Bibliographies

Nachbar, John G. *Western Films: An Annotated Critical Bibiliography*. New York: Garland, 1975.

Nachbar, John G., Jackie R. Donath, and Chris Foran. *Western Films 2: An Annotated Critical Bibliography from 1974 to 1987*. New York: Garland, 1988.

Credits

Lentz, Harris M., III. *Western and Frontier Film and Television Credits, 1903–1995*. Jefferson, N.C.: McFarland, 1996.

Film Adaptations

Hitt, Jim. *The American West from Fiction (1823–1976) into Film (1909–1986)*. Jefferson, N.C.: McFarland, 1990.

Filmography

Eyles, Allen. *The Western*. South Brunswick, N.J.: A.S. Barnes, 1975.

Guides and Encyclopedias

Adams, Les, and Buck Rainey. *Shoot-Em Ups: The Complete Reference Guide to Westerns of the Sound Era*. New Rochelle, N.Y.: Arlington House, 1978.

Buscombe, Edward, ed. *The BFI Companion to the Western*. London: A. Deutsch, 1988.

Garfield, Brian. *Western Films: A Complete Guide*. New York: Da Capo Press, 1982.

Hardy, Phil. *The Western*. London: Aurum, 1991.

————, ed. *The Overlook Film Encyclopedia: The Western*. Woodstock, N.Y.: Overlook Press, 1994.

Holland, Ted. *B Western Actors Encyclopedia: Facts, Photos, and Filmographies for More Than 250 Familiar Faces*. Jefferson, N.C.: McFarland, 1989.

Histories and Interpretations of Westerns (Anglo-American)

Calder, Jenni. *There Must Be a Lone Ranger*. London: Hamilton, 1974.

Cawelti, John G. *The Six-Gun Mystique*. Bowling Green, Ohio: Bowling Green University Popular Press, 1971.

Davis, Robert Murray. *Playing Cowboys: Low Culture and High Art in the Western*. Norman: University of Oklahoma Press, 1991.

Everson, William K. *The Hollywood Western*. Secaucus, N.J.: Carol, 1992.

Fenin, George N., and William K. Everson. *The Western: From Silents to the Seventies*. New York: Penguin Books, 1977.

French, Philip. *Westerns: Aspects of a Movie Genre*. New York: Oxford University Press, 1977.

Kites, Demetrius John. *Horizons West: Anthony Mann, Budd Boetticher, Sam Peckinpah, Studies of Authorship within the Western*. Bloomington: Indiana University Press, 1970.

Lenihan, John H. *Showdown: Confronting Modern America in the Western Film*. Urbana: University of Illinois Press, 1980.

McDonald, Archie P., ed. *Shooting Stars: Heroes and Heroines of Western Film*. Bloomington: Indiana University Press, 1987.

Meyer, William R. *The Making of the Great Westerns*. New Rochelle, N.Y.: Arlington House, 1979.

Nachbar, John G., ed. *Focus on the Western*. Englewood Cliffs, N.J.: Prentice-Hall, 1974.

Parish, James Robert, and Michael R. Pitts. *Great Western Pictures*. Metuchen, N.J.: Scarecrow Press, 1976.

————. *Great Western Pictures II*. Metuchen, N.J.: Scarecrow Press, 1988.

Parks, Rita. *The Western Hero in Film and Television: Mass Media Mythology*. Ann Arbor: UMI Research Press, 1982.

Pilkington, William T., and Don Graham, eds. *Western Movies*. Albuquerque: University of New Mexico Press, 1979.

Rainey, Buck. *The Reel Cowboy: Essays on the Myth in Movies and Literature*. Jefferson, N.C.: McFarland, 1996.

Rothel, David. *Those Great Cowboy Sidekicks*. Metuchen, N.J.: Scarecrow Press, 1984.

Sarf, Wayne Michael. *God Bless You, Buffalo Bill: A Layman's Guide to History and the Western Film*. Rutherford, N.J.: Fairleigh Dickinson University Press, 1983.

Short, John R. *Imagined Country: Environment, Culture, and Society*. London: Routledge, Chapman, and Hall, 1991.

Slotkin, Richard. *Gunfighter Nation: The Myth of the Frontier in Twentieth-Century America*. New York: Atheneum, 1992.

Sullivan, Tom R. *Cowboys and Caudillos: Frontier Ideology of the Americas*. Bowling Green, Ohio: Bowling Green State University Popular Press, 1990.

Thomas, Tony. *The West That Never Was*. New York: Carol Communications, 1989.

Tompkins, Jane P. *West of Everything: The Inner Life of Westerns*. New York: Oxford University Press, 1992.

Tuska, Jon. *The American West in Film: Critical Approaches to the Western*. Westport, Conn.: Greenwood Press, 1985.

———. *The Filming of the West*. Garden City, N.Y.: Doubleday, 1976.

Wright, Will. *Six Guns and Society: A Structural Study of the Western*. Berkeley: University of California, 1975.

Histories and Interpretations of Westerns (European)

Bertelsen, Martin. *Roadmovies und Western: Ein Vergleich zur Genre-bestimmung des Roadmovies*. Ammersbek bei Hamburg: Verlag an der Lottbek, 1991.

Brion, Patrick. *Le Western: Classiques, Chefs-d'Oeuvre et Decouvertes*. Paris: Éditions de La Martiniere, 1992.

De Luca, Lorenzo. *C'era una Volta: Il Western Italiano*. Roma: Istituto Bibliografico Napoleone, 1987.

Di Claudio, Gianni. *Il Cinema western*. Chieti: Libreria Universitaria Editrice, 1986.

Gaberscel, Carlo. *Il West di John Ford*. Tavagnacco: Arti Grafiche Friulane, 1994.

Hanisch, Michael. *Western: Die Entwicklung eines Filmgenres*. Berlin: Henschelverlag, 1984.

Hembus, Joe. *Western-Geschichte, 1540 bis 1894: Chronologie, Mythologie, Filmographie*. Munich: C. Hanser, 1979.

———. *Western-Lexikon: 1272 Filme von 1894–1975*. Munich: Hanser Verlag, 1976.

Jeier, Thomas. *Der Westernfilm*. Munich: Wilhelm Heyne, 1987. Kartseva, E. *Vestern: Evoliutsiia Zhanra*. Moscow: Iskusstvo, 1976.

Kezich, Tullio. *Il Mito del Far West*. Milan: Il Formichiere, 1980.

Leguebe, Eric. *Histoire Universelle du Western*. Paris: Éditions France-Empire, 1989.

Leutrat, Jean Louis. *L'Alliance Brisée: Le Western des Années 1920*. Lyon: Presses Universitaires de Lyon, 1985.

———. *Le Western: Archeologie d'un Genre*. Lyon: Presses Universitaires de Lyon, 1987.

Leutrat, Jean Louis, and S. Liandrat-Guigues. *Les Cartes de l'Ouest: Un Genre Cinematographique, Le Western*. Paris: A. Colin, 1990.

Mauduy, Jacques, and Gerard Henriet. *Géographies du Western: Une Nation en Marche*. Paris: Nathan, 1989.

Morin, Georges Henry. *Le Cercle Brisé: L'Image de l'Indien dans le Western*. Paris: Payot, 1977.

Moscati, Massimo. *Western all'Italiana*. Milan: Pan, 1978.

Seesslen, Georg. *Western: Geschichte und Mythologie des Westernfilms*. Marburg: Schuren, 1995.

———. *Western-Kino*. Reinbek bei Hamburg: Rowohlt, 1979.

Masculinity in Westerns

Mitchell, Lee Clark. *Westerns: Making the Man in Fiction and Film*. Chicago: University of Chicago Press, 1996.

Producers, Directors, Actors

Fraser, Harry. *I Went That-a-Way: The Memoirs of a Western Film Director*. Metuchen, N.J.: Scarecrow Press, 1990.

Place, Janey Ann. *The Western Films of John Ford*. Secaucus, N.J.: Citadel Press, 1974.

Roberts, Randy, and James Olson. *John Wayne, American*. New York: Free Press, 1995.

Seydor, Paul. *Peckinpah: The Western Films*. Urbana: University of Illinois Press, 1980.

Native Americans

Bataille, Gretchen M., and Charles L.P. Silet. *Images of American Indians on Film: An Annotated Bibliography*. New York: Garland, 1985.

Bataille, Gretchen M., and Charles L.P. Silet, eds. *The Pretend Indians: Images of Native Americans in the Movies*. Ames: Iowa State University Press, 1980.

Churchill, Ward. *Fantasies of the Master Race: Literature, Cinema and the Colonization of American Indians*. Monroe, Maine: Common Courage Press, 1992.

Friar, Ralph E., and Natasha A. Friar. *The Only Good Indian*. New York: Drama Book Specialists, 1972.

Hilger, Michael. *The American Indian in Film*. Metuchen, N.J.: Scarecrow Press, 1986.

———. *From Savage to Nobleman: Images of Native Americans in Film*. Lanham, Md.: Scarecrow Press, 1995.

O'Connor, John E. *The Hollywood Indian*. Paterson, N.J.: New Jersey State Museum, 1980.

Silent Westerns

Brownlow, Kevin. *The War, the West, and the Wilderness*. New York: Alfred A. Knopf, 1979.

Langman, Larry. *A Guide to Silent Westerns*. New York: Greenwood Press, 1992.

Singing Cowboys

Rothel, David. *The Singing Cowboy*. South Brunswick, N.J.: A.S. Barnes, 1978.

Spaghetti Westerns

Frayling, Christopher. *Spaghetti Westerns: Cowboys and Europeans from Karl May to Sergio Leone*. London: Routledge & Kegan Paul, 1981.

Weisser, Thomas. *Spaghetti Westerns: The Good, the Bad, and the Violent: A Comprehensive, Illustrated Filmography of 558 Eurowesterns and their Personnel, 1961–1977*. Jefferson, N.C.: McFarland, 1992.

Contributors

ERIC GARY ANDERSON is assistant professor of English at Oklahoma State University, where he teaches American and Native American Literature. His book *Southwestern Dispositions: Native American Literary Relations, 1880–1990* is forthcoming from the University of Texas Press.

ROBERT BAIRD teaches film at, and serves as Multimedia Consultant to, the University of Illinois English Department. He is currently working on two books, *How Movies Scare Us: A Cognitive Poetics of the Threat Scene,* and an expansion of his article published here, tentatively entitled *"Going Indian": Noble Savages, Wannabes, and True Americans through 200 Years of Popular Imagination.* He is now designing Web pages for teaching and publishing. His essay on *Vertigo* can be found at the Web-based film journal *Images:* http://www.qni.com/~ijournal/.

LARRY E. BURGESS, director of the A.K. Smiley Public Library in Redlands, California, is an adjunct professor of history at the University of Redlands and the University of California, Riverside. His books include *Daniel Smiley of Mohonk: A Naturalist's Life.* He is co-author with James A. Sandos of *The Hunt for Willie Boy: Indian-Hating and Popular Culture,* which won the Gustavus Myers Center Award. Current projects include a chapter in a forthcoming book on Southern California's rancho period, as well as work on water resources and the image of Southern California.

TED JOJOLA is associate professor of Community and Regional Planning and former director of Native American Studies at the University of New Mexico. He is widely published on topics related to stereotyping, tribal community development, and technology. His principal area of research and scholarship is the role of image in sustaining community development, particularly as it pertains to the appropriation of indigenous concepts by mainstream America. He has participated in, and sponsored numerous forums related to, image-making, especially in the performing arts, and has advised major production companies on program content. He resides on the Isleta Pueblo Reservation.

MARGO KASDAN is professor of film studies at San Francisco State University. She is co-author with Christine Saxton and Susan Tavernetti of *The Critical Eye: An Introduction to Looking at Movies.* Her article "'Why are you afraid to have me at your side?': From Passivity to Power in *Salt of the Earth*" is included in *The Voyage In: Fictions of Female Development,* edited by Abel, Hirsch, and Langland, and also on the Voyager CD-ROM on the film.

FRANK MANCHEL is professor of English at the University of Vermont, where he teaches film history and criticism. A former associate dean of the College of Arts and Sciences, he was a member of the George F. Peabody Awards Committee for seven years. He is also a member of the editorial boards of the *Journal of Popular Film and Television* and *Film & History.* Of his nineteen published books, the most recent is the four-volume *Film Study: An Analytical Guide.* His most recent articles have been on Woody Strode for *Black Scholar; Schindler's List* for the *Journal of Modern History;* and *The Shining* for *Literature/Film Quarterly.* He is currently working on a book about African-American films in the 1970s.

STEVEN MINTZ, a professor of history at the University of Houston and co-director of the American Cultures program, teaches courses on such topics as film history, slavery, ethnicity, and the history of the family. As a member of the executive committee of H-Net: Humanities On-Line, and founder and co-moderator of H-Film, a scholarly electronic discussion list on the study and uses of media, he plays an active role in the application of new technologies in history teaching and research. His books include *Hollywood's America: Twentieth Century U.S. History Through Film; A Prison of Expectations: The Family in Victorian Culture; Domestic Revolutions: A Social History of American Family Life; Moralists & Modernizers: America's Pre—Civil War Reformers;* and *America and Its Peoples.* Mintz is an editor of The American Social Experience, a series of books published by New York University Press, and has served as a consultant to the National Museum of American History, the Minnesota Historical Society, and the New Jersey Historical Society.

KEN NOLLEY is professor of English at Willamette University in Salem, Oregon, where he teaches literature and film. He has written often on the work of John Ford and Peter Watkins. In 1984 and 1985 he worked with Peter Watkins on research and filming of *The Journey.* He serves as co-moderator, with Stephen Mintz, of *H-Film,* an H-Net film discussion list (SMintz@uh.edu).

JOHN E. O'CONNOR, professor of history at the New Jersey Institute of Technology and Rutgers University, Newark, has been active in the study of visual media since the late 1960s. In 1970 he founded *Film & History: An Interdisciplinary Journal of Film and Television Studies.* In the mid-1970s he brought scholars together at the Rockefeller Foundation; the results were published as *Film and the Humanities.* His *American History/American Film, American History/American Television,* and *Hollywood Indian* have been important texts. His most recent book is *Image as Artifact: The Historical Analysis of Film and Television* with accompanying videodisc/videotape and study guide.

MICHAEL J. RILEY is curator of education at the Roswell Museum and Art Center in New Mexico. His research program focuses on the social and cultural dimensions of art, particularly the relationships between images, cultural identities, and notions of place. He holds a Ph.D. in sociocultural anthropology from the University of Texas at Austin, and has also studied studio art and art history extensively. As an artist/scholar, he has worked and taught at a variety of museums and colleges.

PETER C. ROLLINS is Regents Professor of English and American/Film Studies at Oklahoma State University. A veteran, he has focused many of his articles and film efforts, including a film, *Television's Vietnam,* on the misrepresentation of American servicemen in visual media. He is chief scholar for the Veterans Legacy Group. In association with the Will Rogers Project at Oklahoma State University he produced an award-winning film and an interpretive book on Rogers. He recently assumed the editorship of *Film & History: An Interdisciplinary Journal of Film and Television Studies* (RR 3, Box 80, Cleveland, OK 74020 and http://h net2.msu.edu/ ~filmhis).

HANNU SALMI is associate professor of cultural history at the University of Turku. He has published numerous articles on the history of music in Finland and Germany. He is best known as a historian of film and popular culture and for organizing film historical research in Finland. He has published books on the history of popular culture and the history of technology. His most recent film book is *Elokuva ja historia* (Film and History). He leads a research project called Crisis, Critique, Consensus: The Social History of Finnish Cinema from the 1940s to the 1970s.

JAMES A. SANDOS is professor of history at the University of Redlands. His writings on California Indian history have appeared in such journals as the *American Indian Quarterly* and the *American Historical Review*. He is co-author with Larry E. Burgess of *The Hunt for Willie Boy: Indian-Hating and Popular Culture*, which won a Gustavus Myers Center Award. He is currently working on a history of Indian-White relations in California from the missions era to the Gold Rush, with special attention to the way these relations have been portrayed in film.

PAULINE TURNER STRONG is assistant professor of anthropology at the University of Texas at Austin and associate editor of *Cultural Anthropology*. Her interests center on representations of Indians in American popular culture. Recent publications include articles on Indian identity, tribalism, and nationalism and on museum displays. Forthcoming books include *Captive Selves, Captivating Others: The Practice and Representation of Captivity across the British-Amerindian Frontier, 1575–1775*.

SUSAN TAVERNETTI received her M.A. degree in cinema from the University of Southern California and teaches in the Film/TV Department at De Anza College in Cupertino, California. Working with Margo Kasdan, she prepared the second edition of *The Critical Eye: An Introduction to Looking at Movies*. Since 1988 she has been a film critic for the *Palo Alto Weekly*, which is available to Internet users at http://www.paweekly.com.

JEFFREY WALKER is associate professor of English at Oklahoma State University. He has published extensively on colonial and early nineteenth-century American literature, including books on Benjamin Church and James Fenimore Cooper. As a member of the editorial board for the Cooper Edition, he established the text for *The Spy* with Lance Schachterle and James P. Elliott and is working on an edition of unpublished Cooper letters. A senior bibliographer for the MLA's International Bibliography, he is also associate editor for *Seventeenth-Century News*.

WILCOMB WASHBURN was Senior Historian Emeritus and director of the American Studies Program at the Smithsonian Institution until his death in February 1997. He also taught at George Washington University, American University, and the University of Maryland. He held a Ph.D. from Harvard University. His books include *The Governor and the Rebel: A History of Bacon's Rebellion in Virginia; Red Man's Land/White Man's Land;* and *The Indian in America*. In 1996 he was awarded the Sidney Hook Memorial Award of the National Association of Scholars for work in the cause of academic freedom and the integrity of the academy. He was buried at Arlington National Cemetery with full military honors.

Index

References to illustrations are shown in **boldface**. Films are shown with date of release in parentheses. Television productions, including made-for-television films, are indicated as (television).